THE PROJECTS OF
SKUNK WORKS

Dedication

FOR ALL SKUNKS—PAST, PRESENT, FUTURE

THE PROJECTS OF
SKUNK WORKS

75 YEARS OF LOCKHEED MARTIN'S
ADVANCED DEVELOPMENT PROGRAMS

STEVE PACE
FOREWORD BY ERIC HEHS

VOYAGEUR
PRESS

CONTENTS

Kelly Johnson, father of the Skunk Works Program.

FOREWORD

Eric Hehs
EDITOR, *CODE ONE* MAGAZINE
LOCKHEED MARTIN AERONAUTICS COMPANY

Anyone with even a mild interest in aviation has some knowledge of the Skunk Works. At the most basic level, the term connects with the highly secretive organization that developed and built the SR-71 Blackbird.

Growing up, a plastic kit model of that big black aircraft took the top center position on my bookshelf for many years. That childhood possession may have presaged my eventual career at the company that designed the aircraft—or maybe it was the B-58 Hustler model next to it. Who knows?

The SR-71 Blackbird may have been the most prominent aircraft in the mind of the public, but it was not the first aircraft developed by the Skunk Works. As Steve Pace details in this book, that distinction belongs to the US Air Force's first operational jet-powered fighter, the P-80 (later known as the F-80 Shooting Star). The P-80 was followed by a number of groundbreaking aircraft including the T-33, F-94, F-104, C-130, and U-2, to name a few. The A-12 and YF-12 were direct predecessors to the SR-71.

And the SR-71 was not the last aircraft developed by the Skunk Works. The U-2R, F-117, F-22, and F-35 each have some or most of their roots in the Skunk Works.

These aircraft designations are just mile markers on highways built of details. The details can fill thousands of pages. Pieced together they can tell intricate stories about personalities, international and domestic politics, funding, design decisions, industry consolidation, and technical advances in everything from material science to digital electronics to software engineering.

The United States spent billions on the projects described here. People have devoted their lives to these projects and derived their livelihoods from them. A few of these efforts stretched the known state of the art. Some projects helped win wars. Others helped avoid them.

As someone who has covered Skunk Works topics as more or less an insider, I have a grasp of the editorial challenges the author faced in creating this book. The biggest challenges with writing projects like this tend to involve decisions on what to leave out. There's not enough room for everything.

That filtering process begins before the point of collecting information and anecdotes. Details on some projects (and even entire programs) are withheld from public view primarily for reasons of national security, although corporate competitiveness also plays a role.

As the years progress, more information on these secretive programs becomes available to the public. At the same time, the Skunk Works adds to its long list of accomplishments. Together, these two factors explain why new books on the Skunk Works, like this one, are needed.

Not only does this book expand on the existing history of the Advanced Development Projects of Lockheed Martin, *The Projects of the Skunk Works* also preserves that history. Steve Pace deserves praise for keeping the conversation current and for encouraging new minds to take part in it.

INTRODUCTION

First and foremost, this authoritative work is not a history of the Lockheed Martin Corporation or any of its many predecessor companies. There are numerous other tomes specifically dedicated to those. Instead, this is a seventy-five-year history of the most clandestine entity of the Lockheed Martin Corporation, which is officially named Advanced Development Programs (ADP). Of course, ADP is much better known as the Skunk Works.

Close to seventy-five years ago now, on June 17, 1943, Lockheed Aircraft Corporation chief engineer Hall Livingstone Hibbard and propulsive system engineer Nathan C. "Nate" Price attended a top secret US Army Air Forces (USAAF) Air Technical Service Command (ATSC) meeting in Washington, DC. In attendance were Brig. Gen. Franklin Otis "Frank" Carroll; Cols. Marshall S. Roth, Howard Bogart, and Ralph P. Swofford Jr. (Lt. Col. Jack Carter later replaced Col. Swofford on this program); and then Capt. Ezra Kotcher—project officer and senior aeronautical engineer in the engineering division of the ATSC's Air Materiel Command (AMC). Hibbard and Price were told about gas turbine (turbojet) engine developments during this conference and prompted to submit a proposal for a pursuit (fighter) to be propelled by a single centrifugal-flow type of turbojet engine that had been designed by Maj. Frank Bernard Halford, a propulsive systems designer and engineer serving in the RAF. His engine was being produced at this time by the de Havilland Aircraft Company Limited in Great Britain as the Halford H.1B Goblin. This engine was to be produced as the J36 in the United States under license by the Allis-Chalmers Manufacturing Company.

The Bell Aircraft Corporation had been made aware of the H.1B Goblin engine earlier for use in its single-engine XP-59B derivative of the twin turbojet–powered P-59 Airacomet. The XP-59B was to be built under AMC Secret Project MX-398. It had acquired detailed H.1B specifications and drawings for this program. Bell, however, wouldn't be able to produce the XP-59B in satisfactory time, so the USAAF turned to Lockheed.

The primary reason the USAAF went to Lockheed was that on February 24, 1942, it had received an unsolicited proposal from Lockheed entitled *Design Features of the Lockheed L-133* in a Lockheed report numbered 2571. At that time the L-133 was proposed to be a twin-engine fighter, powered by two Price-designed axial-flow turbojet engines, known in-house as the L-1000. This rather unique airframe and powerplant proposal was turned down, however, and Lockheed continued to manufacture piston-powered and propeller-driven combat and transport aircraft for the war effort.

So, on June 17, 1943, with full knowledge of Lockheed's interest in producing a turbojet-powered fighter, the USAAF correctly surmised that Lockheed would be interested in taking over for Bell. Hibbard was given the specifications and drawings related to the H.1B Goblin engine and headed back home to Burbank, California, where the Lockheed Aircraft Corporation resided. The program became known as AMC Secret Project MX-409.

Upon his return to Burbank, Hibbard and his chief of experimental design, Clarence Leonard "Kelly" Johnson, set their wheels in motion to generate an appropriate airplane. Two Lockheed reports associated with the MX-409 design—numbers 4199 and 4211, respectively—were entitled *Preliminary Design Investigation* and *Manufacturer's Brief Model Specification*. These were taken to the USAAF, and on June 17, 1943, Lockheed received a green light to proceed. On this very same day the USAAF issued Lockheed Letter [of intent to purchase] Contract Number W535 AC-40680. It called for the manufacture of one experimental pursuit airplane designated XP-80. As Lockheed had promised, and now by contract, the XP-80 was to be produced in about six months.

So secret was the MX-409 program that it couldn't be accomplished under normal circumstances, on a factory floor or near any production line. Lockheed found a site near the factory and cordoned off the space in which the XP-80 would be built. It would be highly guarded. The building in question was located next to a putrid-smelling factory.

The Skunk Works was born in the early 1940s, but it wasn't officially called so until a number of years later. Prior to being called Skunk Works it was called Advanced Development Projects (ADP) and then Advanced Development Programs. In the 1940s and 1950s the division generated a number of outstanding aircraft.

The Skunk Works came through again in the 1950s with a number of F-80 Shooting Star spinoffs, including the first dedicated jet-powered trainers—the T-33 T-Bird and the T2V SeaStar—for the US Air Force (USAF) and US Navy (USN), and an all-weather fighter, the F-94 Starfire; the world's first doublesonic fighter, the F-104 Starfighter; and the world's highest-flying airplane, the U-2.

In the 1960s the Skunk Works proved that science fiction could indeed become science fact when it reinvented aircraft design and produced the amazing Blackbird series of triplesonic aircraft. These 2,000-mile-per-hour aircraft included the A-12, M-21/D-21, YF-12, and SR-71. All were way ahead of their time—not only in form, but also in function. It also produced an advanced version of the U-2 with its U-2R.

In the 1970s the Skunk Works created the Have Blue Experimental Survivable Testbed and the F-117 Nighthawk. The *Sea Shadow* and a stealthy cruise missile followed in the 1980s.

Yet another U-2 variant came forth from ADP in the 1980s—a tactical reconnaissance version called the TR-1 that sported improved avionics and engine.

In the 1990s, to answer a call from the USAF for an Advanced Tactical Fighter (ATF), ADP designed the YF-22, which led to the Engineering Manufacturing Design (EMD) phase and then the production of the world's first fifth-generation fighter—the F-22 Raptor air dominance fighter.

The 2000s were rife with manned and unmanned ADP creations, including the X-35 Joint Strike Fighter series of concept demonstration aircraft that led to the System Development and Demonstration phase, which then produced the world's second fifth-generation fighter, the F-35 Lightning II; the flying-wing Polecat unmanned aerial vehicle (UAV); the P-971 hybrid air vehicle; and several other interesting air vehicles.

From the year 2010 on, the Skunk Works continued to challenge the world of advanced aerospace products. During this time, Lockheed Martin ADP has generated a number of unique air vehicles and concepts for future air vehicles. These include ARES, VARIOUS, UCLASS, LBFD, SR-72, TR, LBFD, and the HWB.

At this writing, as we rapidly approach the 75th anniversary of the Skunk Works, some of its newer programs are more than just a little tantalizing. The trouble is that these programs are for the most part classified. To paraphrase the current Skunk Works executive vice president and general manager Rob Weiss, "Eighty percent is classified, twenty percent isn't."

—Steve Pace

®

9

THE 1940s: FORMING THE WINGS TO COME

"Keep it simple, stupid."

—KELLY JOHNSON

The Lockheed Martin Corporation of today can trace its history back to 1912, when the brothers Allan H. and Malcolm Loughead established the Alco Hydro-Aeroplane Company in San Francisco, California. In 1916 Allan and Malcolm moved their enterprise to Santa Barbara, California, and renamed it the Loughead Aircraft Manufacturing Company. The firm went on to produce a few aircraft, namely the Model F-1 flying boat and the Model S-1 sport plane. The latter was of the advanced monocoque design that, due to its prohibitive price tag, couldn't compete. Thus, without any airplane orders, Loughead Aircraft was forced out of business in 1921.

In 1926 Allan Loughead, John Knudsen "Jack" Northrop, and Kenneth "Ken" Jay teamed up and formed the Lockheed Aircraft Company in Hollywood, California (the spelling of *Loughead* was changed to *Lockheed* to prevent mispronunciation). Northrop had joined Loughead Aircraft in 1920 as a draftsman, and it was he who had designed the S-1 sport plane. This new company used the monocoque design features of the S-1 to create the Lockheed Vega.

The company relocated to Burbank, California, in March 1928, and by year's end, it reported sales exceeding one million dollars. From 1926 to 1928 the company produced more than eighty aircraft and employed more than three hundred workers who, by April 1929, were building five aircraft per week.

In July 1929, majority shareholder Fred E. Keeler sold 87 percent of the Lockheed Aircraft Company to the Detroit Aircraft Corporation. In August 1929, Allan Loughead resigned.

The Great Depression ruined the aircraft market, and Detroit Aircraft went bankrupt. A group of investors headed by Walter Varney and the brothers Robert Ellsworth "Bob" Gross and Courtlandt Sherrington "Cort" Gross bought the company out of receivership in 1932. The syndicate bought the company for $40,000. Ironically, Allan Loughead had planned to bid for his own company but had raised only $50,000, which he felt was too small a sum for a serious bid. He should have bid, for he would have won back his company. Famed Hollywood filmmaker Samuel "Billy" Wilder said it best: "Hindsight is always 20/20."

In 1934 Bob Gross was named chairman of the new company, the Lockheed Corporation, which was headquartered at the municipal airport in Burbank. Cort Gross was named cofounder and executive.

The first successful aircraft that was built in any number (141 aircraft) was the Lockheed Vega of 1927, which is best known for its several first and record-

The second of the two XP-80As—nicknamed *Silver Ghost*—in early 1949, when it was being used as an engine testbed for the Lockheed-designed afterburner section for use on the Westinghouse J34 turbojet engine slated for the XF-90 program. *LM Code One*

setting flights by, among others, Amelia Earhart, Wiley Post, and George Hubert Wilkins.

In the 1930s, Lockheed spent $139,400 to develop its Model 10 Electra, a small, twin-engine transport airplane. The company sold forty in the first year of production. Earhart and her navigator, Fred Noonan, flew it in their failed attempt to circumnavigate the world in 1937. Subsequent designs, the Lockheed Model 12 Electra Junior and the Lockheed Model 14 Super Electra, expanded their market.

Also in 1937, Lockheed initiated its multi-engine Excalibur airliner program. Though the design was interesting, it wasn't well received by the airlines.

Throughout the years 1938 and 1939 the Lockheed Aircraft Corporation was in various stages of designing and developing a new 400-plus-mile-per-hour pursuit aircraft, called the P-38 Lightning, for the US Army Air Corps (USAAC). The cutting-edge Lightning was a twin-engine, twin-boom, twin-tail interceptor pursuit aircraft that eventually became a pivotal combat aircraft in World War II.

The design and engineering that went into the P-38 were the handy work of aeronautical engineers Hibbard and Johnson, and the first example, the one-off XP-38, made its first flight on January 27, 1939. It was flown by a USAAC AMC engineering test pilot, 1st Lt. Benjamin Scovill "Ben" Kelsey, who was a fighter project officer in the Engineering Division of the AMC and one of P-38's biggest supporters. In fact, he helped convince the USAAC to procure the type.

In addition to the P-38 Lightning program, Lockheed Aircraft and its Vega Aircraft Corporation subsidiary (formerly the AiRover Company) were busy building advanced trainers under license for North American Aviation (Vega's Vega-35 version of the North American NA-35, which became the AT-6 Texan); the Vega, Electra, and Super Electra airliners; and the Hudson, Ventura, and Harpoon bombers and patrol bombers.

In 1939 Howard R. Hughes Jr.—billionaire and major stockholder in Trans World Airlines (TWA)—put forth an industrywide request for a forty-passenger transcontinental airliner with a range of 3,500 miles. The earlier Lockheed L-044 Excalibur design didn't fit the requirements but lent itself to modification into what became the Lockheed L-049 Constellation.

Lockheed was well established as one of the major airplane production firms in America by the year 1940. But like so many other aircraft manufacturers of that era it was constantly looking for new business to survive and to keep its relatively small workforce intact. On order for fiscal year (FY) 1940 were sixty-five P-38 Lightnings and a single Lightning derivative designated XP-49. These aircraft, ordered by the then USAAC, were a mere handful to produce, and additional orders were highly sought after.

The year 1941 proved much more lucrative due to the expanding wars in Europe and the Pacific. FY 1941 military orders increased dramatically for Lockheed. After December 8, 1941—the date America declared war on Germany and Japan—the floodgates opened and combat and military transport aircraft soon began to stream off the Lockheed and Vega production lines.

Lockheed combat and military transport aircraft production for FY 1942 included P-38E, P-38F, and P-38J Lightnings; F-4 and F-5 Photo Lightnings; C-56, C-57, C-59 and C-60 Lodestars; A-28 and A-29 Hudsons; B-34s and RB-34s; B-37 Venturas; Lockheed/Vega B-17Gs; and C-69 Constellations.

The Lockheed Aircraft Corporation was producing the B-17 Flying Fortress (under USAAF contract, licensed by the Boeing Airplane Company), the C-69 Constellation, the PV-1 Ventura, the PV-2 Harpoon, the experimental XP2V-1 Neptune, the P-38 Lightning, and its new P-80 Shooting Star when 1945 calendars replaced 1944 ones.

World War II ended in Europe on May 8, 1945, though the war in the Pacific raged on for another four-plus months. In the interim, the fledgling Skunk Works was busy trying to improve upon its P-80 series of aircraft while it delved into new designs. It was a time of discord because the US War Department planned to cut back on its numerous high-volume aircraft orders. Wartime aircraft production was about to come to a screeching halt.

For example, on January 7, 1945, North American Aviation, Inc., received a contract to produce one thousand Lockheed-licensed P-80N aircraft (North American Aviation charge number NA-137) at its Kansas City, Kansas, facility for the USAAF (USAAF contract number W535 AC-7717). But the contract was canceled before any production P-80Ns could be built; the reserved USAAF serial numbers 45-6701 to 45-7700 are believed to have been for these one thousand NAA-built P-80Ns.

In any event, inside Kelly's lair the design, development, and engineering on various aircraft projects were constant. And since he was chief research engineer, Johnson was responsible for all of its wants and needs.

With the military market dwindling, it came time for Lockheed to reinvestigate the civilian aircraft market. Its large and elegant Constellation would soon ply the skies throughout the world, but there was a need for smaller, feeder-type airliners to shuttle passengers between major cities.

During this particular time period, the still rather fledgling Skunk Works entered into unprecedented territory with the creation of several interesting aircraft projects. Its aerodynamic, aeronautical, electrical, fuel, hydraulic, propulsive, and thermal engineering staff was rampant with genius minds, and they came up with many successful offerings.

Lightning: The XP-38 and YP-38

If "hindsight is 20/20," then foresight must be all-seeing—or so it would seem when it came to the extraordinary visions of Lockheed Vice President and Chief Engineer Hibbard and Chief Research Engineer Johnson in the late 1930s. These two highly skilled personalities foresaw the creation of the exact advanced fighter to fit the requirements of Circular Proposal X-608 put forth by the USAAC in February 1937. The proposal called for a twin-engine interceptor to pursue and destroy enemy aircraft at high altitude. It also called for a maximum level-attitude flight speed of at least 360 miles per hour and the ability to reach an altitude of 20,000 feet within six minutes. These were unheard-of performance goals at that time in aviation history, and they required the design of an *advanced fighter* in the truest sense of that phrase.

After Hibbard and Johnson settled on the propulsive system for their twin-engine design—two Allison twelve-cylinder, water-cooled, V-1710C Vee-type turbo-supercharged (engine exhaust-driven) 1,500-horsepower piston engines with counter-rotating propellers—Johnson

Above: YP-38 takes flight. *USAF*

Right: Page 1 of patent drawings and information on Lightning, filed by Hibbard and Johnson on June 27, 1939—patent awarded on March 26, 1940. *United States Patent Office*

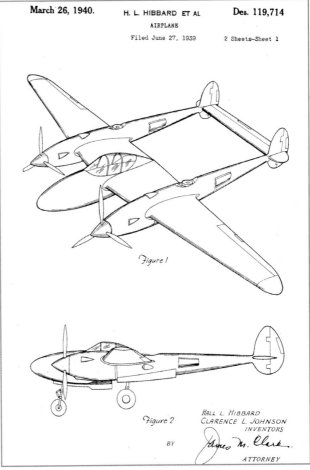

drew up a number of configurations. The configuration that made the most sense to them was frozen. They had settled upon a design to which Lockheed issued Model 22, or Model 22-64-01 to be exact. It featured twin booms outboard of the cockpit gondola and armed nose section to house the engines and to support the horizontal and vertical stabilizer and rudders. The armament, in keeping with the 500- to 1,000-pound maximum weight requirement, was comprised of two .50-caliber Browning M2 heavy machine guns with 200 rounds per gun, two .30-caliber Browning machine guns with 500 rounds per gun, and a single Madsen 23mm T-1 Army Ordnance auto-cannon with a rotary magazine. This arrangement offered concentrated firepower without a need for propeller synchronization.

Lockheed presented it CP X-608 projections to the AMC in April 1937. Lockheed had promised an unheard-of top speed of 400 miles per hour, and its Model 22 was almost immediately accepted. The USAAC ordered a single experimental airplane, designated XP-38 under USAAC contract number AC-9974 (approved on June 23, 1937), and it was issued USAAC serial number 37-457.

13

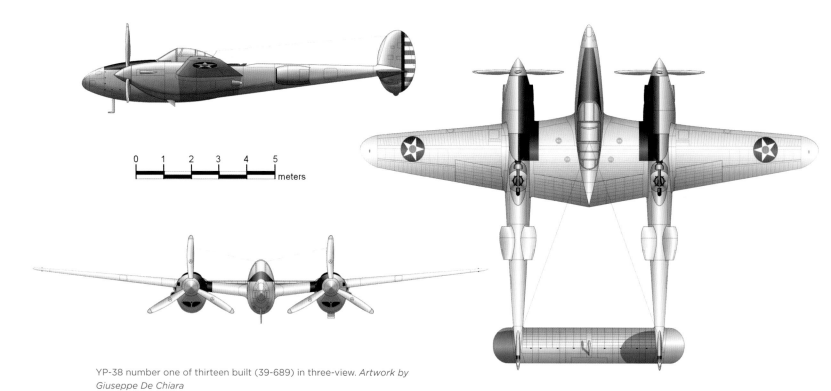

YP-38 number one of thirteen built (39-689) in three-view. *Artwork by Giuseppe De Chiara*

Milo Burcham shows new anti-compressibility dive flap to World War II's and America's still highest-ever-scoring eight-time ace Richard Ira "Dick" Bong (forty kills). *LM via Denny Lombard*

Construction of the XP-38 began in July 1937 and was completed in December 1938, just before the Christmas and New Year holidays. The unavailability of its desired engines had caused the delay in its preparedness. It wasn't armed, and its livery was of polished aluminum with USAAC markings. It was a very good-looking airplane, and it was unlike any fighter design seen to that point.

After the holidays, the one-off XP-38 was prepared for its inaugural test flight out of March Field near Riverside, California. The airplane had been moved there earlier under tight security, and on January 27, 1939, Kelsey—who had sold the airplane to the USAAC as project officer—took it up. Subsequent test hops by Kelsey and Lockheed Aircraft Chief Engineering Test Pilot Marshall E. "Babe" Headle demonstrated a top speed of 413 miles per hour at 20,000 feet. Thus the Lightning—as it was appropriately named—became the first true 400-mile-per-hour airplane on the planet.

The XP-38 wasn't perfect, however, and had demonstrated a few problems, such as wing flap vibrations and wheel brake failures, including one where the airplane wound up in a ditch. These difficulties were systematically addressed and corrected.

The USAAC authorized a transcontinental record demonstration of the Lightning's speed, and on February 11, 1939, Kelsey departed March Field. His destination was Mitchel Field in New York. He made refueling stops in Amarillo, Texas, and Dayton, Ohio. On his final leg, just

XP-38

SPECIFICATIONS

CREW: One (pilot)

PROPULSIVE SYSTEM: Two 1,090-horsepower, turbosupercharged, water-cooled, 12-cylinder, V-1710-11 (L) and V-1710-15 (R) Allison Model C9 piston engines, with inward-rotating, three-bladed propellers

LENGTH: 37 ft 10 in

HEIGHT: 12 ft 10 in

WINGSPAN: 52 ft

EMPTY WEIGHT: 11,507 lbs

GROSS TAKEOFF WEIGHT: 15,416 lbs

MAXIMUM SPEED: NA

MAXIMUM RANGE: NA

SERVICE CEILING: NA

ARMAMENT: None installed

prior to landing at Mitchel Field, the engines lost power and Kelsey made a forced landing due to engine failure on the Cold Stream Golf Course in Hempstead, New York. Kelsey survived the ordeal, but the XP-38 did not.

The P-38 Lightning was a winner. Hibbard and Johnson filed for its patent on June 27, 1939—exactly six months after its first flight—and on March 26, 1940, a fourteen-year patent was granted to them.

As of that time, however, only the XP-38 had flown. The USAAC ordered thirteen prototype YP-38 airplanes in the interim, and it wasn't until September 17, 1940, that the first of these service test aircraft took wing, with Headle at the controls.

The YP-38s, USAAC serial numbers 39-689 to 39-701, were ordered earlier under USAAC contract number AC-12523, which was approved on April 27, 1939. These were assigned Model 122-62-02 and designated YP-38-LO.

On September 20, 1939, the USAAC ordered twenty-nine RP-38s and thirty-six RP-38Ds (USAAC serial numbers 40-744 to 40-761 and 40-763 to 40-773), and one of these (40-762) was completed as the experimental XP-38A, to be evaluated under USAAC Secret Project MX-6. With this third order Lightning production was well on its way.

The XP-38A was created to evaluate the use of a pressurized cockpit, and a second cockpit was inserted into the left-hand boom, where the never-installed General Electric Model B-1 turbosupercharger was to be located.

Orders continued to come in, and by the end of production more than ten thousand Lightnings had been built.

SUMMARY

The P-38 Lightning program gave rise to numerous variants and several spinoffs, including the F-4 and F-5 photographic reconnaissance Lightnings. Two of its spinoffs, the one-off XP-49 and the XP-58 Chain Lightning, are discussed later in this chapter.

While Hibbard and Johnson were responsible for the design of many successful Lockheed-built aircraft, the P-38 Lightning was their first over-the-top invention. It was this airplane that created America's still-highest-scoring fighter aces, and it helped in a big way to bring about the end of World War II.

TDN L-133 and TDN L-1000

Due to World War II, which had been declared by the United States on December 8, 1941, military aircraft orders became epic for Lockheed when compared to past years where it had struggled. It continued to design new, exciting, and futuristic aircraft, including an advanced fighter known in-house as TDN L-133.

As previously mentioned, while working at Lockheed in early 1941 as an aircraft engine supercharger/turbo-supercharger systems engineer on the XP-49 program, Nate Price—who was also an inventor—approached Johnson with a design for a turbojet engine that he had been developing on and off since 1938.

Johnson was impressed, to say the least, and took Price to see Hibbard. Hibbard likewise found it intriguing and went to Lockheed management. Lockheed management—namely Lockheed president Bob Gross—approved the risky project.

Hibbard gave Johnson the green light, and he ordered the development of a high-speed aircraft to use the propulsive system Price had designed. He assigned Willis M. "Willy" Hawkins Jr. to serve as project engineer. Hawkins had joined Lockheed in 1937 as a draftsman.

Price finalized the design of his axial-flow turbojet engine under TDN L-1000, and the Lockheed-built XJ37-1-LO turbojet engine program was born.

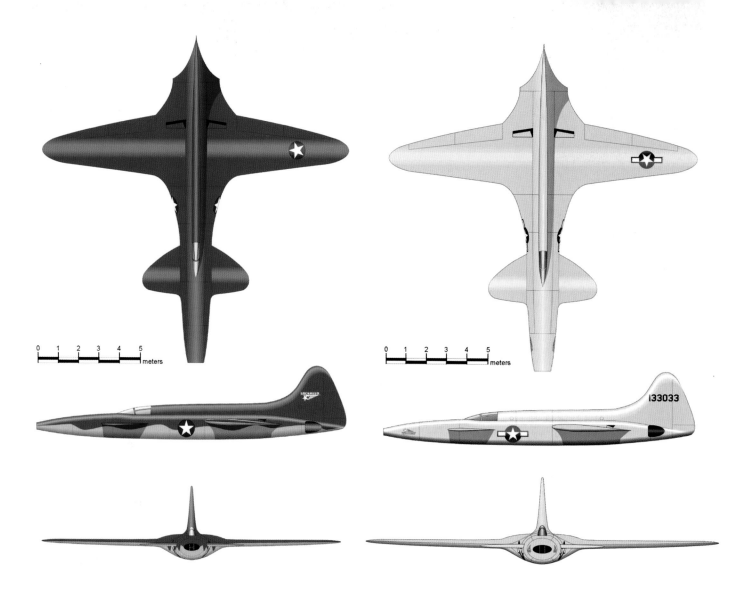

The L-133 in three-view as it might have appeared during USAAF testing. *Artwork by Giuseppe De Chiara*

The L-133 (final configuration TDN L-133-02-01) in three-view as it might have looked when it was first completed. *Artwork by Giuseppe De Chiara*

Lockheed TDN L-133—the proposed high-speed pursuit to utilize the XJ37—was offered to the USAAC on March 30, 1942. Its intended propulsive system, the Lockheed TDN L-1000—the XJ37—was offered to the USAAC at the same time.

The L-133/L-1000 projects were Lockheed's original attempt to build a turbojet-powered airplane. Turbojet propulsion, though in its infancy, was considered by Lockheed to be a practical approach in the attainment of high speeds approaching that of sound. Specific— albeit lofty—design parameters established by Lockheed included the following:

- High speed greater than any high-altitude bomber or pursuit; 600 miles per hour assumed to be required.
- Service ceiling of at least 40,000 feet.

- Firepower sufficient to destroy a well-armored bomber or pursuit at high altitude; four 20mm cannon considered to be adequate.
- Endurance sufficient for the aircraft to serve as a high-altitude patrol defender; three hours at 50 percent power to be sufficient.
- Maneuverability would be sacrificed to obtain the desired high-speed performance.
- Aircraft would be single place, using jet propulsion units of Lockheed design.
- Armor and bulletproofing would be minimal to keep the aircraft as small and light as possible. However, provisions for such items would be included (up to 160 pounds of pilot armor and normal fuel tank bulletproofing).
- No provision for assisted takeoff that would require special airfields or ground equipment.

A depiction of what an operational L-133 may have looked like in aerial combat over Italy. *Artwork by Luca Landino*

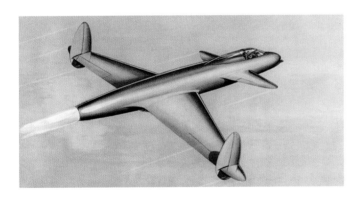

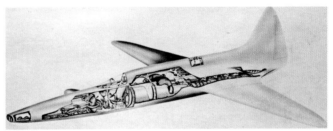

Above: Phantom view of the proposed L-133. *LM via Denny Lombard*

Left: Early artist concept of L-133 design. *LM Code One*

The L-133 was to be powered by two Lockheed L-1000 turbojet engines, and its simple design was to make it adaptable to mass production. It was to be a mid-wing, tail-first airplane with a large area vertical tail aft of the wing. The wings and forward-mounted tail plane, or canard, were to be full cantilever tapered flying surfaces. The fuselage cross-section was to be an ellipse with the major axis horizontal. The cockpit would have formed the leading edge or apex of a long dorsal fin, which was to fair into the vertical tail.

The L-1000 engines would be mounted aft of the pilot, one in each wing-to-fuselage fillet. The bifurcated engine air inlets for the turbojet engines would be in the extreme nose of the airplane. The cockpit, cannon armament, landing gear, fuel tanks, and so on would be contained in the fuselage between the engine air ducts. The ducts for engine air requirements would be *D*-shaped tunnels running aftward down either side of the fuselage. The four 20mm cannon would fire from the center of the engine air inlets, mounted in the extreme nose of the aircraft

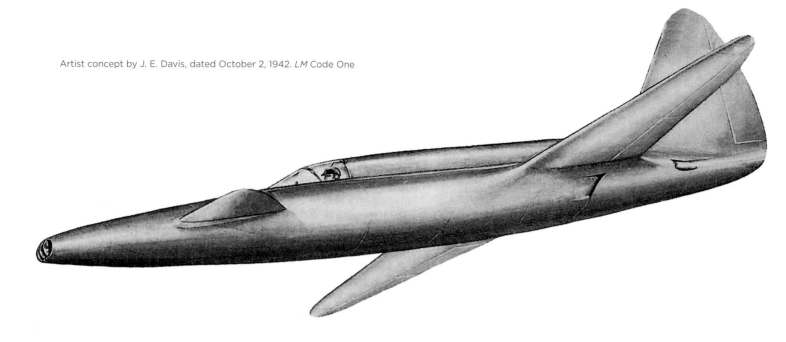

Artist concept by J. E. Davis, dated October 2, 1942. *LM* Code One

(gun gas ingestion might have been a problem with this particular configuration). The landing gear would be of the tricycle type, retracting into the fuselage. Estimated performance data, although high for the proposed aircraft, are as follows:

NORMAL GROSS WEIGHT: 18,000 lbs

OVERLOAD GROSS WEIGHT: 19,500 lbs

FUEL CAPACITY: 500 gal (fuselage only)

HIGH SPEED AT SEA LEVEL: 615 mph

HIGH SPEED AT 20,000 FT: 620 mph

HIGH SPEED AT 40,000 FT: 602 mph

MAXIMUM CLIMB RATE AT SEA LEVEL: 3,740 ft/min

MAXIMUM CLIMB RATE AT 20,000 FT: 5,670 ft/min

MAXIMUM CLIMB RATE AT 40,000 FT: 6,350 ft/min

TIME TO CLIMB TO 40,000 FT: 7.3 minutes

TAKEOFF DISTANCE OVER 50-FOOT OBJECT: 1,885 ft

NORMAL RANGE AT SEA LEVEL: 320 mi

NORMAL RANGE AT 20,000 FT: 350 mi

NORMAL RANGE AT 40,000 FT: 390 mi

TERMINAL VELOCITY AT SEA LEVEL: 710 mph

Had it been produced and met its performance estimates, the L-133 would have really turned some heads; it would be ten more years before any jet fighter exceeded those performance goals.

The proposed powerplant for the L-133, the L-1000 (or XJ37 as it was subsequently designated), is a story in itself. Thus, we will touch on its development as well.

The L-1000 turbojet engine was estimated to provide a whopping 5,500 pound-foot static at sea level—totally unheard of for the day. Lockheed estimated that two of

Nate Price and Hall Hibbard with L-1000 (XJ37) turbojet engine. *Author collection*

these axial-flow turbojet engines would propel the L-133 to a top level-attitude speed of about 620 miles per hour at 20,000 feet. The XJ37 (L-1000) engine featured twin spools, a high compression ratio, and an afterburner section, features that didn't find their way into turbojet engines until the late 1940s.

The L-1000 engine was to be built under license from Lockheed by the Menasco Manufacturing Company in Burbank, California, in 1944 under USAAF AMC Secret Project MX-411, and the patent for the engine was ultimately obtained by Nathan Price and the Curtiss-Wright Corporation in 1946; Curtiss-Wright took over its development from Menasco. Several XJ37s were built, but maximum thrust was a disappointing 2,200 pound-foot.

What finally became of two of these engines is unclear, but the third is on display at the Planes of Fame Air Museum in Chino, California.

Nevertheless, Lockheed's early involvement with the L-133 and L-1000 airframe and powerplant projects clearly indicates why the USAAF went to this inventive firm for the design and development of what became a classic: the Lockheed F-80 Shooting Star.

XP-49

In answer to USAAC AMC Circular Proposal 39-775, issued on March 11, 1939, Lockheed opted to generate a slightly revised version of its P-38 to meet the criteria. In doing so, Lockheed designed an advanced, high-speed, high-altitude interceptor based on the Lightning.

A letter of intent to purchase contract was received by Lockheed on January 8, 1940, and on January 22, 1940, the US War Department officially approved USAAC contract number AC-13476, for a single experimental XP-49 (USAAC serial number 40-3055).

The one-off XP-49 version of the Lightning looked very much like a production P-38—almost identical, in fact, as 66 percent of its airframe structures were interchangeable with the P-38. But it was manufactured with two very different types of turbosupercharged (exhaust-driven) engines and a pressurized cockpit for very-high-altitude operations. It also featured a reshaped cockpit canopy windshield, reshaped vertical tails, beefier landing gear, two rather than one 20mm cannon, and four .50 caliber machine guns.

XP-49

SPECIFICATIONS

CREW: One (pilot)

PROPULSIVE SYSTEM: Two 1,600-hp, inverted-vee, Continental XIV-1430-9L/-11R V-12 piston engines

LENGTH: 40 ft 1 in

HEIGHT: 9 ft 10 in

WINGSPAN: 52 ft 0 in

EMPTY WEIGHT: 15,410 lbs

LOADED WEIGHT: 18,700 lbs

MAXIMUM SPEED: 406 mph at 15,000 ft

MAXIMUM RANGE: 680 mi

RATE OF CLIMB: 3,300 ft/min

ARMAMENT: Two 20mm cannon, four .50-caliber Brown M2 heavy machine guns (proposed; never fitted)

Hibbard appointed aeronautical engineer M. Carl Haddon (who later became chief engineer of Lockheed-California Company) to be the chief project engineer on the XP-49 program. It was designed and engineered under TDN L-106 and later assigned Model 222.

Its original engines were two experimental water-cooled, 1,540 horsepower (on takeoff), inverted-vee, Continental XIV-1430-9L/11-R twelve-cylinder, contra-rotating piston engines. Difficulties with these engines first appeared during ground tests.

The one-off XP-49. *LM Code One*

Lockheed engineering test pilot Joseph C. "Joe" Towle was assigned to head the XP-49 flight test program, and on November 14, 1942, he successfully completed its first flight. Subsequent test hops were performed despite numerous engine problems. These engine difficulties resulted in several groundings until fixes could be applied.

Test flights came to an abrupt halt on January 1, 1943, when Towle experienced troubles and was forced to make an emergency landing at Muroc Army Air Field (AAF) in California. His emergency had been caused by the simultaneous failures of its electrical and hydraulic systems. The airplane was subsequently repaired, and flight testing resumed on February 16, 1943.

In the interim, due to several postcrash modifications, the XP-49 was assigned a new Lockheed model number: Model 522.

As previously discussed, under Secret Project MX-6, a single P-38-LO (USAAF serial number 40-762)—the thirteenth P-38-LO built, was modified to incorporate a pressurized second cockpit on the left-hand engine nacelle. This one-off airplane was designated XP-38A and tested during the last eight months of 1942. The results of these tests had provided invaluable information for the XP-49 program.

The XP-49 was ferried to Wright Field in Dayton, Ohio, on June 26, 1943, for USAAF evaluations. In the end, the XP-49 didn't prove itself to be any better than the latest versions of the P-38, and further development wasn't warranted.

The lone XP-49 was salvaged at Wright-Patterson Air Force Base (AFB) in 1946.

Constellation: The C-69

Although it flew some six months before the Skunk Works was organized, the Model L-049 Constellation program was headed by the same personnel, namely, Vice President and Chief Engineer Hall L. Hibbard and Chief Research Engineer Clarence L. Johnson—the very same persons who had codesigned and copatented the airplane. They applied for its patent on October 5, 1942. They were issued a fourteen-year patent on their design of the "Connie" on September 14, 1943.

Beginning in late 1938, Lockheed had designed its Model 44, which it named Excalibur. It was the result of

Artist concept of the revised Model 44 Excalibur A in its proposed Pan American Airways livery. *LM Code One*

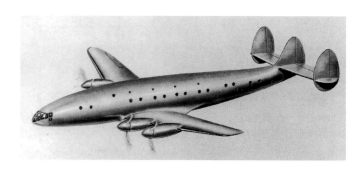

1939 conceptual drawing of what became the Constellation with Type I faired-nose cockpit windows. The final configuration used what was called Type VI single curvature conical cockpit windows. *Author collection*

Lockheed's desire to sell a more modern airliner to the Pan American Airways system specifically, as well as to any other interested airlines.

The Model 44 Excalibur was the first four-engine design from Lockheed and featured twin vertical tail/rudder assemblies. It later received three vertical tail/rudder assemblies and was renamed Excalibur A.

Pan Am was close to ordering the Excalibur A when the project was abandoned by Lockheed so that it could concentrate on its much-improved Model 049 Constellation for TWA, which had ordered it into production.

The Constellation program was created at the behest of William John "Jack" Frye and Howard Hughes for TWA, but the USAAF drafted it and designated it C-69. Frye was president of TWA, which had recently been acquired by Hughes.

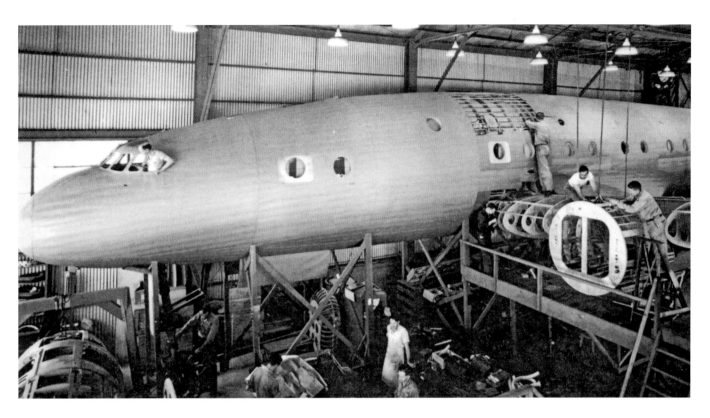

C-69 full-scale engineering mockup being assembled in Burbank. *Author collection*

The gorgeous Lockheed Model L-049 (Civil registration number NX25600) as it appeared on its January 9, 1943, first flight. Also shown in this historic photograph is the one-of-a-kind Vega Model 5C built as the USAAF UC-101 parked alongside (they're just fourteen years apart in development; take note of the giant leap in technology between the two types). *LM via Denny Lombard*

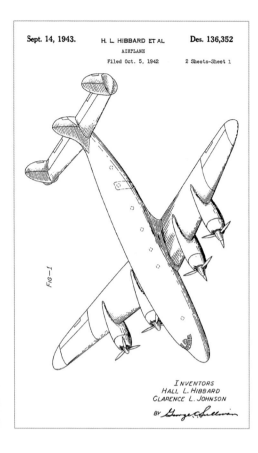

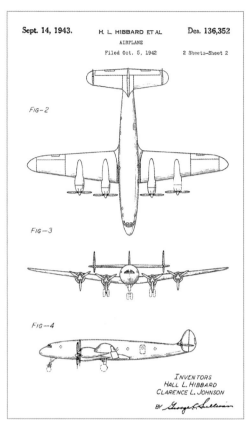

Below and right: Patent drawings and information of Constellation filed by Hibbard and Johnson on October 5, 1942—patent awarded on September 14, 1943. *United States Patent Office*

UNITED STATES PATENT OFFICE

136,352

DESIGN FOR AN AIRPLANE

Hall L. Hibbard, West Los Angeles, and Clarence L. Johnson, Encino, Calif., assignors to Lockheed Aircraft Corporation, Burbank, Calif.

Application October 5, 1942, Serial No. 108,433

Term of patent 14 years

To all whom it may concern:

Be it known that we, Hall L. Hibbard and Clarence L. Johnson, citizens of the United States, residing at West Los Angeles and Encino, respectively, both in the county of Los Angeles and State of California, have invented a new, original, and ornamental Design for an Airplane, of which the following is a specification, reference being had to the accompanying drawings, forming a part thereof.

Figure 1 of the drawings is a perspective view of an airplane embodying the new design as it would appear from a point off to the side and slightly forward and above the airplane while in flight with its main and nose landing wheels retracted:

Figure 2 is a plan view of the subject airplane;
Figure 3 is a front elevational view of the subject airplane;
Figure 4 is a side elevational view thereof.
The airplane of the present design is characterized by the fuselage having a downwardly turned nose and an upwardly turned tail portion as best illustrated by the perspective of Figure 1, and by the side elevational view in Figure 4.
We claim:
The ornamental design for an airplane, substantially as shown and described.

HALL L. HIBBARD.
CLARENCE L. JOHNSON.

In the interim, the Constellation was to serve as a military transport instead of a commercial airliner. On September 20, 1942, the War Department approved USAAF contract number W535 AC-32089, which covered the production of two prototype C-69-LO airplanes (USAAF serial numbers 43-10309 and 43-10310) and seven production C69-1-LO airplanes (43-10311 to 43-10317).

Since Boeing chief engineering test pilot Edmund T. "Eddie" Allen already had flying experience with the XB-29 powered by four of the same engines used by the Constellation, he was loaned to Lockheed for the C-69's first flight. And on January 9, 1943, the famed freelance test pilot completed a successful first flight, from Burbank to Muroc AAF. Several more test hops were flown that very day during which Lockheed chief engineering test pilot Milo Garrett Burcham familiarized himself with the airplane.

Lockheed chief flight test engineer Rudolf L. "Rudy" Thoren was also onboard. This airplane, civilian (civil) registration number NX25600, was an instant favorite of TWA and Hughes.

The Constellation—as the C-69, served well in World War II. After the war some of the C-69s were refitted to serve as airliners for TWA.

Eventually the Constitution morphed into numerous variants to serve all branches of the US military and a plethora of commercial airlines throughout the world.

C-69

SPECIFICATIONS

CREW: Four (pilot, copilot, flight engineer, navigator/radioman)

PROPULSIVE SYSTEM: Four 2,200-hp, 18-cylinder, Wright air-cooled R-3350-35 Cyclone radial engines

LENGTH: 95 ft 2 in

HEIGHT: 22 ft 5 in

WINGSPAN: 123 ft 0 in

EMPTY WEIGHT: 50,000 lbs

GROSS TAKEOFF WEIGHT: 72,000 lbs

MAXIMUM SPEED: 330 mph at 10,000 ft

MAXIMUM RANGE: 2,400 mi

SERVICE CEILING: 25,030 ft

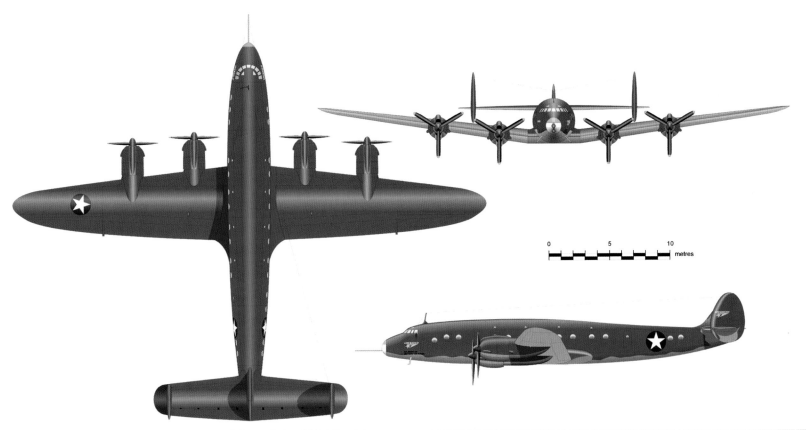

Above: The premier Lockheed C-69-LO Constellation (USAAF serial number 43-10309) in three-view. *Artwork by Giuseppe De Chiara*

Below: The first two C-69-LOs (43-10309/-10310). C-69 number one was retained by Lockheed for numerous tests and received the nickname *Beast of Burbank. Author collection*

The XB-30

The proposed XB-30—initially developed under USAAF AMC Secret Project MX-18, was closely based on the design of the Constellation. The Model L-249-58-01 (the final configuration of the XB-30) never progressed past the design stage, mainly because the Boeing Airplane Company had a huge lead with its XB-29 Superfortress (MX-17).

The XB-30 was to use four of the same Wright R-3350 Duplex-Cyclone radial engines as the Constellation. Only scale wind tunnel models of the XB-30 were ever built. Retaining the wings and tail surfaces of the Model L-049 Constellation, the XB-30 was to have had a slightly revised fuselage with five twin-gun turrets housing ten .50-caliber guns in each turret. The five twin-gun turrets would have been placed two above and two below the modified fuselage, with one more in the nose.

A single 20mm cannon was to be mounted in a tail turret. Two centerline bomb bays—one forward and one aft of the wing carry through structure—were to accommodate four 2,000-pound bombs each.

Above: XP-80 Lulu-Belle posed on Muroc Dry Lake following her first flights on January 8, 1944. *LM* Code One

Left: The one-off XP-80 being readied for her first flight. *USAF*

Shooting Star: The F-80

By early spring 1943 it was apparent that the Bell P-59 Airacomet fighter—America's first and then only turbojet-powered airplane—would never be suitable for combat. It was woefully underpowered and too unstable to be used as a gunnery platform in combat. Worse, during combat-type test maneuvers, it wasn't agile and it lost too much energy (speed) in climbs. A jet-powered fighter was desperately needed to combat jet-powered 500-mile-per-hour Messerschmitt Me-262s in Europe, and the 400-mile-per-hour P-59 wasn't it. Thus, a meeting between Lockheed representatives and the Engineering Division of the USAAF ATSC was scheduled for May 17.

Hibbard and Price represented Lockheed, and USAAF Brig. Gen. Franklin Otis Carroll, chief of the ATSC Engineering Division, chaired the meeting. Also in attendance were USAAF Cols. Howard Bogart, Ralph Swofford, and Marshall S. Roth, Lt. Col. Jack Carter (who had replaced Swofford), and Capt. Ezra Kotcher.

These preliminary discussions generated positive conclusions, and Lockheed was invited to present a fighter proposal based upon the use of a single British-designed de Havilland Halford H.1B Goblin turbojet engine. The Lockheed reps returned to Burbank with the basic H.1B Goblin engine specifications (length, diameter, dry weight, etc.) and immediately put their key personnel to work on what the USAAF AMC called Secret Project MX-409.

Just one month later, on June 17, the USAAF approved the TDN L-140 proposal that Lockheed had offered up in the interim. On June 24, Letter Contract W535 ac-40680 was issued to Lockheed. The one-off airplane was designated XP-80; Lockheed, of its own volition, had agreed to produce the airplane in a mere 180 days.

Earlier, under USAAF contract number W535 AC-26614, Bell was to produce a single XP-59B (Bell Model 29): an experimental fighter powered by a single turbojet engine under USAAF AMC Secret Project MX-398. It quickly became apparent that Bell wouldn't be able to produce its XP-59B in the time desired, so the USAAF canceled the MX-398 project.

This action left the door open for Lockheed, which had met the time frame desired by the USAAF. Thus, the XP-59B was out and Lockheed XP-80 was in.

But 180 days was a very demanding time limit. Gross, Hibbard, and Johnson knew that no company had ever designed and built a prototype airplane in less than a year, let alone in only six months. Moreover, a turbojet-powered airplane was a radical departure from contemporary piston-powered aircraft. Nevertheless, a contract is binding and it was time to move forward.

Gross made Hibbard the overseer of the project, as vice president and chief engineer, and Hibbard established what was called the XP-80 Experimental Group. He appointed XP-80 designer Johnson to the post of chief research engineer on the project. (Due to the secrecy of the XP-80 program, Johnson didn't file for his patent until June 5, 1944. He was issued his fourteen-year patent on February 12, 1946.)

To man the top secret XP-80 Experimental Group, Hibbard and Johnson robbed the best personnel they could find from within the corporation.

These included W. W. "Ward" Beman (aerodynamics and wind tunnel division engineer), E. Donald "Don" Palmer (assistant), Arthur M. "Art" Vierick (managing

The first XP-80A—nicknamed *Gray Ghost*—in flight over Muroc AAF, circa June 1944. *LM* Code One

Restored XP-80 as it appeared when it was donated by Lockheed to the National Air and Space Museum. *LM* Code One

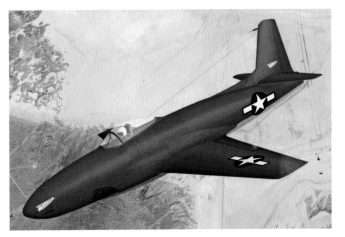

Depiction of *Lulu-Belle* on her second test flight over Muroc AAF on January 8, 1944. *Artwork by Luca Landino*

engineer experimental department/phones), Rudy Thoren (flight test division engineer), William P. "Bill" Ralston (assistant), and Lawrence F. "Larry" Holt (assistant/backup for Vierick).

After this initial group was formed, Johnson hand-picked a number of other aeronautical engineers and draftsmen and gathered 105 airframe and powerplant mechanics, fabricators, and machinists for the job at hand. There's no record of names and duties for these 105 shop

workers, unfortunately, but the names of the engineers and their respective duties are: Walter L. "Wally" Bison (material), Richard H. "Dick" Boehme (fuselage), Arthur "Art" Bradley (hydraulics), Gordon F. Brown (cockpit layout and flight controls), Irven H. "Irv" Culver (fuselage), Henry C. Danielson (wing contours), Edward "Ed" Fife (balance and weights), Willy Hawkins (detail design), David C. "Dave" Hill (landing gear and stress analysis), Richard L. "Bob" Holland (loft-lead draftsman), John A. "Johnny"

Johnson (balancing loads/stress analysis), J. F. "Fred" Kerr (business management), Phillip W. "Phil" McLane (cockpit layout and flight controls), Virgil D. Moss (balancing loads/stress analysis), Joseph "Joe" Newcomer (aft fuselage and tail group), Edward "Ed" Posner (aerodynamic loads/stress analysis), William P. "Bill" Ralston (assistant project engineer), Henry M. Rempt (radio equipment, electrical wiring and power), Charles C. "Charlie" Sowle (wing), Wavey M. Stearman (propulsive system), Joseph "Joe" Szep (aft fuselage and tail group), and A. J. "Al" York (aerodynamic loads/stress analysis). Several additional engineers—Harold L. Benson, Harold R. Bojens, Leonard J. "Len" Bohacek, Gerald W. "Gerry" Gossett, Julius A. "Juge" Jaeger, and R. L. Kirkham—joined soon after.

Controls were fabricated, drawings were drawn, fuel and hydraulic lines were plumbed, aluminum alloy was cut and bent, cables were run, holes were drilled, fasteners were fastened, wiring was bundled, parts were test fit and joined, rivets were bucked, and the airplane was assembled and painted. On October 16, 1943, USAAF contract number W535 AC-40680—which superseded the June 24, 1943, Letter Contract—was approved by the US War Department. It was time to line up a test pilot for the project. And at this time in aviation history, jet airplane pilots were few and far between.

Hired by Lockheed in 1939 as an experimental test pilot, Milo Burcham had by mid-1941 worked his way up to become chief engineering test pilot. He was first choice to be chief test pilot on the XP-80 program. To prepare for this, he spent uncounted hours familiarizing himself with the XP-80 prior to its first flight. He also flew a prototype Bell YP-59A several times in late 1943 at Muroc AAF to acclimate himself to flight with turbojet propulsion.

In early November 1943, *Lulu-Belle* (as the XP-80 had been nicknamed, after a seductive songstress featured in a 1926 play) was removed from its assembly area during the night and secretly trucked to the North Base area of Muroc AAF. On day 139, November 12, 1943, the British Goblin turbojet engine roared to life. On day 143, November 15, 1943, the airplane was accepted by the USAAF as ready for flight. Everything had gone well—too well.

During late evening on the 15th, de Havilland engine expert Guy Bristow gave the H.1B Goblin a final run-up prior to the scheduled flight the next morning. As the engine roared at full power, the engine air intake ducts on both sides of the fuselage sucked inward and collapsed. Before Bristow could shut down the engine, pieces of ducting metal were sucked into the Goblin's maw. A terrible grinding noise preceded engine stop. The damage

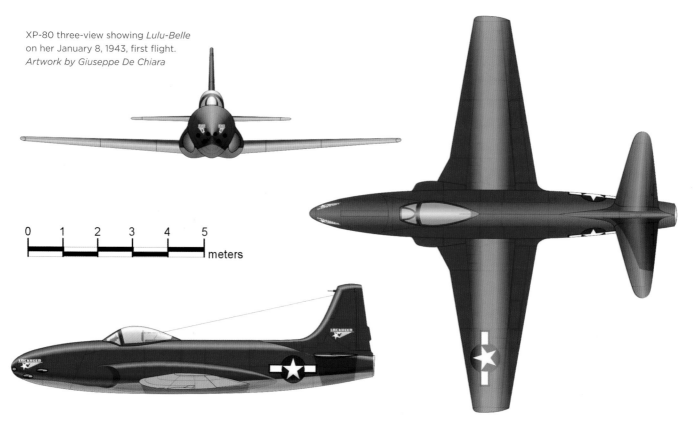

XP-80 three-view showing *Lulu-Belle* on her January 8, 1943, first flight.
Artwork by Giuseppe De Chiara

0 1 2 3 4 5
meters

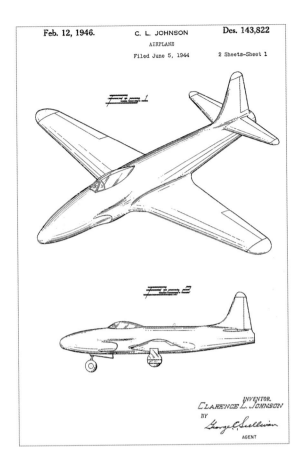

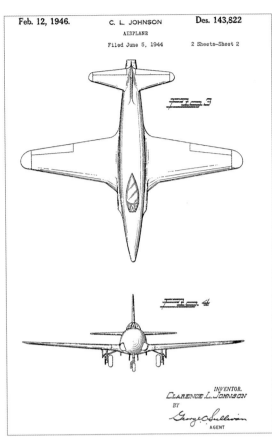

to this rare engine was not repairable, and therefore a replacement engine would have to be delivered from Great Britain before *Lulu-Belle* could fly.

Engine air intake ducting repaired, a new Goblin engine was installed and tested. The XP-80 was now scheduled to fly during the early morning of January 8, 1944, fifty-four days later than originally scheduled.

Just before takeoff, Johnson gave Burcham a last-minute pep talk: "Just fly her, Milo. Find out if she's a lady or a witch. And if you have any trouble at all, bring her back. She's all yours from here. Treat her nice."

Lulu-Belle took off. Burcham initiated a climbing turn during which the wings began to wobble. He immediately nosed her down, came around, and landed on the dry lakebed. After Burcham landed, Johnson asked him, "What's the trouble?" "Overcautious, maybe," Burcham answered. "She felt funny on the ailerons. Pretty touchy." "You've got fifteen-to-one boost and a hot ship that's naturally sensitive—maybe you were overcontrolling," Johnson said. "Could be," Burcham agreed.

Lulu-Belle's engine was restarted, and Burcham lifted off again. This time she climbed straight as an arrow. He made one low pass across the base before climbing up and out of sight. Burcham then came down from high altitude so fast that no one knew he was approaching until he passed overhead and the roar of the Goblin engine was heard. Burcham then came back across the field doing full aileron rolls before landing. Immediately after the flight Burcham said, "You don't fly this airplane—you just hint to it where you want it to go. And it really goes."

At the end of the day, *Lulu-Belle* had flown twice and performed quite well for her first timid outings. The attendees were enthralled with her potential, and even though her maiden flight was a few months late, she had more than made up for lost time.

The handful of USAAF officers in attendance at the XP-80 demonstration flight were both surprised and delighted. They let it be known just how badly they wanted production P-80s—and how very soon.

The de Havilland H.1 Goblin engines, to be manufactured under license in the United States by the Allis-Chalmers Corporation as the J36, would not be available in quantity anytime soon, however. This, of course, posed a serious problem for the USAAF and Lockheed. An answer to this dilemma was at hand though.

27

General Electric had speeded up development and production on its new Model I-40 or J33 centrifugal-flow turbojet engine. It was a larger engine than the Goblin and offered nearly 1,300 pound-foot more power, but it would require a larger and almost new XP-80 airframe to accommodate it. The USAAF asked Lockheed—Kelly Johnson in particular—if it could be done without a great deal of difficulty. "Can do," Johnson replied.

Thus P-80 airframes were enlarged to accommodate the General Electric J33 turbojet engines, and due to their airframe redesign and their new propulsive systems, they were assigned TDN L-141 and then redesignated XP-80A: same contract, amended.

SUMMARY

The XP-80 was later assigned to the 412th Fighter Group for extensive evaluations. The 412th returned it to Muroc AAF, from where it was sent to the Air Training Command (ATC) at Chanute AAF, Illinois.

On November 8, 1946, the one-off XP-80 was donated to the Smithsonian Institution. It was placed in storage in its Silver Hill facility until its restoration by Lockheed in 1978. Today, America's second jet airplane is on permanent display inside the National Air and Space Museum in Washington, DC.

XP-80A

The XP-80A program was launched under MX-409-A, an extension of MX-409 (the XP-80). Two experimental XP-80A airplanes were ordered on amended USAAF contract number W535 AC-40680.

Incredibly, Johnson and his group of engineers and mechanics produced the first XP-80A in just 132 days! It was flown on day 139, June 10, 1944, when Anthony William "Tony" LeVier made a successful first flight on XP-80A number one at Muroc AAF. Because the plane's all-gray livery seemed to vanish against the sky, it was dubbed *Gray Ghost*.

Although it was nearly a ton heavier, *Gray Ghost* was an even more impressive performer than *Lulu-Belle*. This was owed in part, of course, to the increase in power. Where the Goblin put out 2,460 pound-foot, the J33 produced 3,750 pound-foot.

LeVier had joined Lockheed in 1941, first as a ferry pilot and then as an experimental test pilot who performed a great many of the compressibility dive tests and spin tests on P-38s. He had checked out on the XP-80 and quickly showed how he could manhandle any type of aircraft and accurately report any and all of its abilities or inabilities. Johnson came to heavily rely on LeVier's post-flight reports.

This writer asked LeVier if there was a major difference between the Goblin-powered XP-80 airplane and the J33-powered XP-80A aircraft. LeVier responded,

The XP-80A was substantially better than the XP-80 because it had at least 1,500 pound-foot more power after the J33 was developed. That amount of additional power probably doubled the excess engine thrust, which of course really makes a plane perform. The speed increase was about 60 miles per hour, and the rate of climb was increased about 50 percent. The XP-80A was heavier the XP-80 by almost two thousand pounds, as I remember. The plane was larger, held more fuel, had wingtip fuel tanks, and could carry all sorts of armament. The XP-80 did 500 per hour, and the XP-80A was 60 to 80 miles per hour faster than that before it was through testing.

As a matter of interest, recently appointed Lockheed engineering test pilot James F. "Jim" White had made two demonstration flights on the XP-80 that very same day—one before and one after LeVier's XP-80A test flight. He first checked out on the XP-80 on May 24, 1944, and he became heavily involved in the XP-80, XP-80A, and subsequent YP-80A flight test programs.

LeVier successfully piloted XP-80A number two—dubbed *Silver Ghost*, on August 1, 1944. It was clad in polished aluminum. Thus, its name.

XP-80A number two came with a seat behind the pilot's seat for a flight test engineer or a VIP to ride along. It later became an engine testbed for the axial-flow Westinghouse Electric Model 24C or J34 turbojet engine.

Bad luck came to LeVier on March 20, 1945, when he was flight testing the *Gray Ghost* during ongoing ATSC flight test operations. He suffered a structural failure due to an engine fire and was forced to bail out. He parachuted safely to the ground. The impact site of the number-one XP-80A was 6 miles southeast of Rosamond, California. It had been assigned to the USAAF 4144 BU at Muroc AAF at the time.

XP-80A number two had to make a forced landing just after its rotation due to an engine fire on July 9, 1945, at Muroc AAF. It was assigned to the USAAF 412th Fighter

A crew of technicians and pilots rests on the wing of the XP-80A. *NMUSAF*

XP-80A

SPECIFICATIONS

CREW: One (pilot)

PROPULSIVE SYSTEM: One non-afterburning, centrifugal-flow 3,825-lbf General Electric XJ33-GE-7 turbojet engine

LENGTH: 34 ft 6 in

HEIGHT: 11 ft 4 in

WINGSPAN: 38 ft 10 in

EMPTY WEIGHT: 7,225 lbs

MAXIMUM TAKEOFF WEIGHT: 13,780 lbs

MAXIMUM SPEED: 553 mph at 5,700 ft

COMBAT CEILING: 48,500 ft

MAXIMUM RANGE: 1,200 mi

ARMAMENT: Six nose-mounted, .50-caliber Colt-Browning M2 heavy machine guns

PAYLOAD: None

Group, 445th Fighter Squadron at the time, and it was being piloted by USAAF 2nd Lt. Harry Clark Higgins. There were no significant damages to the *Silver Ghost*, and it was returned to flight duties shortly thereafter.

Unfortunately, neither the *Gray Ghost* nor the *Silver Ghost* survived: both were scrapped. The *Gray Ghost* is depicted by a modified early production P-80A, however, and is on display outside the headquarters building of the Skunk Works in Palmdale, California.

YP-80A

The YP-80A—Lockheed Model 080, was developed under USAAF AMC Secret Project MX-409-B and was the immediate follow-on to the XP-80 and XP-80A programs. Thirteen YP-80As were ordered under USAAF contract number W535 AC-2393, which was approved on July 1, 1944 (USAAF serial numbers 44-83023 to 44-83035). Of the thirteen YP-80As ordered, twelve were completed as such, while number two was finished as the one of XF-14 discussed later.

29

The first YP-80A (44-83023) was initially flight tested on September 13, 1944, at Wright Field. It had been completed early on July 1, 1944, and then trucked from Burbank to Wright Field for static tests. After its static testing and several additional test flights at Wright Field, it was ferried back to Burbank, where it was specially instrumented and turned over to the National Advisory Committee for Aeronautics (NACA) Ames Aeronautical Laboratory at Moffett Field in Santa Clara, California, south of San Francisco, for high-speed dive tests. On January 13, 1945, during a NACA test at Muroc AAF, pilot Lawrence A. Clousing crash-landed it on Muroc Dry Lake.

The YP-80A airplanes were closely related to the XP-80A airplanes and used the same propulsive system. They were extensively used for service test and armament trials.

YP-80A number three (44-83025) crashed immediately after a takeoff from Lockheed Air Terminal at Burbank on October 20, 1944, killing Milo Burcham. It was assigned to USAAF ATSC 4035 Base Unit at that time.

Four YP-80As were sent abroad: two to England (44-83026 and 44-83027) and two to the Mediterranean (44-83028 and 44-83029). Of the two sent to England, 44-83026 was fitted with a prototype Rolls-Royce Nene (Model B.41) for flight trials. It crashed to destruction at Bold near Widnes during its second flight out of Burtonwood, England, with the Nene engine, killing its test pilot, Maj. Frederic A. Borsodi. While still in the European Theater of Operations (ETO), the other YP-80A (44-83027) suffered an engine failure on November 14, 1945, and was destroyed in the crash.

Of the two YP-80As that went to the Mediterranean—Italy, in fact, during Operation Extraversion—both flew operational sorties but never encountered enemy aircraft. Both were shipped back to the United States, and one of them (44-83029) was lost in a crash on August 2, 1945, some 2 miles southeast of Brandenburg, Kentucky, killing its pilot, Ira B. Jones III. The other Mediterranean Theater of Operations (MTO) veteran (44-83028) was modified and served as a pilotless drone.

One YP-80A (44-83032), assigned to USAAF ATSC 4144 AAF Base Unit at Muroc AAF, was involved in two mishaps. On March 4, 1945, pilot Donald C. Craig was forced to make a gear-up belly landing 6 miles south of the base due to engine failure. Then, on November 4, 1945, pilot Charles F. Hale also had to make a gear-up belly landing on Muroc Dry Lake due to a fuel system malfunction and engine flameout.

XF-14 (XFP-80)

The one-of-a-kind Lockheed XF-14-LO (Model 080) was a modified YP-80A (number two, USAAF serial number 44-83024) produced as an unarmed experimental photographic reconnaissance and mapping airplane. The XF-14 was manufactured under USAAF contract number W535 AC-2393, approved on July 1, 1944.

After its first flight at Burbank and USAAF acceptance, it was flown to Muroc AAF, where it was assigned to ATSC 4144 AAF Base Unit for its series of evaluations.

On December 6, 1944, it was involved in a nighttime midair collision with a B-25J Mitchell (USAAF serial number 44-29120) some 7 miles south southwest of Randsburg, California. Lockheed test pilot Perry Earnest "Ernie" Claypool Jr. and the four-man crew on the B-25J were all killed. If the XF-14 had survived, it would have been redesignated XFP-80. No other XF-14 (XFP-80) airplanes were built to replace this airplane.

SUMMARY

From the lone XP-80, two experimental XP-80As, thirteen prototype YP-80As, and a one-off XF-14 (XFP-80) sprang forth.

The successes of these aircraft led to the production of several operational variants of the Shooting Star. These included the P-80A, FP-80A, P-80B, and P-80C.

After June 10, 1948, the *P* for "pursuit" prefix became *F* for "fighter," *FP* became *RF* for "reconnaissance fighter," *TP* became *T* for "trainer." Thus, the P-80A, FP-80A, P-80B, and P-80C became F-80A, RF-80A, F-80B, and F-80C respectively. A reconnaissance version of the F-80C was put into service as the RF-80C. And of course the trainer version of the F-80C became the T-33.

Additional versions of the F-80 were designed and proposed to the USAF, but they were not proceeded with due to several fighter aircraft being produced by other airframe contractors that were more applicable.

One such offering was the F-80D in July 1948, Model 680-33-07. It was based upon the F-80C, but faster, with improved instrumentation and a more efficient cockpit layout, and it was to use an afterburning 7,500-pound-foot (with afterburning) Allison J33-A-29 turbojet engine for its propulsive system.

Another design of late 1948 was the F-80E, featuring 35-degree sweptback wings and horizontal tail planes; it was to retain its straight vertical tail. Designed under TDN L-181-1, it was also based upon the F-80C and was to

Above: The F-80 Shooting Star splits the sky. *LM*

be powered by an afterburning 6,500-pound-foot (with afterburning) Allison J33-A-27 turbojet engine to give it a maximum level flight speed of 662-mile-per-hour at sea level.

The F-80 Shooting Star series of fighters, fighter-bombers, and reconnaissance fighters were the first operational turbojet-powered aircraft to serve in these specific roles. And they were all the offspring of *Lulu-Belle*.

Chain Lightning: The XP-58

There were numerous derivatives of the P-38 Lightning, with the subsequent emergence of several major spinoff aircraft. The first of these spin-off types was the one-off XP-49 (TDN L-106, Model 522) that first took wing on November 14, 1942, with Lockheed experimental test pilot Joe Towle at its controls.

Both designs were invented and patented by Hibbard and Johnson. As codesigners of the XP-58, they applied for its patent on October 1, 1943, and a fourteen-year patent was granted on February 12, 1946—nearly four months before the type's first flight on June 6, 1944.

Chief Engineering Test Pilot Tony LeVier with a later version of the *Shooting Star*, a P-80A-1-LO. *NMUSAF*

The one-off XP-58 Chain Lightning (USAAF serial number 41-2670) at Burbank circa summer 1946. *NMUSAF*

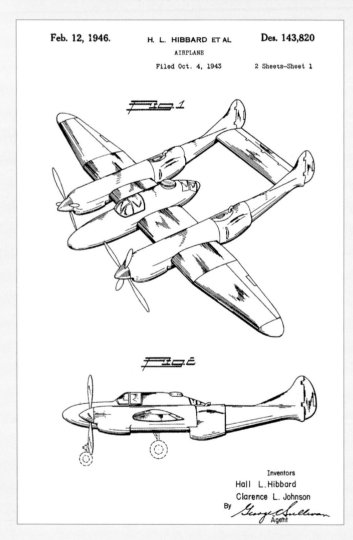

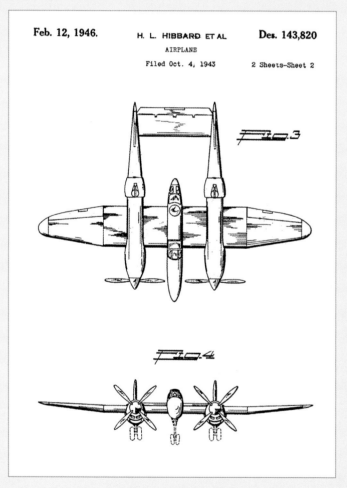

Above left: Page 1 of XP-58 patent application filed on October 4, 1943, by co-inventors Hall Hibbard and Kelly Johnson. They received a fourteen-year patent on February 12, 1946. *United States Patent Office*

Above right: Page 2 of patent.

Extremely rare color view of the XP-58 on an early test hop. *Lockheed Martin, Stephane Beaumort Collection*

Technicians prepare to see what the P80 captured after removing its nose camera.

Saturn: The Model 75

World War II ended the delivery of civilian airliners to the commercial airlines. Airliners continued to be produced, however, to fill the high demand for military transports. Lockheed's own Constellation is a prime example of this, as it was drafted by the USAAF and went to war as the C-69 troop transport.

After the war, the commercial airline market took off again and most airframe contractors clamored for production contracts. Lockheed was no different.

The Constellation became a popular airliner as it began to acquaint itself with civilian passengers. But even with the success of the Connie, Lockheed was interested in marketing to the smaller feeder airlines as well. Feeder airlines fly less distant routes between major hubs to bring passengers to them for transfer.

Don Palmer—who had been a key player in the XP-80 program, was put in charge of the Saturn program as chief engineer. Flying out of Burbank, chief engineering test pilot Tony LeVier successfully completed the first flight on the first of two Saturn prototypes on June 17, 1946.

Beautiful color study of a Saturn in its element, circa 1946. *LM* Code One

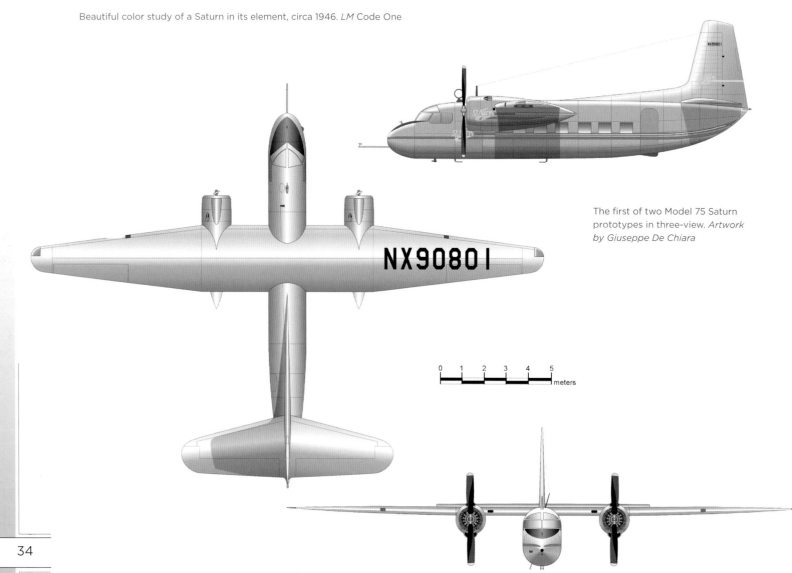

The first of two Model 75 Saturn prototypes in three-view. *Artwork by Giuseppe De Chiara*

NX90801

0 1 2 3 4 5 meters

Lockheed had received provisional orders for 500 Saturn aircraft priced at $85,000 each—more than enough to launch a production program. However, before a production line had been set up, their individual cost rose by $15,000. The customers balked at $100,000 each and opted to buy surplus Douglas C-47s instead.

SUMMARY

The Model 75 Saturn program proved to be a failure that lost money for Lockheed as the glut of war-surplus Curtiss C-46 Commandos and Douglas C-47 Skytrains were gobbled up at relatively low cost. Not until the late 1950s and early 1960s would a new-build, feeder-type airliner be put into service. These included several foreign-built types and Lockheed's own turbopropjet-powered L-188 Electra.

Unfortunately, neither example of the Saturn survived, as they were both salvaged in 1948.

Constitution: The XR6V

The Lockheed Constitution began life in 1942 as a joint study by the USN, Pan American Airways, and Lockheed. The design requirements called for a large transport aircraft to improve upon the USN's fleet of flying boats. Pan Am was involved in the study because such an aircraft had potential use as a commercial airliner.

This very large transport was to carry up to 17,500 pounds of cargo 5,000 miles at a cruising altitude of 25,000 feet and a speed of 300 miles per hour. The aircraft would be fully pressurized and large enough so that most major components could be accessed and possibly repaired in flight. For instance, tunnels led through the thick wings to all four engines.

The aircraft—Lockheed Model 89—was designed by a team of Skunk Works engineers led by Willy Hawkins and Wilfred A. "Dick" Pulver of Lockheed and Cmdr. E. L. Simpson Jr. of the navy. The name *Constitution* was given to the project by Lockheed president Bob Gross.

The Constitution design had a "double bubble" fuselage, the cross-section of which was a figure eight. This unorthodox design, originally created in 1937 by Curtiss-Wright's chief aircraft designer George A. Page Jr. and first introduced with the Curtiss C-46 Commando, utilized the structural advantages of a cylinder for cabin pressurization, without the wasted

Test pilot Joe Towle (bottom) and copilot Tony LeVier preparing for the first flight test on the number-one XR6O-1. *USN*

space that would result from a single large cylinder of the same volume.

The original contract from the Bureau of Aeronautics called for fifty production R6O Constitutions for a total price tag of $111,250,000. On V-J Day, however, the contract was scaled back to $27,000,000 for only two experimental aircraft.

35

Above: Beautiful color study of the number one XR6O-1 on its first flight. *LM Code One*

Below left: Page 1 of patent drawings and information on Constitution filed by Hibbard and Johnson on November 26, 1943—patent awarded on April 10, 1945. *United States Patent Office*

Below right: Page 2 of patent.

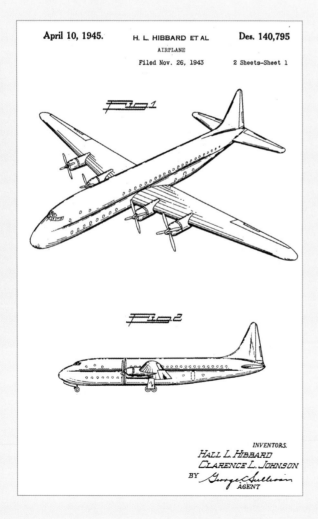

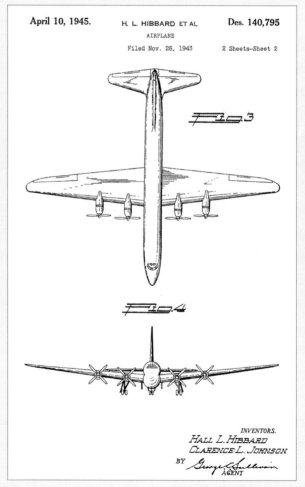

Jet-assisted takeoff (JATO) launch of XR6O-1. *USN*

XR6V-1

SPECIFICATIONS

CREW: Twelve (pilot, copilot, flight engineer, navigator, radioman, and seven attendants)

PROPULSIVE SYSTEM: Four 3,000-hp Pratt & Whitney R-4360-25 Wasp Major radial air-cooled piston engines

LENGTH: 156 ft 1 in

HEIGHT: 50 ft 4.5 in

WINGSPAN: 189 ft 1 in

WING AREA: 3,610 sq ft

EMPTY WEIGHT: 113,780 lbs

GROSS WEIGHT: 184,000 lbs

MAXIMUM SPEED: 300 mph

MAXIMUM RANGE: 5,390 mi

SERVICE CEILING: 28,600 ft

PAYLOAD: 17,500 lbs of cargo

CAPACITY: 169 passengers

Both Constitution airplanes together. *USN*

The first flight on the first XR6O-1 was successful on November 9, 1946. It was piloted by Lockheed test pilot Joe Towle, copiloted by Lockheed test pilot Tony LeVier.

The number-two Constitution made its first flight on June 9, 1948. By this time the Constitution had been redesignated from XR6O-1 to XR6V-1 when the *O* suffix for USN Lockheed aircraft was changed to the suffix *V* for USN Lockheed aircraft.

SUMMARY

The Constitution proved to be underpowered for the weight it was expected to carry, and the program was

37

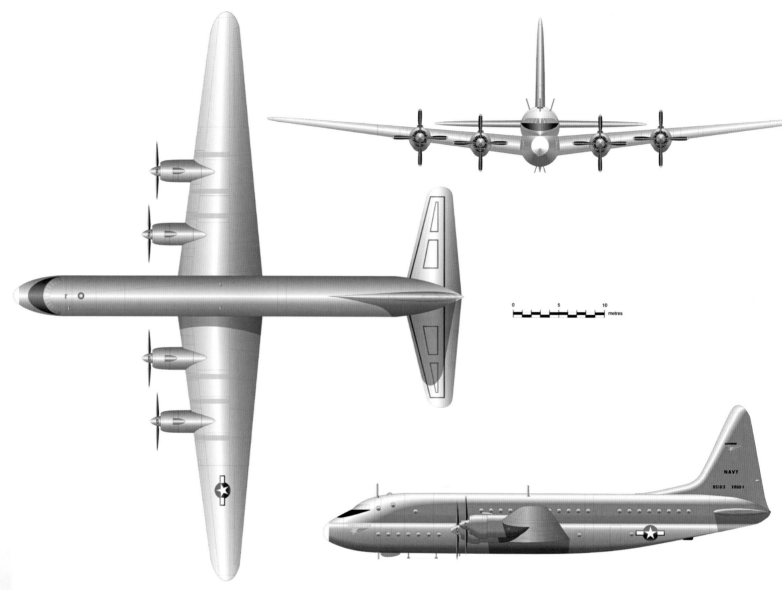

First of two experimental XR6O-1 airplanes in three-view.
Artwork by Giuseppe De Chiara

terminated in 1949. In 1953 the aircraft and thirteen spare engines were offered to US airlines, but none purchased them. Both examples were ultimately scrapped.

Racey: The P-80R

What do get when you modify the one-of-a-kind XP-80B into a dedicated world speed record–setting airplane? The one-off P-80R nicknamed *Racey*, of course.

In 1945, under USAAF contract number W535 AC-2527, Lockheed was authorized to modify its eighty-first production P-80A (a P-80A-11-LO to be specific) airplane into the one-off XP-80B (USAAF serial number 44-85200). The

XP-80B was almost identical to the P-80A but featured a thinner wing to help improve performance. Following its flight test program, it was parked at Lockheed's facility in Burbank.

USAAF commander Gen. Henry H. "Hap" Arnold got a bug to bring the world speed record back to the United States. He therefore prompted Wright Field to set up such a program. Wright Field contacted Lockheed and suggested it modify the XP-80B for this program.

To establish an official world speed record under Fédération Aéronautique Internationale rules the airplane involved had to fly at low "on the deck" altitude (under 100 feet) over a measured 3-kilometer course

The one-off P-80R *Racey* posed on the ramp for this freeze-frame at Muroc AAF in late 1946. It is shown with its original NACA flush-type engine air inlet design. *LM* Code One

The P-80R right after it had established the new world speed record of 623-plus miles per hour on June 23, 1947. Two of the ground personnel are removing the modified low-drag cockpit canopy so that Muroc AAF commander and pilot Col. Albert "Al" Boyd can exit the airplane. Its performance was lackluster with the NACA air inlet system, and its air inlet system was further modified. *LM* Code One

THE 1940S: FORMING THE WINGS TO COME

Above: The P-80R is shown here in its final configuration while taxiing at Muroc AAF in early 1947 with Tony LeVier at its controls. Note revised engine air inlet system. *NMUSAF*

Left: The *USAF* donated the P-80R to the National Museum of the *USAF*, and it was restored by its staff for permanent display. *NMUSAF*

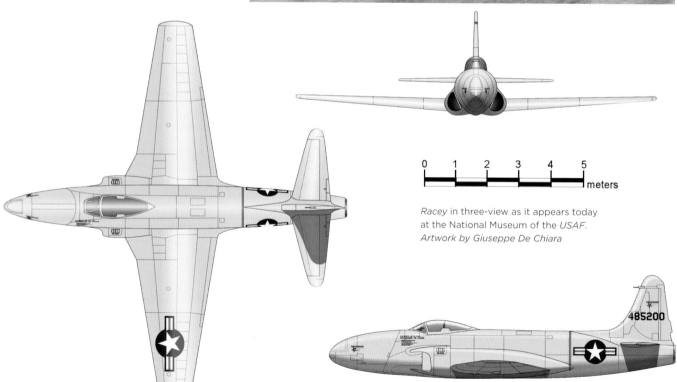

Racey in three-view as it appears today at the National Museum of the *USAF*. *Artwork by Giuseppe De Chiara*

Colonel Al Boyd posed by *Racey* following his record-setting performance. *NMUSAF*

four times to produce its average speed. And of course that average speed had to exceed the previous average speed that had been established by the current world speed record–holding airplane.

The world speed record for turbojet-powered aircraft at that time was 991.000 kilometers per hour or 615.778 miles per hour, held by RAF Group Capt. Edward M. Donaldson of Great Britain. He flew a modified Gloster F.4 Meteor, and his record was established on September 7, 1946.

In the meantime, the one-off XP-80B-LO was modified in Burbank. The modifications included the fabrication of NACA flush-type engine air inlets and the installation of a smaller, low-profile, low-drag cockpit canopy. A standard centrifugal-flow, 3,825-pound-foot General Electric-designed, Allison-built J33-A-17 turbojet engine was used as its propulsive system. The P-80 named *Racey* was born.

An attempt to break the world speed record was made in earnest in October 1946, but *Racey* barely averaged 600 miles per hour, which of course was too slow. The NACA air inlets and the inadequate power from the engine were to blame. The airplane was returned to Burbank for additional work. The engine was replaced by a modified (water/methanol alcohol-injected) centrifugal-flow, 5,400-pound-foot Allison J33-A-35 (Model 400-C13) turbojet engine.

The new *Racey* appeared in late 1946. It now featured cheek-type engine air inlets similar to standard P-80 inlets but with larger area openings to provide more air for the engine.

The weather conditions were right on the morning of June 19, 1947. The P-80R was readied by its ground crew, after which Col. Albert G. "Al" Boyd, the commander of Muroc AAF, climbed aboard and fired it up. The goal was to average any speed higher than 615.80 miles per hour—the more the better. Boyd taxied out and took off.

The measured course was situated about dead center on Muroc Lake. There were synchronized cameras and timers at each end of the 3-kilometer course. Col. Boyd averaged 1,003.810 kilometers per hour, or 623.738 miles per hour. It was a modest 8-mile-per-hour increase in average speed, but it was an official world speed record nonetheless—the first time in many years that the United States had held a world speed record.

The P-80R named *Racey* had succeeded.

SUMMARY

The 623.738-mile-per-hour world speed record established by the P-80R was thrilling but short-lived, as a USN Douglas D-558-1 Skystreak research airplane piloted by Cmdr. Turner F. Caldwell Jr. exceeded it by some 17 miles per hour on August 20, 1947, when it hit 640.66 miles per hour flying over the very same 3-kilometer course at Muroc AAF.

The P-80R *Racey* was a significant addition to aviation history. It was later donated the National Museum of the United States Air Force, where it can be seen today.

T-Bird: The T-33

When a proper airframe and powerplant combination comes along, it lends itself to many derivations. This was the case of the Shooting Star airframe and powerplant marriage, for it evolved into numerous other offspring. One such offshoot was the T-33A, affectionately nicknamed T-Bird.

The T-33A T-Bird began life as the tandem-seat pilot training and transition TP-80C variant that was designed

41

The original two-seat TP-80C-1-LO (48-356) was created in part from a P-80C-1-LO by inserting a 12-inch plug just behind its wing and a 29-inch plug just in front of its wing. It made its first flight on March 22, 1948. *NMUSAF*

TP-80C

SPECIFICATIONS

CREW: Two (student pilot and instructor pilot)

PROPULSIVE SYSTEM: One non-afterburning, centrifugal-flow, 5,400-lbf Allison J33-A-23 (Model 400-C5) turbojet engine

LENGTH: 36 ft 7 in

HEIGHT: 11 ft 3 in

WINGSPAN: 38 ft 9 in

The original prototype TP-80C parked next to a P-80C—the type from which it came. *USAF*

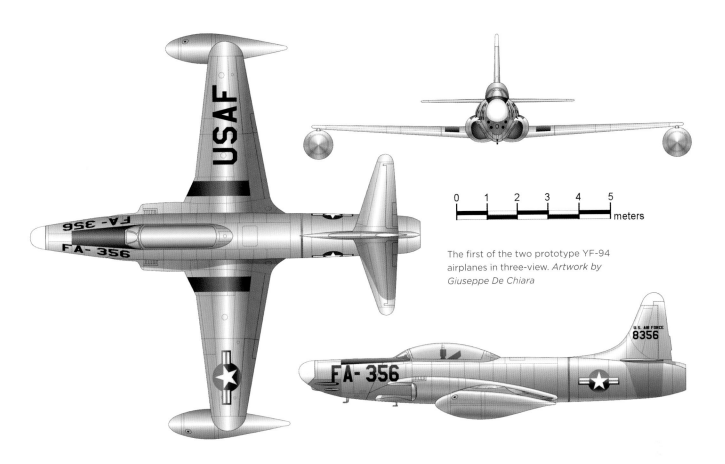

The first of the two prototype YF-94 airplanes in three-view. *Artwork by Giuseppe De Chiara*

Pilot Tony LeVier and flight test engineer Glenn Fulkerson discuss their first flight with crew chief. On June 11, 1948, the TP-80C was redesignated TF-80C; on May 5, 1949, the TF-80C was redesignated T-33A. *NMUSAF*

Secret Project MX-843

Marquardt Aircraft in Venice, California (later the Marquardt Corporation in Van Nuys, California), was a big developer of ramjet engines in the United States through the 1940s and into the late 1960s, and several different types of aircraft were pressed into service to help test them while they were in flight. Marquardt built these in varying diameters: 20-inch, 30-inch, and 48-inch.

One such aircraft was a specially prepared P-80A-1-LO (44-85214) that was evaluated under USAF AMC Secret Project MX-843 in 1948 with wingtip-mounted, 30-inch-diameter ramjets.

An air-breathing ramjet engine won't produce thrust until it reaches a speed of at least 600 miles per hour, at which the air being rammed into it is fast enough for ignition and propulsion.

The knowledge gleaned from these experimental flight tests later played a big part in the development of the ramjet engines and derivative ramjet engines that propelled the Lockheed Skunk Works–engineered X-7A/X-7A-1 "Flying Stovepipe," D-21/D-21B stealth drones, and the Blackbird series of aircraft to be discussed later.

and engineered in the Skunk Works. Twenty TP-80C-1-LO airplanes were ordered and built, and the first two examples were used primarily as demonstration aircraft during USAF service testing.

The first TP-80C made its first flight on March 22, 1948, with LeVier at the controls. Lockheed flight test engineer Glenn Fulkerson was seated behind him.

SUMMARY

The TP-80C was the first dedicated turbojet-powered pilot trainer and transition airplane in air-force service.

Starfire: The F-94

The Lockheed Aircraft Corporation F-94 series of aircraft were built to serve as nighttime (all-weather) fighter-interceptors. With the failure of the F-87 Blackhawk and the delay with the F-89 Scorpion, the USAF became hard-pressed to fill its immediate need for all-weather fighter-interceptors. Since the Lockheed T-33A (TF-80C until May 5, 1949) was already in production, and it was a two-seater with adequate room for the required electronic equipment and weapons, it became a natural choice for a stopgap measure.

YF-94 (ETF-80C, ET-33A)

Two two-place, tandem-seat TF-80C airplanes (USAF serial numbers 48-356 and 48-357) were used as the service test aircraft for the F-94 program. The first of these (48-356) was initially flight tested on April 16, 1949, by LeVier with Fulkerson in the back seat.

These TF-80C airplanes, as service test F-94s, were initially designated ETF-80C. After the TF-80C was redesignated T-33A, they became ET-33As. They were never officially designated YF-94 but are recognized as such.

YF-94A

On July 1, 1949, the first production F-94A made its first flight out of Burbank. Like the prototype YF-94s, the F-94A was the first to enter service (December 1949).

YF-94B

The second production F-94A-5-LO (USAF serial number 49-2497) was selected to serve as the service test YF-94B under USAF contract number AF-1847, which was approved on August 26, 1949.

YF-94C (YF-97A)

A single YF-94C (formerly YF-97A) was ordered on USAF contract number AF-11205, approved on July 21, 1950 (USAF serial number 50-955). It was created from the last production F-94B-1-LO.

LeVier made a successful first flight on the YF-97A on January 18, 1950, at Edwards AFB. Its designation was changed to YF-94C on September 12, 1950. The F-94C was the first version of the F-94 to bear the name *Starfire* on an official basis.

YF-94D

The F-94D was to be a dedicated fighter-bomber version of the F-94C fighter-interceptor with tremendous firepower for ground target strafing. The proposed F-94D featured an eight-gun nose fitted with eight .50-caliber machine guns. The F-94D program was terminated, however, before any orders were received. Two demonstrators

were created with scabbed-on F-94D type nose sections from modified F-94B-5-LOs (51-5500 and 51-5501). A dedicated prototype YF-94D (51-13604) was nearly complete when the program was cancelled on October 15, 1951.

SUMMARY

The F-94 Starfire series of aircraft worked in unison with the F-89 Scorpion series until the advent of dedicated all-weather, all-missile- and/or all-rocket-armed interceptor aircraft.

It is a rare occasion indeed when a powerplant and airframe combination is so good that it lends itself to the creation of several other aircraft. This was certainly the case of the Shooting Star, which evolved into no fewer than three other versions, with as many different missions. These included the T-33 T-Bird, T2V SeaStar, and the F-94 Starfire.

As previously discussed, after Lockheed had successfully sold its two-seat pilot trainer and transition concept to the USAF as a turbojet-powered advanced trainer in

YF-94

SPECIFICATIONS

CREW: Two (pilot, flight test engineer)

PROPULSIVE SYSTEM: One centrifugal-flow afterburning 6,000 lbf (with afterburning) Allison J33-A-33 turbojet engine

LENGTH: 40 ft, 1 in

HEIGHT: 12 ft, 8 in

WING SPAN: 38 ft, 11 in

EMPTY WEIGHT: 10,000 lbs

GROSS WEIGHT: 13,000 lbs

MAXIMUM SPEED: 600 mph

MAXIMUM RANGE: 1,000 mi

ARMAMENT: Four .50 caliber machine guns

YF-94B

SPECIFICATIONS

CREW: Two (pilot, flight test engineer)

PROPULSIVE SYSTEM: One centrifugal-flow afterburning 6,000 lbf (with afterburning) Allison J33-A-33A turbojet engine

LENGTH: 40 ft, 1 in

HEIGHT: 12 ft, 8 in

WING SPAN: 38 ft, 11 in

EMPTY WEIGHT: 10,064 lbs

GROSS WEIGHT: 13,475 lbs

MAXIMUM SPEED: 600 mph

MAXIMUM RANGE: 975 mi

ARMAMENT: Four .50-caliber machine guns and 2,000 lbs of bombs

The second of two prototype YF-94 airplanes (*USAF* serial number 48-373) taxiing at Burbank. Tony LeVier (pilot) and Glenn Fulkerson (flight test engineer) are onboard. *USAF*

August 1947, the USAF ordered twenty first-run TP-80C-1-LO production airplanes for service test (USAF serial numbers 48-356 to 48-375), Lockheed factory serial numbers 580-5001 to 580-5020. The USAF contract for these aircraft (AC-19283) was approved on April 7, 1948.

The USAF had for the most part transformed its various fleets of piston-powered, propeller-driven fighters into turbojet-powered combat aircraft by this time. And although it had a number of dedicated all-weather (nighttime) turbojet-powered interceptors in the pipeline, their operational debuts were considered to be too far off to be practical. So there came a need to acquire a temporary fill-in, and the first goal was to replace the current piston-engine all-weather fighter: the North American F-82 Twin Mustang.

All-weather fighter-interceptor aircraft of that era required a second crewman to operate the radio- and radar-guidance systems and the fire-control system. Since the new TP-80C was already two-seater, the USAF approached Lockheed with its scheme to transpose this airplane into a stopgap all-weather interceptor. Its plan was to install the Hughes E-1 fire-control system, Sperry

A-1C computing gunsight, AN/APG-33 radar system, and appropriate armament into the tandem-seat TP-80C.

Lockheed jumped on this opportunity, and since it was a rush-rush program, management turned it over to the ADP department. In turn, Hibbard gave it to Johnson, who handed it off to James Russell "Russ" Daniel, whom he had appointed project engineer on what became known as the Model 780. Dallas Burger (who later became project engineer on the F-104 program) served as assistant project engineer.

On October 8, 1948, the USAF issued an official General Operational Requirement (GOR) to acquire a turbojet-powered, all-weather (nighttime) interceptor as soon as possible. The Lockheed program was approved by Secretary of Defense James Vincent Forrestal in November 1948. Lockheed received a letter of intent to purchase contract in January 1949 to modify two TF-80C (formerly TP-80C) airplanes to the prototype interceptor aircraft initially designated XTF-80C.

Among the other turbojet-powered all-weather fighter candidates were the North American YF-86D Sabre,

Fabulous full-color photograph of the premier YF-94. *USAF*

Curtiss XF-87 Blackhawk, and Northrop XF-89 Scorpion of the USAF, and the Douglas XF3D-1 Skyknight of the USN. One other consideration was the North American YF-93A of the USAF which, for a time, was also a contender in the USAF Penetration Fighter program.

In any event, the F-86D, F-89B, and F3D-1 didn't enter service until, respectively, March 1953, June 1951,

and February 1951. The F-87 and F-93 programs were canceled in 1948 and 1950 respectively.

Two TF-80C-1-LO airplanes—number one and number eighteen (48-356 and 48-373), were used to serve as the demonstration airplanes. These were also known as ETF-80Cs, then ET-33As (the prefix *E* meaning "exempt"), and finally the two prototypes were unofficially dubbed YF-94s.

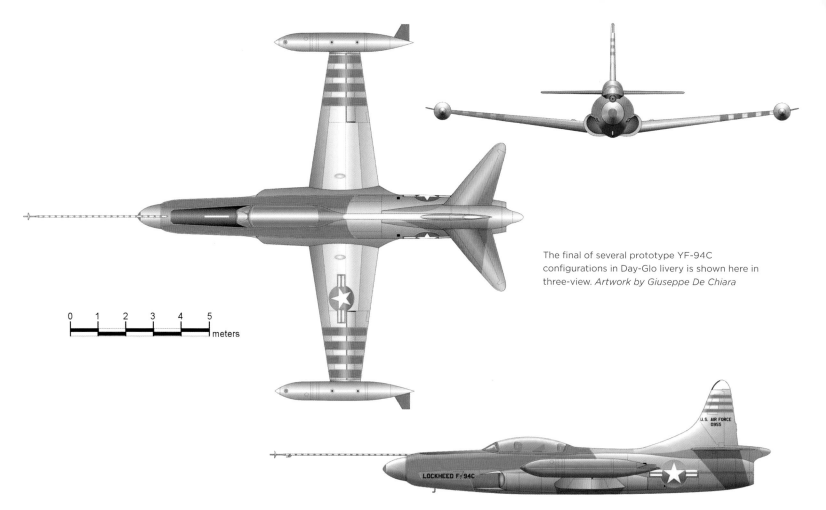

The final of several prototype YF-94C configurations in Day-Glo livery is shown here in three-view. *Artwork by Giuseppe De Chiara*

(Note: On June 11, 1948, the TP-80C became the TF-80C, and on May 5, 1949, the TF-80C was redesignated T-33A. The prefix *TP* for "trainer pursuit" was changed to *TF* for "trainer fighter. Then the *TF* prefix was changed to *T* for "trainer.")

Flight testing on the two demonstrators found them adequate for the mission, and two dedicated prototypes were tapped for further radar-intercept and armament demonstrations. The first example, still using 48-356, became the YF-94A, and a second YF-94A example (48-357) went to work.

On April 16, 1949, LeVier and Fulkerson made a successful first flight on the former TF-80C, now known unofficially as the prototype YF-94 (48-356).

To help clear things up in reference to the TF-80C-cum-F-94 (Model 780), USAF serial number 48-356 began life as a two-seat tandem derivative of the F-80C-1-LO (Model 080). As such it was designated TF-80C-1-LO (Model 580) and served as the prototype TF-80C, making its first flight as such on March 22, 1948. Following its modification to serve as the solicited USAF all-weather fighter prototype YF-94, this airplane made its *second* first flight on April 16, 1949.

The prototypes did well enough to warrant production, and the USAF ordered an initial batch of seventeen service test F-94A-1-LOs on USAF contract number AF-1847, which was approved on August 26, 1949. In addition, on the same contract, it ordered ninety-three F-94A-5-LOs (USAF serial numbers 49-2496 to 49-2588). The second F-94A-5-LO example (49-2497) was to be completed as the prototype YF-94B-LO.

F-80C, TF-80C, and F-94A aircraft production ran concurrent on the same production line in Burbank. The first F-94A was delivered to the USAF in December 1949, and the USAF began using them in April 1950.

Now known as the first of two YF-94As, 48-356 was involved in a landing accident at Edwards AFB on August 29, 1950, with pilot John A. Margwarth at the controls.

THE EYF-94B

The F-94B version was created to improve upon the F-94A version. To create a prototype B-variant, Lockheed modified the nineteenth production F-94A-1-LO (49-2497). It was designated EYF-94B and made its first flight on September 28, 1950.

This airplane is known to have had two mishaps at

Wright-Patterson AFB, Ohio, during its Air Research and Development Command (ARDC) All-Weather Division flight test evaluations. The first of these came on May 5, 1951, when pilot Ralph W. Broeske experienced an engine fire and aborted his takeoff. The second event was on January 16, 1953, when a taxiing accident caused a ground loop. The pilot was William S. Ross, assigned to the ARDC Flight Operations Branch at Wright-Patterson AFB.

THE F-94C

As designed and engineered by the Skunk Works, the F-97A version of the F-94 series of aircraft would primarily feature the use of an all-rocket armament and fire-control system, and a different propulsive system: a single centrifugal-flow Pratt & Whitney Model JT7, which the US Department of Defense (DOD) designated J48.

It was developed under TDN L-188, whereby a redesigned thin wing and revised empennage (aft fuselage section and tail group) would be attached to a modified F-94A temporarily dubbed "F-94B." This was first offered to the USAF in July 1948, but excitement was low. So Lockheed opted to build a prototype demonstrator using in-house funds.

The prototype YF-97A—essentially a J48 engine testbed—was built without armament and originally assigned civil registration number N94C. As such it first took wing at Muroc AFB on January 18, 1950 (according to USAF documentation), with LeVier at the controls. This flight and subsequent flights proved its airworthiness.

On March 7, 1950, the USAF published a Characteristics Summary (CS) dealing with the Lockheed F-97A fighter. This CS described the F-97A in limited detail, as the program was still in its infancy. However, this CS did say that the F-97A would feature the use of a rocket nose, XA-1 radar (two-man), Sperry instrument landing system with a zero reader indicator, high-pressure oxygen system, F-5 autopilot, thermal anti-icing system, Hughes collision course sight, thin wing, jettisonable canopy and seats, AN/APX-6 radar identification equipment (with Identify Friend or Foe), and a maximum fuel capacity of 747 gallons. It would be powered by a single afterburning 8,750-pound-foot (with afterburning) Pratt & Whitney J48 turbojet engine of an undetermined dash number.

The centrifugal-flow Pratt & Whitney J48 engine was a licensed US-built version of the British Rolls-Royce Tay developed under USAF ARDC Project MX-1447. Two dash

YF-97A

SPECIFICATIONS

CREW: Two (pilot, radar operator)

PROPULSIVE SYSTEM: One afterburning centrifugal-flow 8,750-lbf (with afterburning) Pratt & Whitney J48-P-5 turbojet engine (dash number of engine unknown at the time of writing); provision for two 12-second-burn, externally mounted 1,000-lbf Aerojet JATO units

LENGTH: 41.5 ft

HEIGHT: 12.7 ft

WINGSPAN: 37.6 ft

WING AREA: 238 sq ft

(No other details were listed at the time of writing.)

numbers (J48-P-1 and J48-P-3) were developed under MX-1447. As it turned out, the airplane was eventually powered by the -5 version of the J48.

On July 21, 1950, the DOD approved USAF contract number AF-11205 for a single prototype YF-97A (USAF serial number 50-955), and the N94C demonstrator received this serial number. At the same time, on the same contract, the USAF ordered 108 production F-97As (50-956 to 50-1063). The USAF—its air-defense sector in particular—was pretty sure of the F-97A being a worthy purchase.

A dedicated prototype was built as an all-rocket-armed nighttime (all-weather) demonstrator carrying two dozen 2.75-inch-diameter, folding-fin aerial rockets (FFARs) within its "Rocket Nose Installation." It was created from a late-production F-94B-1-LO (USAF serial number 50-877).

The Rocket Nose Installation (as it was entitled on the patent application) was yet another invention of Kelly Johnson's, along with coinventor William A. Reed. They applied for a fourteen-year patent for their invention on January 26, 1950.

On September 12, 1950, the YF-97A and F-97A aircraft were redesignated YF-94C and F-94C respectively.

The name *Starfire* was coined by someone in Lockheed public affairs, and it was officially adopted by the USAF for its fleet of F-94Cs. Neither the F-94A nor the F-94B were so named.

The first YF-94C (50-955) was involved in two mishaps at Edwards AFB, on October 12, 1950, and January 9,

FOUNDING FATHER: KELLY JOHNSON AND THE BIRTH OF THE SKUNK WORKS

Clarence Leonard "Kelly" Johnson joined the Lockheed Aircraft Corporation in 1933 at the age of twenty-two. His first assignment was tool maker.

Johnson was born on February 17, 1910, in Ishpeming, Michigan. Some of his school chums teased him about his name, calling him "Clara" on occasion. He got fed up with that girly-sounding nickname and one day, when one of these chums called him "Clara," he tripped him. The boy fell down so hard he broke his leg. From then on his classmates called him "Kelly," after a then popular song entitled "Kelly with the Green Neck Tie," since he had proved he was not a pushover.

In 1989 Johnson's autobiography, entitled *Kelly: More Than My Share of It All*, was published by Smithsonian Books. In it he shared, "For some time I had been pestering Gross and Hibbard to let me set up an experimental department where the designers and shop artisans could work together closely in the development of airplanes without the delays and complications of intermediate departments to handle administration, purchasing, and all the other support functions. I wanted a direct relationship between design engineer and mechanic and manufacturing. I decided to handle this new project [the XP-80] just that way."

Thus, what became the Skunk Works was born.

Irv Culver, a self-taught aeronautical engineer, designer, and inventor, had joined Lockheed in 1938 as a draftsman. He was one of the engineers handpicked by Hibbard and Johnson for the XP-80 program. A few days into the program—the exact date isn't clear—a telephone rang out. It was a call from the USN intended for Dick Pulver, the project engineer working on the Lockheed XR6O-1 Constitution transport program, but apparently the caller had misdialed. Culver was seated at the desk upon which the telephone was ringing, so he answered, "Skonk Works, inside man Culver." Surely that

caller on the other end of the line didn't know what in the hell the guy was talking about and most likely hung up on him.

In that era, the "Skonk Works" was a rundown Dogpatch factory in the *Li'l Abner* newspaper comic strip where "Kickapoo Joy Juice" was brewed from old smelly shoe leather and other putrid inclusions. Al Capp's comic strip was most likely a favorite of Culver's. In any case, Culver is credited with the naming of the famed Skunk Works.

1952. The first of these was a minor takeoff accident with Russell M. "Rusty" Roth at the controls. The airplane was assigned to Headquarters Squadron, 3077th Evaluation Group, at Edwards AFB at that time. The second mishap was a gunnery accident at Edwards AFB, with Lockheed test pilot Herman R. "Fish" Salmon in the front seat.

On March 7, 1950, the USAF published its preliminary CS dealing with the then secret Lockheed F-97A all-weather, all-rocket-armed, turbojet-powered fighter program. Its preliminary specifications called for the use of a single centrifugal-flow, afterburning, 8,750-pound-foot (with afterburning) Pratt & Whitney J48 turbojet engine and a pair of 1,000-pound-foot Aerojet 12AS1000D4 jet-assisted takeoff (JATO) units, mounted on either side of its aft fuselage section. It was to have a two-man crew, seated on jettisonable seats under a single-piece jettisonable cockpit canopy, and a rocket nose housing twenty-four folding-fin-type 2.75-inch diameter unguided projectiles. Four armament bays surrounded the nose, and each bay was to hold six of these projectiles; no guns or cannon would be carried.

SUMMARY

The USAF eventually procured 109 F-94As, 355 F-94Bs, and 387 F-94Cs, for a total of 851 production airplanes. These were preceded by the two prototype YF-94s, two prototype YF-94As, one prototype YF-94B, and the two prototype YF-94Cs.

Penetration Fighter: The XF-90

On April 11, 1946, Lockheed received teletype authorization to proceed on its part of the Penetration Fighter program. The date of contract was June 20, 1946.

The Lockheed Aircraft Corporation XP/XF-90 was the direct competitor to the McDonnell XP/XF-88 during the USAAF-cum-USAF Penetration Fighter competition. The North American YF-93A was a late entry, but it also participated.

Lockheed investigated numerous XP-90 configurations under several temporary design numbers (TDN) which included TDN L-153, L-167, and L-169. It was TDN L-153 that was built.

Lockheed XP-90 proposal number one called for two afterburning 4,900-pound-foot (with afterburning)

51

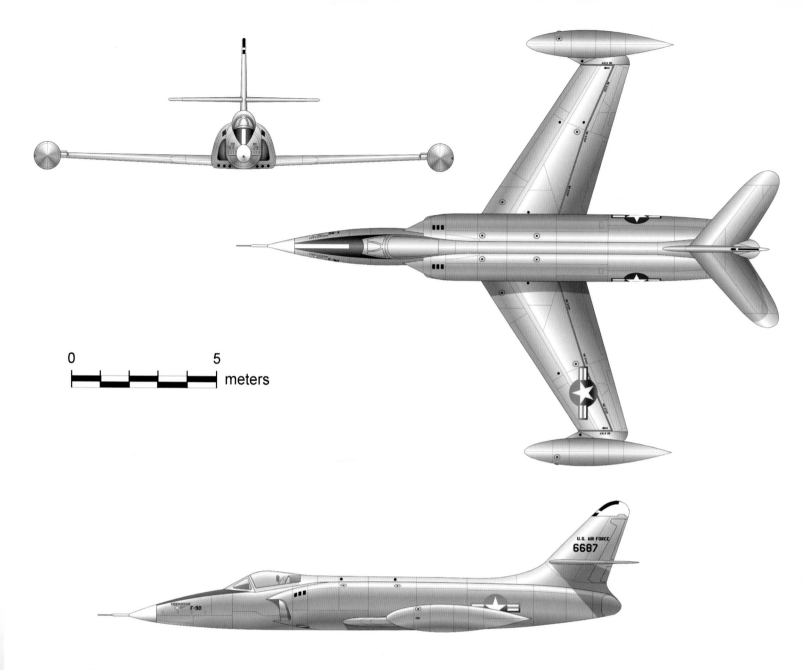

The first of the two XF-90 airplanes (USAF serial number 46-687) in three-view. *Artwork by Giuseppe De Chiara*

Westinghouse axial flow XJ34-WE-32 US Navy–type turbojet engines. Number two (alternate) featured two afterburning axial-flow 6,100 pound-foot (with afterburning) Westinghouse XJ46-WE-2 USN-type turbojet engines. Neither one of these engines were ever used, however.

XP/XF-90

On April 11, 1946, Lockheed received teletype authorization to proceed on its long-range fighter program. On June 5, 1946, Lockheed received a letter contract to purchase two XP-90 airplanes under USAAF AMC Secret Project MX-812; USAAF contract number

AC-14563. Lockheed offered its TDN L-169-1 design on December 20, 1946.

A full-scale engineering XP-90 mockup was built and given a preliminary inspection by the USAAF on June 1, 1947. The full and final USAAF 689 Engineering Board inspection of the XF-90 (as designated after June 11, 1948) mockup was completed in April 1949. Following the engineering inspection, the order for two XF-90 airplanes was finalized under USAAF AMC Secret Project MX-812. USAAF contract number AC-14563 was approved by the DOD on January 25, 1949. The projects had already been issued USAAF serial numbers 46-687 and 46-688. The estimated first flight date was June 1948.

The first of the two experimental XF-90 airplanes, depicted during one of its many dive tests at Edwards AFB. *Artwork by Luca Landino*

XF-90 number two (46-688) in the foreground, flying in formation with number one—clean configuration (no wingtip fuel tanks). *LM via Denny Lombard*

The first XF-90 (46-687) made its first flight on June 3, 1949, at Muroc AFB with Tony LeVier at the controls. The second XF-90 (46-688) made its first flight at newly named Edwards AFB in March 1950.

XF-90A

Both XF-90 airplanes were redesignated XF-90A after they were refit with afterburner-equipped 4,200-pound-foot (with afterburning) J34-WE-15 turbojet engines. The maximum speed attained in level attitude flight by an XF-90A was 0.90 Mach or 668 miles per hour.

SUMMARY

The first year and a half in the life of the Skunk Works gave birth to the first operational fighter in the United States powered by a turbojet engine. By the end of 1944, the P-80A—the first production version of the Shooting Star—had entered into production.

The rather unique design of the P-80 lent itself to the creation of other aircraft types, such as photographic reconnaissance and pilot trainer/transition variants, which

the Skunk Works pursued with vigor. But the Shooting Star wasn't the only aircraft program this new entity of the Lockheed Aircraft Corporation was working on.

Diversity became a way of life, and in the fall of 1944 a wholly different type of aircraft was in the works. This aircraft, at first known as TDN-146, would evolve into the Model 75 Saturn—a small piston-powered, propeller-driven, feeder-type airliner that will be discussed in Chapter 2.

This diversity became status quo within the Skunk Works, a fact that remains true today. As of this writing, the Skunk Works has created a vast assortment of machinery, including manned and unmanned aircraft, missiles and rockets, seacraft and spacecraft. This diversity is the biggest factor in the continuing triumphs of the Skunk Works.

As seen from the foregoing, the Skunk Works began in 1943 but took root several years earlier in a number of interesting aircraft programs developed under company security blankets. This was status quo then, now, and will remain to be so throughout the years to follow.

Above: XF-90 number one in her element during an early test in mid-1949. *LM via Denny Lombard*

Left: Page 1 of XF-90 patent application—although it's not the final configuration—as it was filed on November 30, 1950—patent awarded to its designer/inventor Kelly Johnson on January 15, 1952. F-94C Starfire "rocket nose" style is noteworthy. *United States Patent Office*

Below: Page 2 of patent.

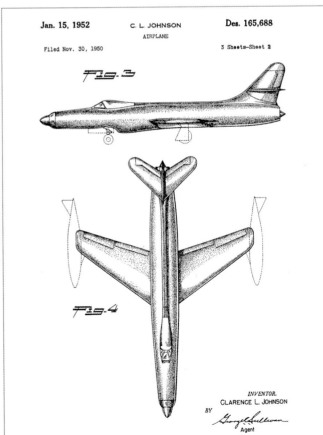

Jan. 15, 1952 C. L. JOHNSON Des. 165,688
AIRPLANE
Filed Nov. 30, 1950 3 Sheets-Sheet 2

Fig.3

Fig.4

INVENTOR.
CLARENCE L. JOHNSON
BY
Agent

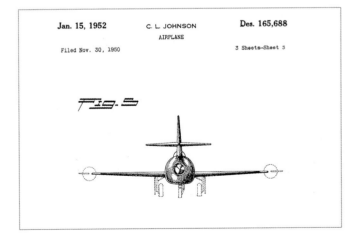

Jan. 15, 1952 C. L. JOHNSON Des. 165,688
AIRPLANE
Filed Nov. 30, 1950 3 Sheets-Sheet 3

Fig.5

THE 1950s: FORTHCOMING TECHNOLOGIES

"That damned Swede can actually see air!"

—HALL HIBBARD TO BEN RICH, IN REFERENCE TO KELLY JOHNSON

The Lockheed Aircraft Corporation was full of activity as the 1940s ended and the 1950s began. It was manufacturing two different fighter aircraft, a commercial airliner, a military transport, a patrol bomber, and two types of advanced pilot trainer and transition aircraft.

The United States had gone back to war to help the people of South Korea counter the unprovoked invasion of North Korea on June 25, 1950. Thus, even more combat aircraft were needed from Lockheed and aircraft production orders increased accordingly.

Beginning in January 1950, just six years after the one-off XP-80 took flight, the fledgling Skunk Works was attempting to sell an advanced version of its F-94 to the USAF. The F-97, as it was first designated, promised to be a big improvement over its predecessor F-94A day fighter aircraft, for it was to be an all-rocket-armed nighttime (all-weather) fighter.

Moreover, as the new decade began, the Skunk Works was swamped with innovation as the demands for faster aircraft—supersonic and doublesonic—and higher-flying aircraft—up to 70,000 feet—came to the forefront. What

was once science fiction was becoming science fact, and the Skunk Works was deeply involved with not only current but also forthcoming technologies.

Flying Stovepipe: The X-7A and the XQ-5 Kingfisher

The X-7A program began in 1946 with a USAAF request for an unmanned, 2,000-mile-per-hour (Mach 3) air vehicle for various test purposes. The X-7A evolved into the XQ-5 when the need arose to test US antiaircraft systems such as the US Army Nike Ajax and Nike Hercules, and the USAF Bomarc. The program was initiated under USAAF AMC Secret Project MX-883. On February 10, 1955, the DOD approved USAF contract number AF-28692 for seven X-7A air vehicles.

The pilotless X-7A "Flying Stovepipe" was a dedicated research air vehicle created to investigate missile guidance systems and the use of Wright Aeronautical and Marquardt ramjet engines for high-speed aircraft propulsive systems. An experimental target drone version designated XQ-5 and named Kingfisher was used to help perfect US air defenses against attacking enemy bombers.

The X-7 (formerly designated PTV-A-1) was carried aloft under the left inboard wings of the Boeing B-29

Suntan refueling a Suntan. *Artwork by Jozef Gatial*

The X-7A-3 attached to a pylon under the left wing of this B-29 carrier aircraft prior to takeoff and test. *USAF*

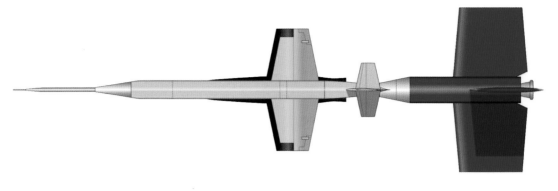

The X-7A-1 (nicknamed the "Flying Stovepipe") in three-view. *Artwork by Giuseppe De Chiara*

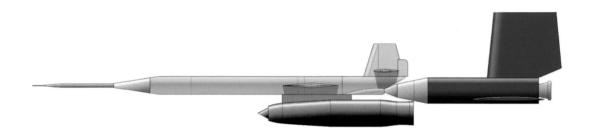

X-7A-1

SPECIFICATIONS

CREW: None

PROPULSIVE SYSTEM: One 105,000-lbf Alleghany Ballistics Laboratory X202-C3 solid-fuel booster rocket engine and various Marquardt ramjet sustainer engines, including the XRJ43-MA-3

LENGTH: 32 ft 9 in

HEIGHT: 7 ft 0 in

WINGSPAN: 12 ft 0 in

GROSS LAUNCH WEIGHT: 8,000 lbs

MAXIMUM SPEED: Mach 4.31 (2,844 mph)

SERVICE CEILING: 106,000 ft

PAYLOAD: Various test equipment

XQ-5

SPECIFICATIONS

PROPULSIVE SYSTEM: Two 50,000-lbf Thiokol XM-45 (Model S-KS-50000) solid-fuel booster rockets and one Marquardt XRJ43-MA-3 ramjet sustainer engine

LENGTH: 38 ft 1 in

HEIGHT: 6 ft 11 in

WINGSPAN: 9 ft 10 in

GROSS LAUNCH WEIGHT: 7,937 lbs

MAXIMUM SPEED: Mach 4.3 (2,838 mph)

MAXIMUM RANGE: 130 mi

SERVICE CEILING: 98,000 ft

PAYLOAD: None

and B-50 mother planes from which it was launched. After launch the booster ignited and propelled it to an approximate speed of 1,000 miles per hour, at which point the ramjet engine took over. The first powered X-7 launch, although unsuccessful, took place on April 27, 1951. After its mission profile was flown, the X-7 returned

to terra firma via parachute. The X-7 ultimately reached a maximum speed of Mach 4.31 (2,844 miles per hour) which was at that time a world record speed for an air-breathing propulsive system propelling an air vehicle. A total of 130 test flights on the X-7A were flown between April 1951 and July 1960.

The X-7A—made of nickel alloy (fuselage) and stainless steel (wings)—also evaluated the use of High Energy Fuel-2 and Hi Cal-3 Zip Fuel for several proposed aircraft, including the North American B-70. Only 28 X-7 air vehicles were built.

The XQ-5 Kingfisher, similarly constructed, was a dedicated target drone version of the X-7A. The XQ-5 was redesigned AQM-60 in September 1962.

The XQ-5 program began officially on September 10, 1957, when the DOD approved USAF contract number AF-29268 for one XQ-5. Although five XQ-5 air vehicles were ordered, only two were built.

SUMMARY

Only 30 X-7s (28) and XQ-5s (2) were built, but their contributions to ramjet engine propulsion, missile guidance systems, and antiaircraft defense technologies made them valuable assets to US security during the warming Cold War of the 1950s. Kelly Johnson designed them and used them as the basis for his future triplesonic masterpieces: the Blackbird series of aircraft.

SeaStar: The T2V

Between 1945 and 1954, the USN bought fleets of contemporary turbojet-powered fighters with many advanced follow-on types in the pipeline. It therefore required an aircraft carrier–suitable advanced pilot training and transition aircraft but had few options at the time. So, beginning in 1949, the USN—its Naval Air Training Command (NATC) in particular—used a near-identical version of the USAF T-33A, designated T-33B, for land-based turbojet-powered advanced pilot training. The T-33B was designated TO-2 before the June 11, 1948, aircraft redesignation system went into effect, and then TV-2 afterward.

The T-33B wasn't carrier-suitable, however, and its pilots had to learn simulated carrier takeoffs and landings from specially prepared ground-based landing strips, complete with catapult-launch and cable-type aircraft recovery systems like those found on aircraft carriers.

The continuing need for a dedicated carrier-compatible advanced trainer led to a more advanced design development of the F-80/T-33 family that evolved into the Lockheed Model L-245, which was designated T2V-1.

The USN released a request for proposals (RFP) for an advanced pilot trainer to the industry, and after

Titanium Alloy

In the early 1950s Lockheed received a USAF contract for the "Development of Titanium Aircraft and Missile Structures" under ARDC Secret Project MX-1136. Titanium is a relatively rare and expensive commodity, and in the early 1950s it was only known to exist in a few places on Earth, including Russia. To acquire this then rare chemical element from a Cold War adversary, while keeping the MX-1136 program secret, Lockheed set up a few dummy non-aviation-related companies to procure the raw material, smelt it, and manufacture the end product in various sizes, shapes, and thicknesses for use.

At this particular time in aviation history, no manned air vehicles required this exotic metal alloy—only very-high-speed missiles and rockets. In fact, there weren't even many of those that needed its benefits. The benefits of metals created from titanium alloys include high strength (strong as some steels), light weight (lighter than aluminum), and the ability to take high heat without becoming too malleable. Airframe and powerplant contractors use three types of titanium alloy: A-A110AT, B-120VCA (the most frequently used), and C-120AV. These early investigations into the use of titanium alloy proved invaluable later, when the Blackbird series of aircraft (made of about 85 percent titanium) were built using B-120VCA.

The SeaStar demonstrator (TDN L-245/Model 1080) made its first flight on December 15, 1953, with test pilot Tony LeVier at the controls. *LM via Denny Lombard*

The T-1A (formerly T2V-1) SeaStar was the first dedicated turbojet-powered advanced trainer for USN and USMC carrier-based combat pilots. *LM via Denny Lombard*

considerable evaluations of all entries it selected the Skunk Works–developed Lockheed L-245, which the DOD designated T2V-1. The name *SeaStar* was Lockheed's suggestion, which the USN readily endorsed.

The SeaStar's design was based on the TV-2 (formerly TO-2) but evolved into an entirely new airframe. For aircraft carrier operations it featured an arresting hook, strengthened landing gear, large-area speed brakes, flaps, and wings.

Lockheed's company-owned demonstrator L-245 first flew on December 16, 1953, with Tony LeVier at the controls; production deliveries to the NATC began in 1956 and operations in 1957.

Compared to the TV-2, the T2V was almost totally re-engineered for carrier landings and at-sea operations with a redesigned tail; naval standard avionics; a strengthened undercarriage (with catapult fittings) and lower fuselage (with a retractable arrestor hook), and power-operated leading-edge flaps (to increase lift at low speeds) to allow carrier launches and recoveries; and an elevated rear (instructor's) seat for improved instructor vision, among other changes. Unlike other USN-operated F-80/T-33 derivatives, the Lockheed Model 1080 T2V-1 could withstand the shock of landing on a pitching carrier deck and had a much higher ability to withstand seawater-related aircraft wear from higher humidity and salt exposure.

In-flight study of an early production T2V-1 SeaStar. *LMSW*

SUMMARY

The T2V-1 was redesignated T-1A in September 1962, when the Tri-Service redesignation system went into effect. The T-1A SeaStar served into the 1970s and was eventually replaced by the T-2 Buckeye.

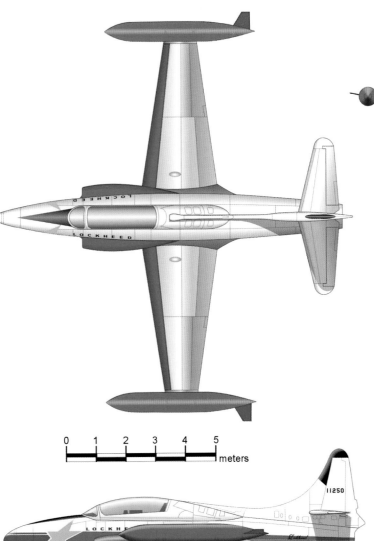

Left and above: The L-245 SeaStar (USN bureau number 11250) in three-view. *Artwork by Giuseppe De Chiara*

T2V-1 company demonstrator (civil registration number N125D) flies with USN T-33B, which it ultimately replaced. *LM* Code One

Naval Air Test Center (NATC) Flight Test (FT) T2V-1 (later T-1A) (USN bureau number 142266) is shown here making its first takeoff from an aircraft carrier. *LMSW*

T2V-1 (T-1A)

SPECIFICATIONS

CREW: Two (student pilot and instructor pilot)

PROPULSIVE SYSTEM: One non-afterburning, centrifugal-flow, 6,100-lbf Allison J33-A-24/24A turbojet engine

LENGTH: 38 ft 6.5 in

HEIGHT: 13 ft 4 in

WINGSPAN: 42 ft 10 in

WING AREA: 240 sq ft

EMPTY WEIGHT: 11,965 lbs

GROSS TAKEOFF WEIGHT: 16,800 lbs

MAXIMUM SPEED: 580 mph

MAXIMUM RANGE: 970 mi

SERVICE CEILING: 40,000 ft

Starfighter: The F-104

In mid-1950, after the Lockheed Aircraft Corporation XF-90 was eliminated from the USAF Penetration Fighter competition, Lockheed went to work on an all-weather fighter-interceptor, which it studied under Temporary Design Number 265 (TDN 265). This fighter was to be powered by a single afterburning, 15,000-pound-foot (with afterburning) General Electric J53 turbojet engine, but the project did not proceed.

In May 1952 Lockheed was offered a contract to build two fighter-interceptor prototypes with a gross take-off weight of 32,000 pounds, powered by two Wright Aeronautical J65 turbojet engines. Lockheed declined to participate because the USAF had insisted on a contract stipulation forfeiting all patent rights, thus permitting the government to give production rights to any air-frame contractor.

Another reason Lockheed refused was that its Skunk Works was then under contract to develop test data and design aids on the Douglas X-3 Stiletto, which it had received from the USAF. Moreover, it was developing TDN CL-246, an uncomplicated single-seat, single-engine fighter with a thin, straight wing. As an unsolicited proposal, this design was submitted to the USAF on an official basis by none other than Kelly Johnson—its designer—in November 1952.

The USAF did not have a requirement for the enticing CL-246 design. However, its seductiveness was enough for the USAF to invent a GOR calling for a new lightweight air-superiority type of day fighter to ultimately replace the F-100, beginning in 1956. To be fair, competitive bids for this GOR were invited from all airframe contractors.

Lockheed had already met all USAF requirements for a high-speed, lightweight fighter by designing an aircraft with an empty weight of just 11,500 pounds. It was a lean machine, with every ounce of extra weight stripped from its airframe and equipment, and proved to be half the weight of the aircraft proposed by the participating airframe contractors. Moreover, the Skunk Works had concentrated its efforts on a fighter plane with a high thrust-to-engine-weight ratio because of the supersonic speed regime in which it would fly and fight. It was to be, in the truest sense, a star fighter—thus its official name.

Under Weapon System 303A, USAF ARDC Secret Project MX-1853, the USAF ordered two experimental XF-104 prototypes on March 12, 1953 (USAF contract number AF-23362; USAF serial numbers 53-7786 and 53-7787). The full-scale engineering mockup was inspected and approved on April 30, 1953, clearing the way for the production of the two prototypes.

In order to obtain the best possible speed from its airframe, Lockheed chose to propel its XF-104 aircraft (Model 083-92-01) with a single Buick Motor Company–built, axial-flow, afterburning Wright Aeronautical J65 turbojet engine rated at 15,000 pound foot (with

The second of the two XF-104 airplanes is depicted here during an early 20mm T-171 Vulcan cannon-firing trial. *Artwork by Luca Landino*

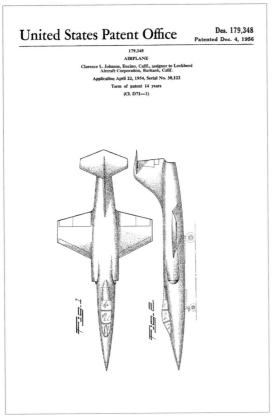

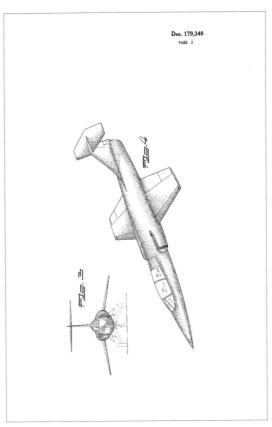

Des. 179,348
PAGE 2

Far left: Patent application filed by F-104 designer/inventor Kelly Johnson on April 22, 1954—14-year patent awarded on December 4, 1956. *United States Patent Office*

Left: Page 2 of patent.

The first of the two experimental XF-104 airplanes (53-7786, Model 083-92-01) in three-view. *Artwork by Giuseppe De Chiara*

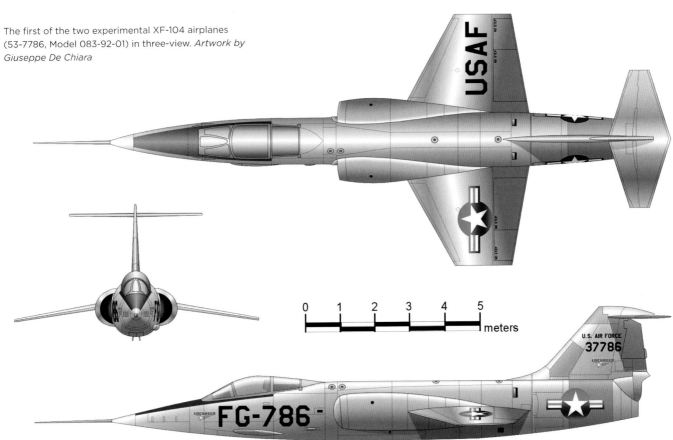

63

XF-104 number one slowing down after a high-speed taxi run in late February 1954 with its drag chute deployed. *NMUSAF*

afterburning). The J65 was an Armstrong Siddeley Sapphire of British design, produced in the United States under license. Initially, however, only the non-afterburning 10,200-pound-foot version of the J65 was available to the XF-104 program.

After being secretly trucked during the nighttime from Burbank to Edwards AFB in late January 1954, the number-one XF-104 was prepared for its initial flight test activities. A high-speed taxi run followed by a short test hop was scheduled for February 38, 1954, with ace test pilot Tony LeVier at the controls. As scheduled, he reached rotation speed and pulled back on the stick, raising the aircraft some 5 feet off the dry lakebed, and the Starfighter flew—but unofficially. Its first official flight wasn't until March 4, 1954. During this first flight of some 20 minutes at low speed, the landing gear had refused to retract. LeVier landed. After some adjustments were made, LeVier took off again and once more the landing gear would not retract.

As it turned out, the landing gear problem was caused by low pressure in the hydraulic system and was soon corrected. LeVier made flights three and four on March 26, 1954, without landing gear difficulties. Further flight tests found that the premier XF-104—powered by the non-afterburning J65-B-3 turbojet engine—could not exceed Mach 1 in level flight. But in a shallow dive, without aerodynamic discrepancies, the XF-104 easily exceeded the speed of sound.

The afterburning 10,200-pound-foot Wright Aeronautical J65-W-7 turbojet engine was installed in XF-104 number one in July 1954. Its performance

dramatically increased. It could attain Mach 1.49 in level flight at 41,000 feet and Mach 1.6 in a dive, and it could zoom climb to 55,000 feet.

Fitted with the J65-W-7 from the start, the second XF-104 made its first flight on October 5, 1954, with Lockheed test pilot Herman Salmon under its cockpit canopy. On March 25, 1955, powered by the J65-W-7, XF-104 number two reached a top speed of Mach 1.79 (1,324 miles per hour) at 60,000 feet. Lockheed test pilot Raymond J. "Ray" Goudey made this flight.

Earlier, seventeen service-test YF-104As had been ordered to be built to fully investigate the assets of the Starfighter. They were assigned USAF serial numbers 55-2955 to 55-2971 under USAF contract number AF-27378, approved March 30, 1955.

Seven preproduction F-104A-1-Los (USAF serial numbers 56-730 to 56-736), along with the seventeen YF-104As and two XF-104s, were revised in various ways during testing to solve different problems revealed during the long-running test program, including armament, pitch-up, low-speed handling, and engine problems. Thus, twenty-six aircraft participated in the Starfighter growth program to mature the F-104 enough for full-scale production of Block 5 F-104A-5-LO Starfighters. The seven additional test F-104A-1-LOs were ordered on USAF contract number AF-30756, approved March 2, 1956.

When the wraps were finally taken off the Starfighter some two years after it had first flown, Lockheed rolled out the second service test YF-104A built for public viewing on February 16, 1956. When it appeared publicly for the first time, people were listening to a new sound

XF-104 number two (53-7787) is shown here on March 5, 1954, during assembly. *LMSW*

called rock 'n' roll—and the Starfighter rocked those in attendance at its unveiling. Attending air enthusiasts were astounded by what they saw. At first glance, it didn't look like it had any wings. Moreover, it had covers faired over the engine air intakes on either side of the fuselage to hide its half-cones (these covers were immediately dubbed *flight falsies* and today might remind us of singer Madonna's bullet-shaped brassieres). It featured downward-angled wings and a high T-tail, and its rocket-like fuselage was much longer than its wingspan was wide. In truth, it looked more like a missile with a cockpit than an airplane. And it looked like it was going very fast indeed, just sitting there on the ramp.

XF-104S DOWN

Unfortunately both XF-104s were lost during their flying careers. Test Pilot Herman Salmon was flying a cannon-firing mission at China Lake, California—a USN aircraft test facility—with XF-104 number two (53-7787) on April 19, 1955. His flight was out of Palmdale, California, some 70 miles north of China Lake. While flying at 47,000 feet, Salmon fired a short burst of 20mm rounds from the T-171 Vulcan cannon. He heard several

The original downward-firing emergency ejection seats installed on the XF-104s proved to be a big no-no and were eventually replaced with upward-firing seats. *LMSW*

65

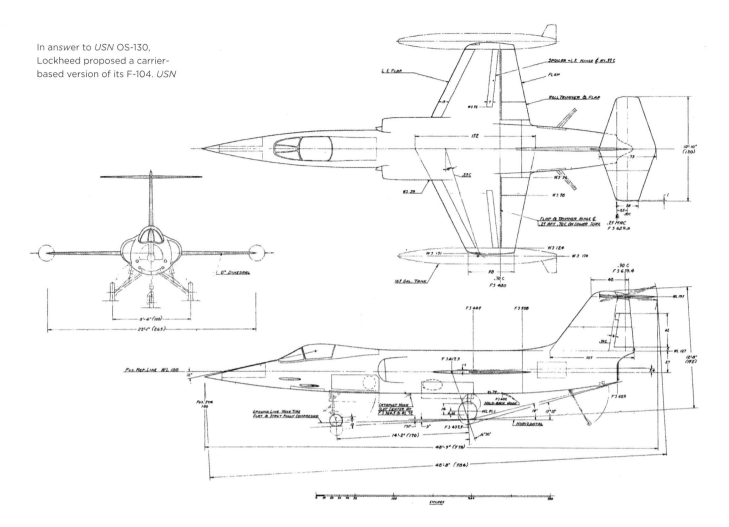

In answer to *USN* OS-130, Lockheed proposed a carrier-based version of its F-104. *USN*

"clunks," and to his shock the emergency ejection hatch under his seat blew off. This caused sudden decompression in the cockpit and a terrific amount of turbulence, which partially inflated his pressure suit. The windscreen on his helmet fogged up until he could barely see, and he elected to make an emergency bailout. He ejected at about 15,000 feet and parachuted to the ground below. He landed about two miles from the aircraft impact area several miles south of the China Lake facility and was found some 2 hours later by a Piasecki HUP-2 Retriever USN search-and-rescue helicopter and its crew. A preliminary medical exam determined that he had survived the ordeal uninjured.

On July 11, 1957, XF-104 number one (53-7786) was lost. With more than 1,000 flying hours registered in its log book, this XF-104—bailed back to Lockheed from the USAF to be used as a pilot check-out, transition, and chase plane in the Starfighter program—was flying a chase mission with an F-104A (55-2957) near Bakersfield, California. This F-104A was being flown by Lockheed test pilot Robert "Bob" Mayte.

XF-104

SPECIFICATIONS

PROPULSIVE SYSTEM: One Buick-built, axial-flow, afterburning, 7,330-lbf Wright Aeronautical J65-B-3 turbojet engine (XF-104 #1 only); One Wright Aeronautical-built, 7,500-lbf J65-W-7 turbojet engine (both XF-104s after XF-104 #1 was refitted with the -7 engine)

LENGTH: 49.17 ft

HEIGHT: 13.49 ft

WINGSPAN: 21.94 ft (without wingtip fuel tanks)

EMPTY WEIGHT: 11,500 lbs

GROSS TAKEOFF WEIGHT: 16,700 lbs

MAXIMUM SPEED: Mach 1.79 (1362.6 mph) (attained)

MAXIMUM RANGE: 500 mi

ARMAMENT: One 20mm T-171E-3 (later M61A1) Vulcan cannon (XF-104 #2 only)

Rare photograph of XF-104 number one posing alongside YF-104A number one. *USAF*

During this particular chase mission, flown out of Air Force Plant 42 in Palmdale, California, the XF-104 was being piloted by Lockheed engineering test pilot William C. "Bill" Park. At 12,500 feet, while flying at high subsonic speed, an unsecured fuel tank cap suddenly came off and struck the vertical stabilizer. The damage was enough to cause severe tail flutter and an immediate loss of control, forcing Park to make an emergency bailout.

The XF-104 impacted the ground some 12 nautical miles south southwest of Bakersfield. Park experienced some difficulty in his attempt to eject, but he did exit safely. He landed about a ½ mile southeast of the impact site. Park was taken to hospital for a general checkup and found to be okay.

SUMMARY

The Lockheed Aircraft Corporation F-104 Starfighter was a bona fide hot rod in its day. It literally earned its catch phrase: "The Missile with a Man in It." It was very light, ultra-sleek, and extremely powerful. When some other fighters were struggling to exceed Mach 1 in level-attitude flight, the F-104 easily blazed past Mach 2 on the level. And it could zoom climb to altitudes heretofore unreached by its contemporaries. Its engine-power-to-airframe-weight ratio was outstanding, and it established numerous speed, altitude, and time-to-climb records.

YF-104A: RISE OF THE STARFIGHTER

We discussed the birth of the F-104 above, but its story was cut short while the Skunk Works waited for its design engine—the Mach 2–rated General Electric J79—to become available.

YF-104A number two (56-2956) was used for the roll-out ceremony. *LMSW*

To evaluate the true potential of the J79-powered Starfighter, the USAF ordered seventeen prototype YF-104A aircraft for service testing. These were manufactured under Lockheed Model 183-93-02.

The former experimental XF-104 aircraft were evocative machines but lacked the high performance required of the type. The YF-104A promised to vastly improve upon that shortcoming. And did it ever.

Completed in February 1956, the first prototype YF-104A was secretly trucked to the special-access North Base part of Edwards AFB. On the very next day, February 17, 1956, with Salmon at the controls, YF-104A number one made its first flight. On February 28, that very Starfighter exceeded Mach 2, becoming the first fighter in the world capable of flying at twice the speed of sound in level-attitude flight.

On October 14, 1956, the USAF ordered the doublesonic Starfighter into production. The first thirty-five of these production F-104As, in addition to the seventeen prototype YF-104As, were all used for service test activities.

67

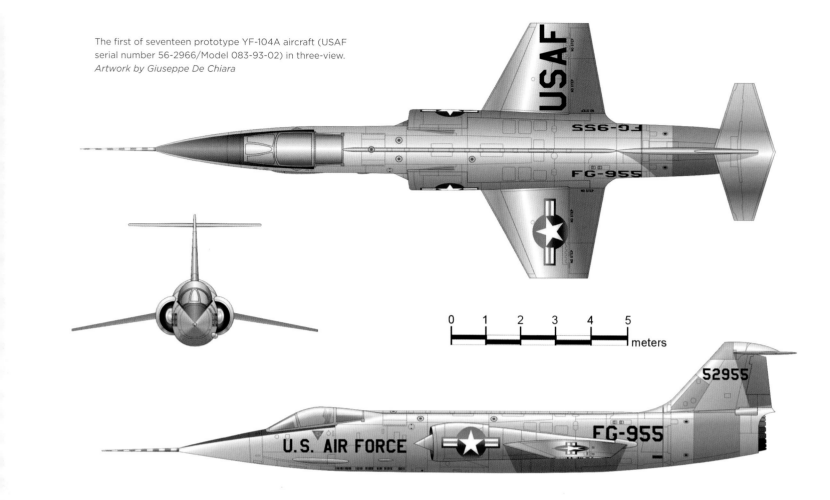

The first of seventeen prototype YF-104A aircraft (USAF serial number 56-2966/Model 083-93-02) in three-view.
Artwork by Giuseppe De Chiara

YF-104A

SPECIFICATIONS

CREW: One (pilot)

PROPULSIVE SYSTEM: One experimental axial-flow, afterburning, 14,800-lbf (with afterburning) General Electric XJ79-GE-3 turbojet engine initially; also tested production J79-GE-3/-3A/-3B turbojet engines

LENGTH: 54 ft, 8 in

HEIGHT: 13.49 ft

WINGSPAN: 29 ft, 9 in

EMPTY WEIGHT: 12,561 lbs

GROSS TAKEOFF WEIGHT: 24,584 lbs

MAXIMUM SPEED: Mach 2.3-plus (1750.8 mph)

MAXIMUM RANGE: 1,400 mi

COMBAT CEILING: 55,000 ft

ARMAMENT: One General Electric 6-barrel T-171 Vulcan rotary-action (Gatling-type) 20mm cannon; Two AIM-9 Sidewinder air-to-air missiles

SUMMARY

It's a real shame that neither of the experimental XF-104s survived for future viewing, for they were historic in the truest sense of that word.

The prototype YF-104As and F-104A service test aircraft played a pivotal role in the success of the overall Starfighter program, and many additional examples were manufactured in Burbank for the USAF Air Defense Command (ADC; after 1968 Aerospace Defense Command), Tactical Air Command (TAC), ATC, and the Air National Guard. These included the 17 single-seat YF-104As, 153 single-seat F-104As, 26 tandem-seat F-104Bs, 77 single-seat F-104Cs, 21 tandem-seat F-104Ds, and 30 tandem-seat F-104Fs—324 in all.

Tony LeVier, who knew as much about flying the F-104 as anyone and who loved the "Zipper," as it was affectionately nicknamed by USAF pilots, said, "If it hadn't been for aircraft like the F-104, which was strategically targeted at key Russian facilities, and the U-2, which let us know everything the communists were doing, there may very well have been a World War III."

Lockheed/NASA NF-104A

Three F-104A Starfighters were modified to serve NASA as high-altitude trainers (USAF serial numbers 56-0756, 56-0760, and 56-0762). The Aerospace Research Pilots School (ARPS) was created at Edwards AFB to provide this training. The Starfighters were designated NF-104A and called AeroSpace Trainers, or ASTs. Optimized for astronaut training, they were powered by both a turbojet engine and a liquid-fueled rocket motor. The former was an axial-flow, afterburning, 14,800-pound-foot (with afterburning) General Electric J79-GE-3B turbojet engine; the latter was a 6,000-pound-foot (maximum power) Aerojet Rocketdyne AR2-3 (LR121) rocket motor. The rocket motor could be throttled from 3,000 lbf to 6,000 pound foot, and its maximum burn time was 2 minutes, or 120 seconds. A reaction control system for flight in the upper atmosphere was also provided.

The trio of NF-104A AST aircraft were all highly modified F-104A-10-LO airplanes. They measured 54 feet 9 inches long and 13 feet 6 inches high, with a wingspan of 25 feet 9 inches and a wing area of 212.8 square feet. Their empty weight was 13,500 pounds, and their maximum takeoff weight was 21,400 pounds. Their top speed is listed at Mach 2.2 to 2.4 (1674.7 to 1826.9 miles per hour).

The trio established numerous zoom-climb records, including to 118,860 feet on October 23, 1963, and to 120,800 feet on December 6, 1963, both with USAF Lt. Col. Robert W. "Bob" Smith at the controls. These flights were flown on NF-104A number one. Smith was the primary pilot assigned to the NF-104A program.

On December 10, 1963, the second NF-104A (56-0762), with ARPS Commandant Charles E. "Chuck" Yeager—then a USAF colonel—on its controls, went out of control at an altitude of 104,000 feet and entered into a flat spin. Yeager managed to eject successfully but was badly burned on his face by the rocket motor of his ejector seat. The aircraft was destroyed in the ensuing crash. An investigation later showed that the cause of the crash was a spin that resulted from excessive angle of attack and lack of aircraft response. The excessive angle of attack was caused not by pilot input but by a gyroscopic condition set up by the J79 engine spooling after shutdown for the rocket-powered zoom-climb phase.

The highly successful NF-104A AST program ended in 1971. One survivor—NF-104A number one (56-0760)—is mounted on a pylon outside the USAF Test Pilot School on Edwards AFB.

Left: The CL-361 program was an attempt to make emergency ejection from a distressed F-104 safer. The entire rocket-powered nose section was to separate and, once safely away from the aircraft, parachute to the ground. *USAF*

Below: The premier XF-104 is shown here on its first official takeoff from Edwards AFB on March 5, 1954. *USAF*

Vertical Riser: The XFV-1

The USN released a secret request for bids on July 21, 1950, under its OS-122 program, calling for the creation of a VF Convoy Fighter—the acronym VF meaning "vertical takeoff and landing (VTOL) fighter." Five airframe contractors bid: Goodyear, Martin, Northrop, Convair, and Lockheed. Since it was a secret program, it was pursued within the Skunk Works.

All five bids were received by the USN on December 1, 1950, and on February 2, 1951, both Convair and Lockheed were approved to proceed.

Two experimental Lockheed XFO-1 airplanes were ordered on April 19, 1951—USN contract number NOas 51-1123. The Lockheed project engineer was Arthur Erman "Art" Flock Jr. Two XFV-1 aircraft were built under Lockheed model number 081-40-01, but only the first example was actually flown.

Promoted by Lockheed as the "Vertical Riser," the XFV-1 was named Salmon by Lockheed to honor the only person to fly it, Lockheed engineering test pilot Herman R. "Fish" Salmon. After all, this aircraft went directly upstream (like a spawning salmon) before it could fly in normal fashion. The first of two examples (BuAer number 138657) is shown here during a taxi test. *LM* Code One

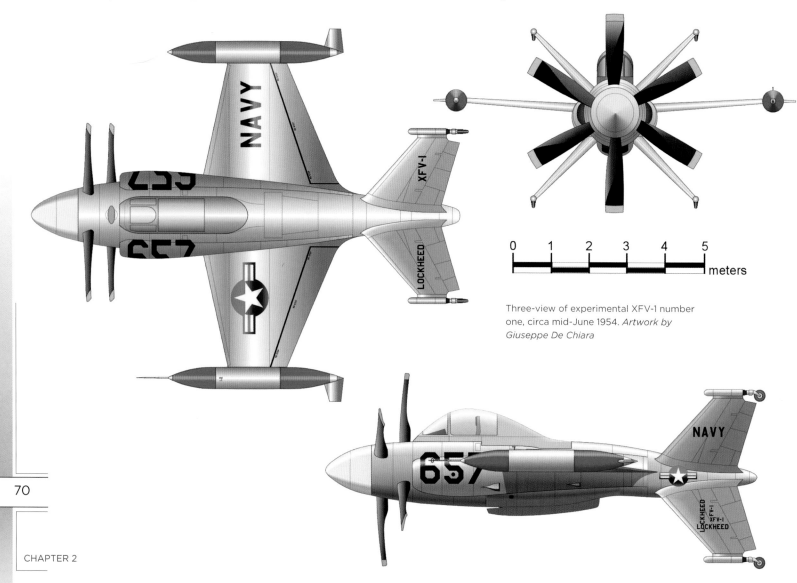

Three-view of experimental XFV-1 number one, circa mid-June 1954. *Artwork by Giuseppe De Chiara*

USN contract NOas 51-1123, dated July 16, 1951, called for the creation of two experimental Class VF (Convoy Fighter) VTOL aircraft designated XFV-1 (previously XFO-1). Artist concept of FV-1s taking off straight up. *Author collection*

Below: Salmon climbed ladder to ingress XFV-1 number one prior to its first flight on June 16, 1954. *USN*

Above: Full-color study of XFV-1 number one. *LM Code One*

Below: USN Design Specification SD 483-0-1 called for the Aerodynamic/Structural prototype airplane (XFV-1 number one) to be armed with four 20mm cannon with 600 rounds of 20mm ammunition (150 rounds per gun) in two two-gun pods mounted on either wingtip. Chief engineering test pilot Herm Salmon posed near "Salmon" number one. *LM via Denny Lombard*

THE 1950S: FORTHCOMING TECHNOLOGIES

XFV-1

SPECIFICATIONS

CREW: One (pilot)

PROPULSIVE SYSTEM: One axial-flow 5,850-shp Allison XT40-A-6 turbopropjet engine

LENGTH: 36 ft 2 in

WINGSPAN: 30 ft 6.34 in

WING AREA: 246 sq ft

EMPTY WEIGHT: 11,314 lbs

GROSS TAKEOFF WEIGHT: 15,960 lbs

MAXIMUM SPEED: 525 mph at 35,000 ft

MAXIMUM RANGE: 45 min endurance

SERVICE CEILING: 47,000 ft

ARMAMENT: None (prototype); four 20mm cannon (600 total rounds 20mm ammunition—150 rounds per cannon) or 48 2.75-inch FFARs (production)

PAYLOAD: None

First flight on XFV-1 number one with ungainly but adequate temporary landing gear for conventional takeoffs and landings. *USN*

Salmon in cockpit. *USN*

The design engine for dedicated VTOL flight test activities, the 7,100 shaft horsepower (shp) YT40-A-14, was never produced.

Eugene C. "Gene" Frost invented what he called a Parachute Means of Landing Aircraft to be used on the XFV-1. On May 22, 1951, he applied for a patent, and on March 23, 1954, he received a fourteen-year patent on this invention. As designed, a large-diameter parachute was to be installed onto a stationary shaft within the propeller spinner. In an emergency during vertical takeoff or landing, the parachute could be deployed to help lower the aircraft back down safely for a four-point landing on its tail wheels.

A follow-on production XFV-2 version was offered (Model 181-43-02) for operational use, but it didn't proceed. It was to be powered by the larger and more powerful Allison T54-A-16 turbopropjet engine, which never materialized. It would have featured armor plating around the cockpit, a bulletproof cockpit canopy windscreen, and a radar dish inside the non-rotating part of the propeller spinner. Its armament was to be comprised of four 20mm cannon—two inside each wingtip pod. Each one of these pods, interchangeably, could have carried twenty-four unguided 2.75-inch diameter "Mighty Mouse" FFARs.

SUMMARY

The USN canceled the Lockheed XFV-1 program after thirty-two flights on June 16, 1955, and its entire VTOL turbopropjet-powered VF Convoy Fighter program outright in 1956. Neither Lockheed nor Convair received further funding on their respective XFV "Rising Star" and XFY "Pogo" projects. (The name *Rising Star* was proposed by Lockheed but wasn't accepted by the USN; the name *Pogo* was also unofficial.)

In any event, due to inadequate propulsive system power, neither design would have been able to exceed 600 miles per hour as had been hoped. Moreover, the piloting skills needed to operate such an aircraft were far too demanding. Thus, neither design ascended from terra firma again.

The first XFV-1 was donated to the US Naval Air Museum in Pensacola, Florida, but it now resides at the Sun 'n Fun Campus Museum at Lakeland Linder Regional Airport in Lakeland, Florida. The second XFV-1, slated for static structural tests, is on display at Los Alamitos Army Airfield near Los Alamitos, California.

Years later, to honor the only person to fly the XFV-1, Lockheed memorialized Fish Salmon by naming the XFV-1 after him. After all, salmon do swim upstream.

Hercules: The YC-130

Not all of the aircraft coming out of the Skunk Works are beautiful triplesonic air vehicles that fly nearly 20 miles above our planet. Most are exceptional airplanes nonetheless. One such airplane is the esteemed medium-class C-130 cargo transport called Hercules.

The C-130 series of aircraft has been produced since 1955, when it first entered into full-scale production. No other series of aircraft has enjoyed such a long production run. C-130s are still in production, with no end in sight, and more than seventy versions of it have been produced, operating out of more than sixty countries.

This sixty-seven-and-more-year production run would not have taken place if not for Willy Hawkins, who designed the "Herc," as the remarkable C-130 is fondly nicknamed.

Dick Pulver was appointed chief engineer on the TDN-206 project, later the Model 82 program, from which the still-growing fleet of C-130s was born. The 130-page proposal for the RFP was prepared and submitted in January 1951. Lockheed won the tactical medium-class cargo airplane competition on July 2, 1951, and the USAF ordered two prototype YC-130 airplanes under USAF ARDC Project MX-1704, contract number AF-30543, approved on August 12, 1953 (USAF serial numbers 53-3396 and 53-3397).

The second of these was the first to fly, as the number-one YC-130 served as the structural static test article. This came about on August 23, 1954, when pilot Stanley A. "Stan" Beltz and copilot Roy E. Wimmer flew YC-130 number two (53-3397) after taking off from the Lockheed Air Terminal in Burbank. Richard "Dick" Stanton and Jack G. Real were respectively the flight engineer and flight test engineer, and the airplane landed at Edwards AFB after sixty-one minutes in the air for additional flight test activities.

The first of the two prototype YC-130s (53-3396) made its first flight on January 21, 1955. The flight, Burbank to Edwards, was flown by pilot Roy Wimmer, copilot Joseph F. "Joe" Ware Jr., and flight test engineer Jack Real.

Earlier, on October 1, 1953, inventors Kelly Johnson, Willy Hawkins Jr., and Gene Frost had applied for its patent. On September 7, 1954—less than a month after first

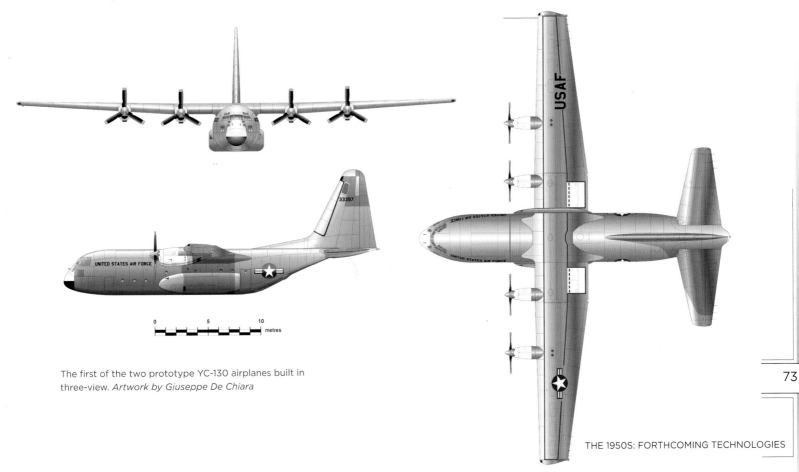

The first of the two prototype YC-130 airplanes built in three-view. *Artwork by Giuseppe De Chiara*

73

YC-130 (Model 082-44-01)

SPECIFICATIONS

CREW: Three (pilot, copilot, and flight test engineer)

PROPULSIVE SYSTEM: Four axial-flow, 3,250-shp Allison T56-A-1 turboprojet engines spinning three-bladed Curtiss Electric propellers

LENGTH: 90 ft 2.5 in

HEIGHT: 38 ft 0 in

WINGSPAN: 132 ft 6 in

EMPTY WEIGHT: 57,500 lbs

MAXIMUM TAKEOFF WEIGHT: 124,200 lbs

MAXIMUM SPEED: 383 mph at 20,400 ft

MAXIMUM RANGE: 3,215 mi

MAXIMUM CEILING: 41,300 ft

Below left: Designers/inventors Kelly Johnson, Willis M. Hawkins, and Eugene C. Frost applied for their patent on October 1, 1953; their fourteen-year patent was grated on September 7, 1954. *United States Patent Office*

Below middle: Page 3 of patent.

Below right: Page 4 of patent.

flight—they received a fourteen-year patent.

The C-130J Super Hercules or "Super Herc" is the current production version and is enjoying great success. Only the two YC-130s were produced in Burbank, with more than 2,500 others being built at the Lockheed Martin facility in Marietta, Georgia. Lockheed Martin has delivered C-130s to sixty-three nations.

SUMMARY

The turboprojet-powered and propeller-driven C-130 Hercules and Super Hercules series of tactical medium-class airlifters are operated by all branches of the US Armed Forces, as well as numerous US allies and friends.

The C-130 is a time-proven airframe propelled by a time-proven powerplant. The Herc began life in the Skunk Works and grew up throughout the world, both at home and abroad. It is an invaluable asset to numerous air forces and navies everywhere on the planet, and it will continue to be the vital multipurpose aircraft it is for many years to come.

The C-130 was "designed right the first time," as Hawkins said, and it truly was and is a Herculean aircraft.

On December 11, 2015, Lockheed Martin delivered its

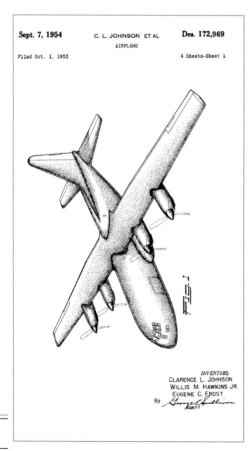

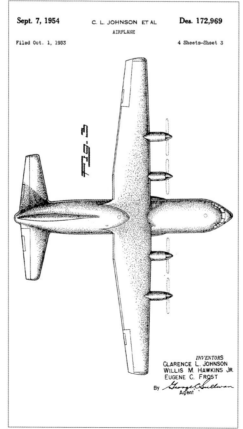

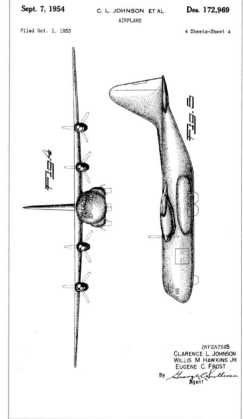

Above: Inboard engine startup on YC-130 number two (*USAF* serial number 53-3397) prior to its first flight on August 23, 1954. *NMUSAF*

Left: First takeoff of YC-130 number two—first to fly—from Burbank to Edwards AFB. YC-130 number one (USAF serial number 53-3396) served as the static structural test article. *LM* Code One

DISSIMILAR PARALLELS

The US government, especially the five branches of the US Armed Forces, has uncountable networks for its operations. Some of these operations are unclassified, but a lot of them are classified, highly classified, secret, top secret, black, and blacker than black.

In the early 1950s the USAF began to look into the feasibility of using liquid hydrogen gas as a fuel source for its aircraft. Hydrogen gas produces water when it's burned. The word *hydrogen*, in Greek, means "water-former."

In early 1956 the USAF created a highly classified project it dubbed Suntan. Project Suntan would be the USAF's effort to develop a hydrogen-gas-fueled airplane with performance superior to the U-2, which had just recently taken wing.

In the spring of 1956 the USAF secretly ordered two prototype CL-400 aircraft under the super-secret Suntan program, and the first example was to fly eighteen months later in the fall of 1957. Before the ink on this contract had dried, the USAF added six production airplanes to the classified document. Lockheed never assigned a model number to its TDN CL-400 series of designs, and the USAF never allocated a designation to the version of the CL-400 it had ordered.

Following a short competition between General Electric and Pratt & Whitney, the latter was selected to produce the propulsive system for the CL-400. The engine, like the air vehicle, was not issued a designation and was only known as the Model 304-2.

2,500th production Hercules: an HC-130J Combat King II (13-5782), marking fifty-nine years of continuous production. The first Hercules delivered was a C-130A (53-3129), and it was delivered on December 9, 1956.

Suntan: TDN CL-400

There were two interesting Skunk Works programs that overlapped one another. These intersecting programs—both designed to create high-altitude, liquid-hydrogen-fuel-burning reconnaissance aircraft—were as similar as they were dissimilar. No smoke and mirrors here: it's just the way it worked out for all of the parties involved with these two programs. And both were intertwined with several others under Project Bald Eagle.

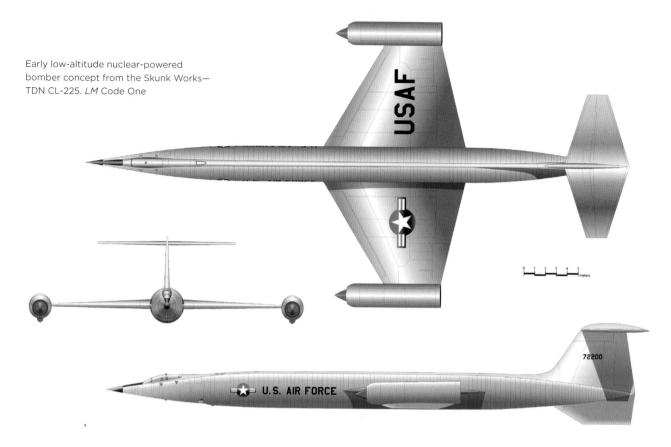

Early low-altitude nuclear-powered bomber concept from the Skunk Works—TDN CL-225. *LM Code One*

CL-400

LENGTH	160'
SPAN	83'9"
T.O.G.W.	69,955 LB
PAYLOAD	1,500 LB
CREW	2

Lockheed TDN CL-400-10 configuration was preferred over the -11, -12, -13, -14, and -15JP examples, among others. *LM via Denny Lombard*

As ordered, the CL-400 was to be capable of Mach 2.5 (1,850 miles per hour) cruise speed at 99,410 feet. It had a fuselage diameter of 9.84 feet, a length of 160.76 feet, and it was to hold 21,473 pounds of liquid hydrogen fuel. Its range was to be 2,530 miles. This gave it a radius to target of just 1,265 miles (the USAF wanted a minimum range of 3,480 miles and a radius to target of 1,740 miles), which would eventually prove to be a significant breakdown in the program. It featured a retractable ventral fin on centerline to improve its stability during high-speed flight.

The Pratt & Whitney Model 304-2 engine was to produce 9,442 pound foot at sea level and 6,070 pound foot at Mach 2.5 (1903 miles per hour) and 95,144 feet; engine weight was 6,283 pounds each.

There were to be three fuel tanks within the CL-400 aircraft: the forward tank, 17,699.5 gallons; the center (sump) tank, 3,962.6 gallons; and the aft tank, 14,265.3 gallons.

In appearance the CL-400 closely resembled the earlier CL-325 design and was reminiscent of the F-104 Starfighter in that it had a similar cockpit canopy, single T-tail, and straight, thin wings. Its engines were to be mounted one on either wingtip. With an overall length of more than 160 feet, it would have covered more than half of a football field.

As previously mentioned, the Suntan program was highly classified. Very few persons were privy to its existence, and even though the program was terminated before any air vehicle was built, it led directly to the creation of the first rocket engine that burned liquid hydrogen fuel (LH2) with liquid oxygen and actually went into service powering the Atlas-Centaur upper stage system in 1962.

THE CL-325 AND THE REX SERIES OF ENGINES FIASCO

In late 1955 a British-born aeronautic, thermodynamic, and propulsive systems engineer was working for the Garrett Corporation in Los Angeles, California. Randolph Samuel "Randy" Rae had designed a different type of non-air-breathing engine, which he simply called a "Jet Power Unit for an Aircraft," that would burn liquid hydrogen instead of kerosene-based jet petroleum fuel. He named his rather unique turborocket engine design the *Rex-I*. At the time of his employment, the Garrett Corporation was a manufacturer of small aircraft engines, flight control systems, gyroscopes, and various other aircraft, missile, and rocket components.

The Garrett Corporation was a strong advocate for Rae's engine designs. So much so, in fact, that it purchased the rights to his patent, formed the Rex Engine division, and made Rae chief engineer. The opening paragraph in Rae's patent application of November 22, 1954, states, "This invention relates to a jet power unit for an aircraft and more particularly to a non-air-breathing jet motor which utilizes separate supplies of low temperature liquid fuel and liquid oxygen carried by the aircraft. The liquid oxygen for the jet motor is continually produced during the flight of the aircraft by liquefying oxygen from atmospheric air so that no more liquid oxygen need be carried by the aircraft than is required for continuous operation of the jet power unit."

The Summers Gyroscope Company, for which Rae had worked, contacted the ARDC in Baltimore, Maryland. The Garrett Corporation acquired Summers Gyroscope Company in the interim. Thus, by proxy, Rae now worked for the Garrett Corporation.

The ARDC liked what Mr. Rae had proposed, and an appointment was set up for Rae to meet with Wright Air Development Center officials at Wright Field in Dayton, Ohio. On March 24, 1954, he presented his firm's brochure for what was entitled "Rex-1, A New Aircraft System."

Rae's division proceeded to develop several versions of the Rex liquid-hydrogen-fueled engine. By late 1955 there were three versions: Rex-I, Rex-II, and Rex-III. Rex-I was the non-afterburning jet-propulsion variant of a hydrogen expansion engine; Rex-II was an afterburning hydrogen expansion engine; and Rex-III was a hydrogen expansion engine with heat exchangers and burners to augment thrust.

Lockheed showed its two CL-325 designs to Wright Field on February 15, 1956. The first of these designs, known as CL-325-1, featured a very long, cylinder-shaped fuselage with thin straight wings and a single internal liquid hydrogen tank. The second of these designs, known as CL-325-2, was similar to the CL-325-1 but had jettisonable external wing tanks in addition to a smaller internal tank, and it was smaller than the -1 version. Both designs had single T-tails similar to those found on F-104 Starfighters. Both featured the use of wingtip-mounted Garrett Rex-III engines.

On October 16, 1958, the USAF directed that all work on the Lockheed CL-325 air vehicles and the Garrett Rex series of engines be terminated.

CL-325-1

SPECIFICATIONS

CREW: Two (pilot and reconnaissance systems operator)

PROPULSIVE SYSTEM: 2 4,500-lbf (takeoff and climb) Garrett Rex-III hydrogen expansion engines; 3,750 lbf (at 100,065 ft altitude)

LENGTH: 153 ft 3 in

HEIGHT: 28 ft 6 in

WINGSPAN: 79 ft 9 in

WING AREA: 2,250 sq ft

EMPTY WEIGHT: 29,436 lbs

MAXIMUM TAKEOFF WEIGHT: 45,704 lbs

MAXIMUM SPEED: Mach 2.25 (1712.7 mph) cruise

MAXIMUM RANGE (RADIUS TO TARGET): 1,738 mi

PAYLOAD: 1,500 lbs

CEILING: 100,065 ft

CL-400-10

SPECIFICATIONS

CREW: Two

PROPULSIVE SYSTEM: Two P&W 304-2 engines

LENGTH: 164 ft 10 in

HEIGHT: 30 ft 0 in

WINGSPAN: 83 ft 9 in

WING AREA: 2,400 sq ft

EMPTY WEIGHT: 48,515 lbs

GROSS WEIGHT: 69,955 lbs

FUEL LOAD: 21,440 lbs

PAYLOAD: 1,500 lbs

Conceptual illustration showing a Suntan serving as a tanker as it refuels another Suntan. *Artwork by Jozef Gatial*

CL-400-11

SPECIFICATIONS

CREW: Two

PROPULSIVE SYSTEM: Two P&W 304-2 engines

LENGTH: 206 ft 8 in

HEIGHT: 36 ft 0 in

WINGSPAN: 77 ft 6 in

WING AREA: 3,000 sq ft

EMPTY WEIGHT: 66,508 lbs

GROSS WEIGHT: 116,508 lbs

FUEL LOAD: 50,000 lbs

PAYLOAD: 1,500 lbs

CL-400-12

SPECIFICATIONS

CREW: Two

PROPULSIVE SYSTEM: Four P&W 304-3 engines

LENGTH: 272 ft 0 in

HEIGHT: 50 ft 0 in

WINGSPAN: 110 ft 0 in

WING AREA: 6,000 sq ft

EMPTY WEIGHT: 140,530 lbs

GROSS WEIGHT: 115,000 lbs

FUEL LOAD: 115,000 lbs

PAYLOAD: 1,500 lbs

SUMMARY

The Suntan program proved to be a colossal waste of time and money, but it was an interesting project nonetheless. Johnson, not wanting to butt heads any longer with stubborn government officials over Suntan requirements—especially its range requirement of 2,800 miles—demanded that the program be terminated, for he knew that even on its best day, 2,200 miles would be the maximum range of Suntan. In February 1959 the Suntan program officially ended.

By this time, however, the Gusto program—renamed Oxcart on September 29, 1959—was at the forefront, and the Suntan program was relegated to the corporation's history.

USAF Neptune: The RB-69A

The USAF RB-69A aircraft were modified USN P2V-7 Neptune airplanes. The service test Lockheed YP2V-7 (Lockheed Model 726-45-14; USN Bureau Number 135544) made its first flight on April 26, 1954, out of Burbank, California, where the Neptune assembly line was located. The -7 was the last version of the P2V (P-2 after September 1962) ordered and produced.

In late 1954 the Central Intelligence Agency (CIA) obtained five newly built P2V-7s and had them converted, by Lockheed's Skunk Works at Hangar B5 in Burbank,

CL-400-13

SPECIFICATIONS

CREW: Two

PROPULSIVE SYSTEM: Two STR-12 engines

LENGTH: 296 ft 6 in

HEIGHT: 68 ft 0 in

WINGSPAN: 84 ft 0 in

WING AREA: 6,500 sq ft

EMPTY WEIGHT: 213,150 lbs

GROSS WEIGHT: 376,000 lbs

FUEL LOAD: 162,850 lbs

PAYLOAD: 1,500 lbs

CL-400-14

SPECIFICATIONS

CREW: Two

PROPULSIVE SYSTEM: FourSTR-12 (85% scale) engines

LENGTH: 290 ft 0 in

HEIGHT: 52 ft 3 in

WINGSPAN: 98 ft 0 in

WING AREA: 5,500 sq ft

EMPTY WEIGHT: 178,500 lbs

GROSS WEIGHT: 358,500 lbs

FUEL LOAD: 180,000 lbs

PAYLOAD: 1,500 lbs

CL-400-15JP

SPECIFICATIONS

CREW: Two

PROPULSIVE SYSTEM: Two P&W J58 engines burning jet petroleum fuel

LENGTH: 144 ft 6 in

HEIGHT: 36 ft 0 in

WINGSPAN: 56 ft 6 in

WING AREA: 1,800 sq ft

EMPTY WEIGHT: 53.620 lbs

GROSS WEIGHT: 158,620 lbs

FUEL LOAD: 104,000 lbs

PAYLOAD: 1,500 lbs

into P2V-7U/RB-69A variants for its private fleet of covert electronic intelligence (ELINT)/ferret aircraft. Later to make up P2V-7U/RB-69A operational losses, the CIA obtained and converted two existing USN P2V-7s, one in September 1962 and one in December 1964, to P2V-7U/RB-69A Phase VI standard, and also acquired an older P2V-5 from the USN as a training aircraft in 1963. Test flights were done by lead aircraft at Edwards AFB from 1955 to 1956, with all the aircraft painted a dark sea-blue color with USAF markings. In 1957 one P2V-7U was sent to Eglin AFB in Florida for testing of aircraft performance at low level and under adverse conditions. The initial two aircraft were sent to Europe, based at

Wiesbaden, West Germany, but withdrawn in 1959 when the CIA reduced its covert aircraft assets in Europe. The CIA sent the other two P2V-7U/RB-69As to Hsinchu Air Base, Taiwan, where by December 1957 they were given to a "black ops" unit, the 34th Squadron (better known as the Black Bat Squadron) of the Republic of China Air Force (ROCAF/Taiwan). They were painted with ROCAF/Taiwan markings. The ROCAF/Taiwan P2V-7U/RB-69A's mission was to conduct low-level penetration flights into mainland China for ELINT/ferret missions, including mapping China's air-defense networks, inserting agents via airdrop, and dropping leaflets and supplies. The agreement for plausible deniability between the US and Republic of China governments meant the RB-69A would be manned by ROCAF/Taiwan crew while conducting operational missions and by CIA crew when ferrying RB-69A out of Taiwan or other operational area to the United States.

The P2V-7U/RB-69A flew with the Black Bat Squadron over China from 1957 to November 1966. All five original aircraft were lost with all hands on board (two crashed in South Korea, three were shot down over China). In January 1967, the two remaining RB-69As flew back to Naval Air Station (NAS) Alameda, California, and were converted back to regular USN P2H/P2V-7 ASW aircraft configurations. Most of the 34th Squadron's missions remain classified by the CIA, although a 1972 CIA internal draft history, "Low-Level Technical Reconnaissance over mainland China (1955–66)," reference CSHP-2.348, covering CIA/ROCAF/Taiwan 34th Squadron's black operations, is known to be in existence but would not be declassified by the CIA until after 2022.

The electronic intelligence–gathering mission was designed from the outset to "listen" to military communications being emitted by all potential adversaries. The P2V-7U version of the USN Neptune patrol bomber was selected for the mission. Seven of these were transferred to the USAF. The CIA opted for these specially modified airplanes to complete its fleet of "special purpose" RB-69As.

The Lockheed RB-69A program remains to be somewhat mysterious. It is known, however, that the seven USAF RB-69A airplanes were former USN P2V-7U Neptune aircraft that were transferred to the USAF during FY 1954, and that they were used for ELINT operations in Southeast Asia under CIA Secret Project Cherry, soon changed to Project Wild Cherry so as to not be confused with Project Cherry, a different secret operation in which the CIA trained and deployed US Army teams of assassins.

Skunk Works personnel, headed by Kelly Johnson and program manager Luther McDonald, modified five new-build P2V-7s and two prior-service P2V-7s throughout 1954 and 1955. As each example was completed it was parked on the P2V-7 flight line for preflight testing. They blended in very well with the other Neptune airplanes, so nobody became suspicious of their true nature. Only their USAF markings and various ELINT equipment bulges hinted at anything all that different from their USN counterparts.

During the 1954 and 1955, the latest USAF bomber was the Douglas RB-66A Destroyer. The Radioplane/ Northrop XB-67 Crossbow air-launched, anti-radar/decoy missile wasn't a bomber at all and was later redesignated XGAM-67 to make that clear; the Martin XB-68 was to be a doublesonic tactical bomber, but it was canceled and replaced by the Martin XB-68 Titan intercontinental ballistic missile (ICBM), which was, ironically, temporarily and erroneously considered to be a strategic bomber. The modified USN P2V-7 Neptune antisubmarine patrol bombers were given the USAF designation RB-69A and never received an official name or unofficial nickname.

After their respective ground tests and contractor flight tests, they were flown some hundred miles northeast of Burbank to the North Base area of Edwards AFB for equipment calibrations and flight crew training. Operational evaluations were then performed at Eglin

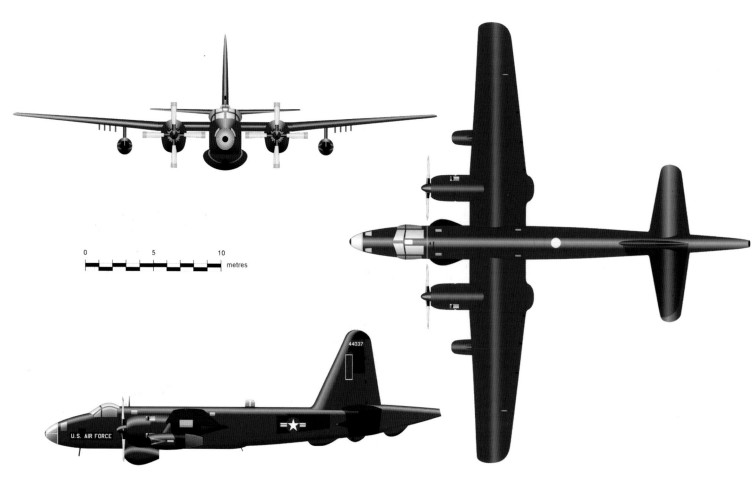

0   5   10
                metres

Left-hand side view of first RB-69A. *NMUSAF*

AFB, after which they were ferried from Florida via the southern route to North Africa and then north to their base of operations in Germany.

During 1955 and 1956, while based in Wiesbaden, Germany, the RB-69As were operated along the western border of Russia, in part to catalog its power grid. Beginning in early 1957, while based at Hsinchu Air Base, the RB-69As operated along the eastern border of China and elsewhere in Southeast Asia.

When RB-69A operations ended, the surviving aircraft were mothballed at the Aircraft Maintenance and Regeneration Center in Kingman, Arizona. Project Wild Cherry had been a stopgap operation while the CIA waited for the U-2 to become operational.

OPERATIONS

Very little is known on an official basis about the actual CIA operations of these RB-69A aircraft. It is known that they began secret operations in 1955 in Germany, followed by covert operations in 1957 in Taiwan. What is acknowledged is as follows.

An undisclosed RB-69A successfully penetrated the airspace of the People's Republic of China on December 15, 1958, and completed its mission.

Another CIA/USAF/ROCAF RB-69A (USAF serial number 54-4040; USN BuNo 140442) crashed into a hillside on March 25, 1960. It happened during a low-level ferry flight from Hsinchu AB, Taiwan, to a staging area in Kunsan, South Korea, and all fourteen of its crewmembers were killed.

On November 6, 1961, another fourteen crewmembers were lost when a CIA/USAF/ROCAF RB-69A (USAF serial number 54-4039; US Bureau Number 140440) crashed to destruction after it was shot down by an SA-2 Guideline surface-to-air missile while flying a low-level penetration flight over Shantung province, People's Republic of China.

A CIA/USAF/ROCAF RB-69A (USAF serial number 54-4038; USN Bureau Number 140438) crashed into the Korean Bay on January 8, 1962, while conducting an ELINT and leaflet-dropping mission. The reason for its crash remains a mystery, but all fourteen crewmembers were lost.

On August 1, 1962, another thirteen crewmembers were lost when an undisclosed CIA/USAF/ROCAF RB-69A was shot down over the People's Republic of China.

On June 14, 1963, a CIA/USAF/ROCAF RB-69A (USAF serial number 54-4041; USN Bureau Number 141233) was

81

Top: Three-quarter rear view of first RB-69A. *NMUSAF*

Above: Rear view of first RB-69A. *NMUSAF*

shot down near Nanchang in the People's Republic of China, killing its crew of fourteen. The aircraft was shot down by a People's Liberation Army Air Force (PLAAF) MiG-17PF Fresco flown by Wang Wenli. Other accounts say this incident happened on June 19 or 20.

A CIA/USAF/ROCAF RB-69A (USAF serial number 54-4037; USN Bureau Number 135612) was shot down on June 11, 1964, near Yantai, Shantung Peninsula, killing its thirteen crewmembers. This nighttime interception was made by a PLAAF MiG-17F Fresco, aided by an Iluyshin Il-28 Beagle that dropped flares to light up the airplane.

SUMMARY

For the most part the CIA RB-69A program—Secret Project Cherry-cum-Wild Cherry—remains classified. It's one of most shielded programs from the CIA and the Skunk Works. What these aircraft did, where they did it, and for whom has not been publically disclosed at this writing. No official RB-69A program documentation has surfaced that this writer is aware of. Pertinent information, such as its primary command (Strategic Air Command [SAC], TAC, or ADC), user unit(s), and the names of crewmembers, remains unknown. Still, as reported in other references, the program was for the most part successful.

RB-69A

SPECIFICATIONS

CREW: Fourteen (pilot, copilot, flight engineer, navigator/radioman, and ten ELINT systems operators)

PROPULSIVE SYSTEM: Two air-cooled, 3,500-hp Wright R-3350-32W Cyclone 18-cylinder, turbo-compound, radial piston engines; two axial-flow, non-afterburning, 3,400-lbf Westinghouse J34-WE-36 turbojet engines

LENGTH: 91 ft 8 in

HEIGHT: 29 ft 4 in

WINGSPAN: 103 ft 10 in

WING AREA: 1,000 sq ft

EMPTY WEIGHT: 49,935 lbs

GROSS TAKEOFF WEIGHT: 79,895 lbs

MAXIMUM SPEED: 400 mph at 14,000 ft (all engines)

SERVICE CEILING: 22,400 ft

MAXIMUM RANGE: 3,750 mi (estimated)

ARMAMENT: None

PAYLOAD: Classified

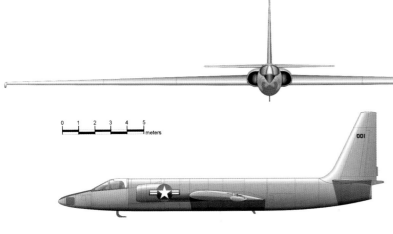

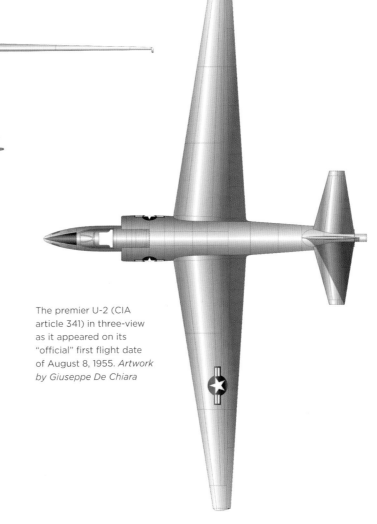

Aquatone: The U-2

In July 1953 the Bell Aircraft Corporation and the Fairchild Engine and Aircraft Corporation received study contracts to develop an entirely new high-altitude reconnaissance aircraft. In addition, the Glenn L. Martin Aircraft Company was asked to examine the possibility of improving the already exceptional high-altitude performance of the B-57 Canberra. By the end of January 1954, all three firms had submitted their proposals under what was called Project Bald Eagle, under ARDC Project MX-2147.

Martin's design was a big-wing version of the twin-engine B-57 called the Model 294, which was to cruise at 64,000 feet. Fairchild's entry was a single-engine airplane known as the Model M-195, which had a maximum altitude potential of 67,200 feet. Bell's offering was a twin-engine airplane called the Model 67, which had a maximum altitude possibility of 69,500 feet.

In March 1954, USAF Maj. John Seaberg—a former Chance Vought Aircraft aeronautical engineer—and other USAF engineers at Wright Field, having evaluated the three contending designs, recommended the adoption of both the Martin and Bell proposals. They considered Martin's big-wing version of the B-57 an interim project that could be completed and deployed rapidly while the more advanced concept from Bell was still being developed. Fairchild's M-195 entry fell by the wayside.

Since the big-wing B-57 already had a *B* for "bomber" designation, the special version was simply identified as the D version of the RB-57 reconnaissance bomber. The Model 67 to be built by Bell, however, needed an inconspicuous designator, so the designation X-16 (the *X* prefix meaning "dedicated research") was applied to it to hide its true mission. Thus, the Martin RB-57D and Bell X-16 would be the USAF's dedicated high-altitude reconnaissance aircraft.

Or would they?

The premier U-2 (CIA article 341) in three-view as it appeared on its "official" first flight date of August 8, 1955. *Artwork by Giuseppe De Chiara*

Article 341 was transported partially disassembled for transport from Burbank to Area 51 onboard a Douglas C-124D Globemaster II. *LM Code One*

83

Reassembled Article 341 (tail number 001) posed at Area 51 prior to flight testing. *LM Code One*

NEW KID ON THE BLOCK

As Bell and Martin were moving forward on their respective high-altitude reconnaissance aircraft programs, the Lockheed-California Company got wind of the program. Suddenly there was a new kid on the block who wanted to play. And in early March 1954, as directed by Lockheed-California management, P-38, F-80, and F-104 designer Kelly Johnson came up with Lockheed Temporary Design Number-282, or TDN CL-282. It was immediately submitted to Wright Field as an unsolicited proposal in early April.

Major Seaberg first saw the proposal in mid-May 1954. After he and his engineering fraternity had carefully evaluated the CL-282 proposal, they turned it down. One of the main reasons for their unanimous rejection was Johnson's desire to use the unproved General Electric J73-X52 (formerly J47-21) turbojet engine. They favored the Pratt & Whitney J57 turbojet engine. Another reason was the use of non-conventional landing gear. Finally, it was a single-engine design, whereas a twin-engine design was preferred. The CL-282 proposal was officially rejected on June 7, 1954. It appeared that nobody wanted to play with the new kid.

Nevertheless, Johnson had great faith in his CL-282 design and simultaneously continued to refine it while he looked for potential customers.

In September 1954 the Bell Aircraft Corporation received a contract to produce twenty-eight X-16 airplanes. The first example was to fly in the spring of 1956.

The CL-282 project was authorized in November 1954 and given the USAF code name Oarfish and CIA

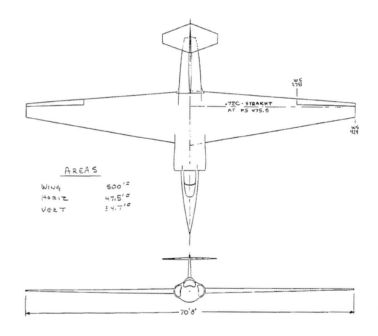

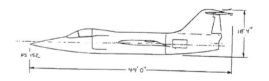

Johnson's original submission (TDN CL-282) was largely based on his F-104 design and was to be powered by a single General Electric J73 turbojet engine. *LM Code One*

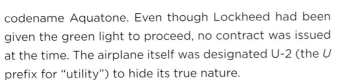

Above: Armed versions of the U-2 were indeed considered, as shown here with this wind tunnel model loaded with various types of ordnance. *LM Code One*

Left: U-2A (USAF serial number 56-6706) cockpit dashboard. *NMUSAF*

codename Aquatone. Even though Lockheed had been given the green light to proceed, no contract was issued at the time. The airplane itself was designated U-2 (the *U* prefix for "utility") to hide its true nature.

Project Oarfish/Project Aquatone became a joint USAF/CIA program, and on December 22, 1964, Lockheed received a Letter Contract for twenty single-seat airplanes and a single two-seat trainer airplane, plus spares. The USAF would supply the engines; the unproven General Electric J73 engine was Johnson's choice from the onset, but it was decided to use a special high-altitude version of the Pratt & Whitney J57 Turbowasp instead—the J57-P-13. A formal CIA contract, number SP-1913, was signed on March 2, 1955, and called for the first U-2 delivery in July 1955 and the last in November 1956, with the first four by December 1, 1955. And, by Johnson's own guarantee, the first flight was to occur no later than August 2, 1955.

The X-16 program was canceled in the late summer of 1956, leaving the big-wing RB-57D to carry the torch until the new kid—the "Super Glider" from Johnson and his Skunk Works—moved in.

THE BELL X-16

Under contract number AF33 (600)-29780, the USAF ordered twenty Bell Model 67 airplanes designated X-16 (USAF serial numbers 56-552 to 56-579). The X-16 itself was designed by Frank William "Bill" Kux, who applied for a fourteen-year patent on June 4, 1956, and received it on April 15, 1958. Bell appointed R. C. Smith as X-16 project engineer. A full-scale engineering mockup was built

and inspected. The first example was about 80 percent complete when the X-16 program was terminated.

BACK TO THE U-2

Referred to as the "Angel" in the Skunk Works, and as the "Article" by the CIA, the U-2 was created to meet stringent CIA requirements under a highly classified top-secret program. The development and operation of the U-2 were critical to US national security and enjoyed a top-priority status.

Once onsite at Area 51, the first U-2—or Article 341 as it was officially called—was reassembled and ground tested in preparation for initial taxi tests and subsequent flight tests. On July 27, 1955, preliminary taxi runs were performed. LeVier took it to 50 knots. A second taxi run was made on August 1, during which LeVier took it to 70 knots to initiate aileron tests. LeVier subsequently performed one more taxi test, and it was agreed that the U-2 was ready for flight.

On August 4, 1955, LeVier took off on an unofficial first flight to see if the "Angel" was a lady or a tramp before CIA and USAF dignitaries were around. Then, on August 8, 1955, with CIA and USAF dignitaries in attendance, the official first flight was made. LeVier took Article 341 up to 32,000 feet and made a near-perfect demonstration flight before landing.

Lockheed Skunk Works test pilot Robert L. "Bob" Matye was the second U-2 pilot. He expanded the U-2's altitude envelope to its maximum operational ceiling. He became chief engineering test pilot on the F-104A/B/C/D programs after his U-2 assignment.

85

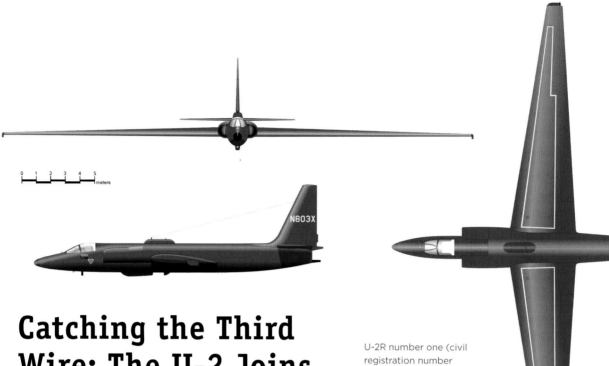

meters
0 1 2 3 4 5

N803X

Catching the Third Wire: The U-2 Joins the US Navy

The early U-2s didn't have limitless range and often couldn't be based close enough for certain overflights. Thus the CIA and USN initiated a program called Project Whale Tail in the early 1960s to investigate the feasibility of operating U-2s from the angled decks of the largest aircraft carriers then in service.

During Project Whale Tail several U-2s were fitted with arresting hooks so that they could snag one of several cables—preferably the third cable—strung across the decks of these aircraft carriers. In action these hooks were to grab a cable to "arrest" the U-2 and bring it to a fast, complete stop; these hooks were good for as many as twenty landings.

Like all carrier-borne aircraft, these U-2s featured beefier landing gear units to address their violent on-deck captures. Since U-2s have a tendency to glide during their landing maneuvers, they were also equipped with special wing spoilers to reduce lift. To take less storage room aboard ship, later U-2s had folding wingtips.

On August 5, 1963, the first U-2 took off from an aircraft carrier. It launched from the relatively new USS *Kitty Hawk* (CVA-63) which was sailing off the West Coast near San Diego, California. On March 2, 1964, the first U-2 landing was made onboard the *Forrestal*-class USS *Ranger* (CVA-61).

Since aircraft carriers need lots of time to sail long distances, U-2 carrier operations were rather sparse. By the time the U-2 would arrive on scene—up to several weeks after the need for their reconnaissance flights—the urgency could very well be null and void.

Q-TIP

The inside windshields on early U-2s had a tendency to fog up, limiting the pilots' forward visibility. U-2 pilots, wearing their cumbersome pressure suits, couldn't reach the windshields to wipe them clean.

This problem was addressed with a simple remedy: the pilots carried along sticks with cloth pads wrapped around one end, like large cotton swabs. These ingenious "Q-tips" allowed the U-2 drivers to clean their windshields during flight.

SUMMARY

Many more examples of the U-2 would be built before its production ended in 1989. Many of these were modified and retrofit to perform all sorts of new duties and types of clandestine missions.

The U-2 is an invaluable aerial Intelligence, Surveillance and Reconnaissance (ISR) platform, and it continues to

U2A

SPECIFICATIONS

CREW: One (Pilot/RSO)

PROPULSIVE SYSTEM: One non-afterburning, axial-flow, 11,000-lbf Pratt & Whitney J57-P-37A turbojet engine

LENGTH: 50 ft 0 in

HEIGHT: 15 ft 0 in

WINGSPAN: 80 ft 0 in

EMPTY WEIGHT (ZERO FUEL): 13,071 to 14,250 lbs, depending on equipment

GROSS TAKEOFF WEIGHT: 22,542 to 24,150 lbs depending on equipment

MAXIMUM CRUISE SPEED: 460 mph at 65,000 ft

SERVICE CEILING: 70,000-plus ft

CRUISE DURATION: 8 hr

ARMAMENT: None

operate at this writing, but beginning in 2014 there was a movement afoot to retire the entire fleet of U-2s. The USAF wanted them gone in favor of less expensive, unoccupied RQ-4 Global Hawks. But, for the time being, the Dragon Lady continues to soar.

U-2R: Rebirth of the U-2

Even though the Blackbird was tearing up even higher altitudes at more than three times the speed of sound, the development of the lower-altitude, subsonic U-2 continued.

Skunk Works test pilot Bill Park was the first to fly the new U-2R version of the Dragon Lady, on August 28, 1967, out of the restricted North Base facility on Edwards AFB. Carrier trials got underway on November 21, 1969, with Park still in the cockpit. He was operating N812X off the USS *America* (CVA-66).

SUMMARY

The U-2R was about 40 percent larger than its predecessor family of U-2s and could therefore carry more equipment within its fuselage and underwing pods. This helped to make the U-2R a more capable reconnaissance platform than its earlier counterparts.

Project Rainbow

The U-2 proved to be highly susceptible to Soviet radar detection. So, beginning in August 1956, just two months after the U-2 became operational, under Secret Project Rainbow, the Lockheed Skunk Works, with the assistance of the Massachusetts Institute of Technology's Lincoln Laboratory, tried to cure this susceptibility with various anti-radar treatments. These treatments included thin film-like veneers called "wallpaper" and external structures called "wires."

During its first Project Rainbow test flight on April 4, 1957, the premier U-2—nicknamed "Dirty Bird" (Article 341)—crashed to destruction, and its pilot, Robert Seiker, was killed. One other Dirty Bird (Article 344) was used in the Project Rainbow program.

The project to reduce the radar cross-section of the U-2 proved unsuccessful and was abandoned in May 1958. It was replaced with Project Gusto, which is described in the next chapter.

U-2R

SPECIFICATIONS

CREW: One (pilot)

PROPULSIVE SYSTEM: One axial-flow, 17,000-lbf Pratt & Whitney J75-P-13B turbojet engine or one axial-flow, 18,000-lbf General Electric F118-GE-101 turbofan engine

LENGTH: 62 ft 10.5 in

HEIGHT: 16 ft 0 in

WINGSPAN: 103 ft 0 in

EMPTY WEIGHT: Classified

GROSS TAKEOFF WEIGHT: Classified

MAXIMUM SPEED: 450 mph

MAXIMUM RANGE: 3,000-plus mi

SERVICE CEILING: 70,000-plus ft

PAYLOAD: Many combinations of intelligence gathering equipment, most of which are classified

NASA ER-2 (NASA number N806NA/USAF serial number 80-1063) on a flight out of Edwards AFB. *NASA*

TR-1A: The Ultimate U-2

The U-2 program proved to be a very successful venture for Lockheed, and the U-2R and its predecessor variants continued to perform their respective duties very well indeed, even up to this writing. But U-2R production was nearing its end, and the Skunk Works came up with an advanced version to sell in hope of generating additional funds for the Lockheed Aircraft Corporation.

To get the program rolling the USAF ordered three aircraft—one designated ER-2 and two designated TR-1B. The single ER-2, the TR-1A program testbed airplane (USAF serial number 80-1063), was first flown at Palmdale on May 11, 1981, with Skunk Works engineering test pilot Arthur Joseph "Art" Peterson at the controls. It was delivered to the National Aeronautics and Space Administration (NASA) as N706NA after its contractor/USAF flight test and equipment evaluations. (The prefix *ER* means "Earth resources.")

The first military-equipped TR-1A was completed in Palmdale in July 1981. Skunk Works engineering test pilot

TR-1A/-1B

SPECIFICATIONS

CREW: TR-1A, one (pilot/tactical reconnaissance systems operator); TR-1B, two (pilot/instructor, student pilot)

PROPULSIVE SYSTEM (ORIGINAL): One axial-flow, afterburning, 17,000-lbf (with afterburning) Pratt & Whitney J75-P-13B turbojet engine

PROPULSIVE SYSTEM (LATER): One axial-flow, afterburning, 18,000-lbf (with afterburning) General Electric F118-GE-101 turbofan engine

LENGTH: 62 ft 10.5 in

HEIGHT: 16 ft 0 in

WINGSPAN: 103 ft 0 in

WING AREA: 1,000 sq ft (overall)

EMPTY WEIGHT: 16,000 lbs

GROSS TAKEOFF WEIGHT: 40,000 lbs

MAXIMUM SPEED: 450 mph

MAXIMUM RANGE: 3,000-plus mi

CEILING: 70,000-plus ft

ARMAMENT: None

PAYLOAD: 5,000 lbs

Above: NASA's other ER-2 (NASA number N809NA/USAF serial number 80-1097). Just two ER-2s were built on the TR-1A production line. *NASA*

Below: U-2S (formerly TR-1A) over USAF Plant 42 on April 16, 2002. *LMSW photo by Denny Lombard*

Kenneth M. "Ken" Weir was the first person to fly the airplane on August 1, 1981.

Peterson made the first flight on the first of the two-seat TR-1B aircraft from Palmdale on February 23, 1982. The pair of two-seat TR-1B aircraft (80-1064/-1065) were subsequently delivered to the USAF. The thirty-seventh and last production TR-1 was delivered on October 3, 1989.

SUMMARY

All single-seat TR-1As and the two-seat TR-1Bs were redesignated U-2R and U-2RT respectively in 1991; U-2S and U-2ST respectively in 1994.

JetStar

In 1956 the USAF put out an RFP to the industry for a dual-purpose aircraft to meet its experimental utility transport (UCX) and experimental utility trainer (UTX) requirements. Two airframe contractors became the finalists—North American and Lockheed—and their entries were respectively named Sabreliner and JetStar. Two demonstrators of each type were ordered.

Several versions of the JetStar were investigated with two and four engines mounted in the wing roots. The

JETSTAR

SPECIFICATIONS

CREW: Two (pilot and copilot)

PROPULSIVE SYSTEM: Two axial-flow, non-afterburning, 4,520-lbf Bristol Siddeley Model 701 Orpheus turbojet engines

LENGTH: 58 ft 10 in

HEIGHT: 20 ft 6 in

WINGSPAN: 53 ft 8 in

EMPTY WEIGHT: 15,139 lbs

GROSS TAKEOFF WEIGHT: 38,841 lbs

MAXIMUM SPEED: 613 mph at 36,000 ft

SERVICE CEILING: 38,000 ft

MAXIMUM RANGE: 2,300 mi

final offering featured two aft-mounted engines on either side of the fuselage. This Skunk Works JetStar offering, the Model CL-329, was patented on August 31, 1954, by Johnson and Hawkins.

The twin-engine CL-329 JetStar featured sweptback flying surfaces and accommodation for a pilot, copilot, and ten passengers.

The original JetStar posed on the lakebed at Edwards AFB following its first flight. *LM* Code One

Above: The livery of the prototype JetStar was changed several times. This is a later, more attractive scheme. *LM* Code One

Below: First flight photograph of the premier JetStar. *LMSW*

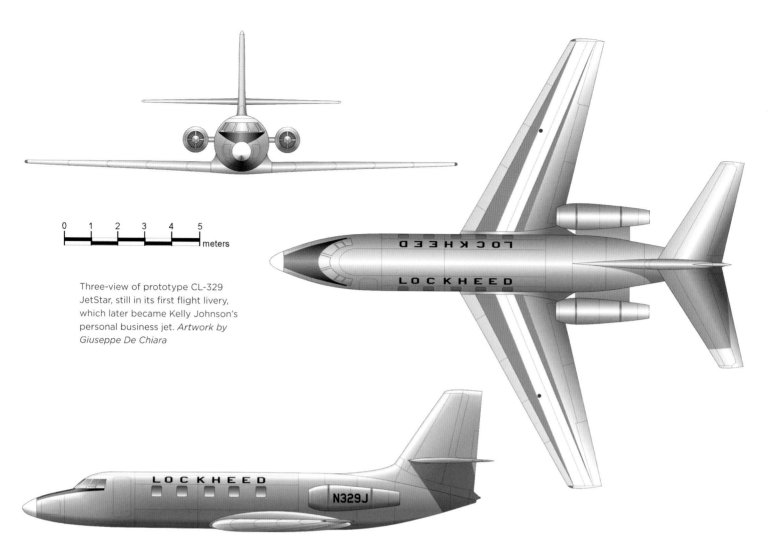

Three-view of prototype CL-329 JetStar, still in its first flight livery, which later became Kelly Johnson's personal business jet. *Artwork by Giuseppe De Chiara*

This is believed to be the final livery of the prototype JetStar when it was Johnson's personal business jet. *LMSW*

On September 4, 1957, Lockheed engineering test pilot Ray Goudey successfully piloted the Lockheed Model CL-329 prototype JetStar out of Burbank, California, and landed at Edwards AFB. His copilot was Lockheed test pilot Robert "Bob" Schumacher. The flight test engineer was Ernest L. "Ernie" Joiner.

Subsequent flight tests went smoothly, and the JetStar was well received—but not by the USAF. Several JetStars were delivered to the USAF as C-140s, but the type was ultimately rejected for further production. Lockheed management decided to put the aircraft into production using its own funds as a full-fledged business jet, and numerous orders for four-jet versions were forthcoming.

The first of the two CL-329 prototype JetStar airplanes was retained by the company and became Kelly Johnson's personal transport. The second CL-329 JetStar prototype was likewise retained by the company.

SAMOS: Satellite Missile Observation System

The WS-117L Satellite Missile Observation System (SAMOS) program traces back to 1945, when intensive studies were initiated in hope of using Earth-orbiting satellites for military purposes. In 1947 it was determined that satellite launchings were feasible, and the DOD became convinced that they could indeed possess military usefulness. It therefore started official go-ahead action on March 16, 1955, by issuing GOR 80 (SA-2C).

WS-117L SAMOS was a result of USAF ARDC Secret Project MX-2226. On October 31, 1956, Lockheed received a Letter Contract, USAF contract number AF 04(647)-97. This program quickly morphed in the Corona program discussed next.

Corona Reconnaissance Satellite System

On August 18, 1960, a Fairchild C-119 Packet cargo transport airplane of the USAF recovered in-flight a Corona satellite's reconnaissance capsule containing photographic film photographed by the satellite's panoramic camera system. This event marked the first mission success of the Corona orbiting satellite reconnaissance spacecraft system, which began as a joint USAF and CIA venture to survey denied territories from Earth orbit.

This particular Corona spacecraft, known as the model Corona C and designated KH-1, was launched

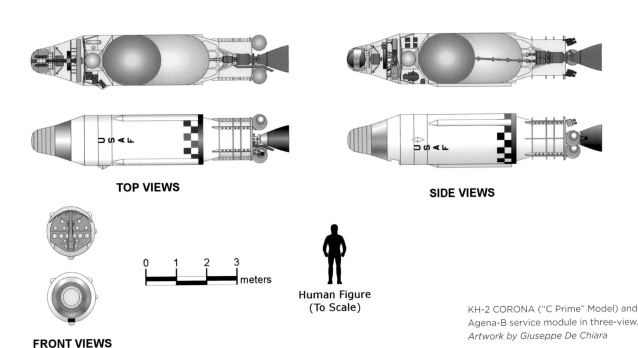

TOP VIEWS

SIDE VIEWS

FRONT VIEWS

0 1 2 3 meters

Human Figure (To Scale)

KH-2 CORONA ("C Prime" Model) and Agena-B service module in three-view.
Artwork by Giuseppe De Chiara

93

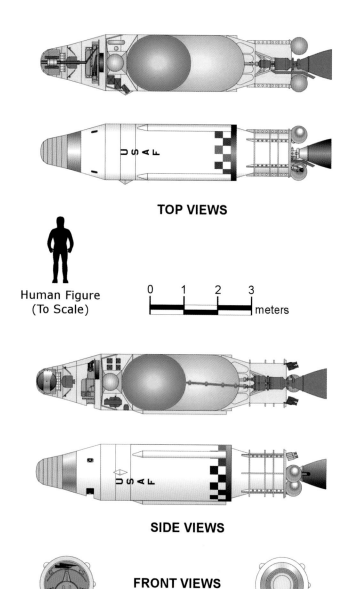

TOP VIEWS

Human Figure
(To Scale)

0   1   2   3

meters

SIDE VIEWS

FRONT VIEWS

Above: KH-3 CORONA ("C Triple Prime" model) and Agena-B service module in three-view. *Artwork by Giuseppe De Chiara*

Opposite top: KH-4 CORONA ("MURAL" Model) and Agena-D service module in three-view. *Artwork by Giuseppe De Chiara*

Opposite middle: KH-4A CORONA ("J1" Model) and Agena-D service module in three-view. *Artwork by Giuseppe De Chiara*

Opposite bottom: KH-4B ("J3" Model) with Agena-D service module in three-view. *Artwork by Giuseppe De Chiara*

into space with a Thor-Agena rocket system, which was comprised of a Douglas PGM-17 Thor first stage and a second-stage Lockheed RM-81 Agena booster that lofted the KH-1 service module into low Earth orbit. The prefix *KH* stood for "Key Hole," which was the CIA code name for the Corona program.

In an August 25, 2010, Lockheed Martin press release marking the 50th anniversary of the Corona program, Joanne Maguire, executive vice president of Lockheed Martin Space Systems Company, said, "The successes achieved by the Corona team were monumental in protecting our nation and advancing aerospace technology." She added, "Having worked with our government partners on such a vitally important ground-breaking program is a source of tremendous pride for the team. Corona paved the way for far more sophisticated systems that today are providing unprecedented new capabilities for both government and commercial customers around the globe."

The Corona program was the brainchild of Skunk Works engineers. It was then passed on to Lockheed Missiles and Space Company (LMSC) in Sunnyvale, California. Willis Hawkins, who had started with the Corona program when he was still in the Skunk Works, was appointed first president of LMSC. In 1956 LMSC received the Corona prime contract for the entire system except for the Douglas-built Thor booster rocket.

The USAF, its ARDC in particular, assigned weapon system number 117L (WS-117L) to the Satellite Reconnaissance System; the *L* suffix means "reconnaissance."

The Corona series of spacecraft were later operated by the National Reconnaissance Office—established in 1961—and, once in their orbits, flew pole-to-pole at some 115 miles out from Earth. The returning film canisters held up to 2.1 million feet of undeveloped film. The Corona program lasted twelve years, during which 145 missions were flown, producing more than 800,000 images. This once highly classified program was declassified by President William J. Clinton in 1992.

SUMMARY

From piston- to turbojet- to turbopropjet- to ramjet-powered aircraft and pilotless air vehicles, the 1950s produced many new types of aircraft, including astronaut trainers, cargo transports, an exotically fueled monster, a fighter-interceptor, a propulsive system test vehicle, reconnaissance bombers, aerial platforms, orbiting space satellites, a target drone, a VIP transport, an early warning aircraft, and a vertical takeoff and landing airplane. This incredible decade of achievement for the Skunk Works opened the door for even more exciting aircraft programs to come. And the Skunk Works put these forthcoming technologies to good work, as we'll see in following chapters.

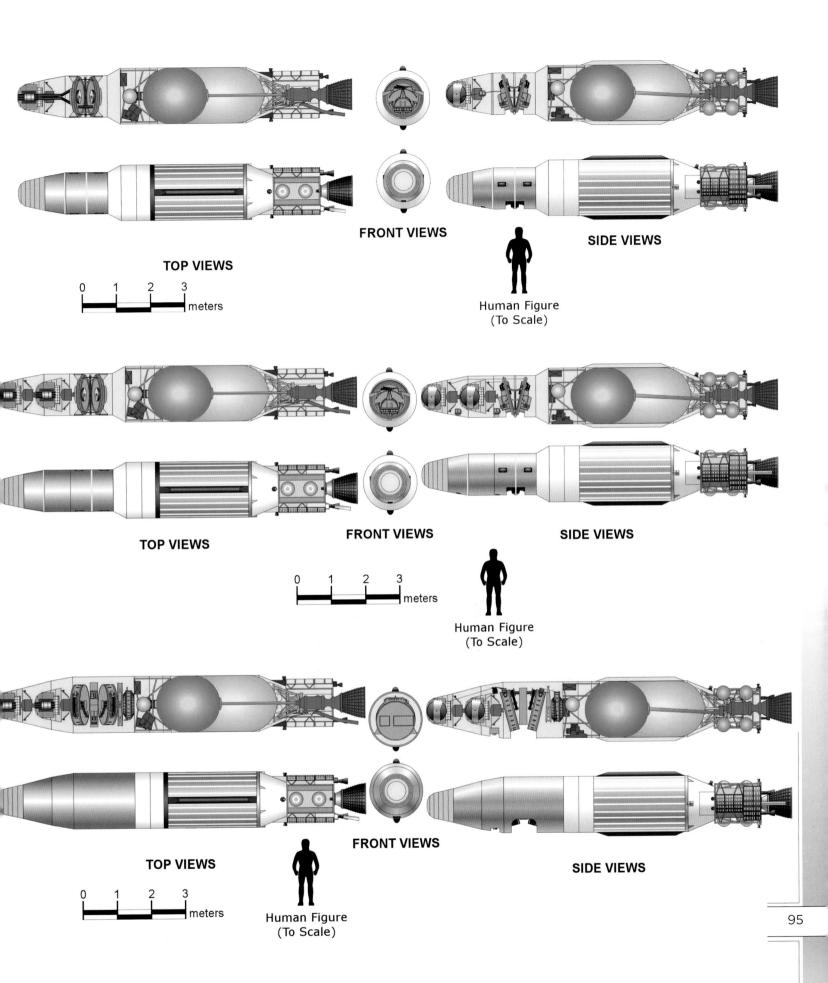

FRONT VIEWS

TOP VIEWS

0 1 2 3
meters

SIDE VIEWS

Human Figure
(To Scale)

TOP VIEWS

0 1 2 3
meters

FRONT VIEWS

SIDE VIEWS

Human Figure
(To Scale)

TOP VIEWS

0 1 2 3
meters

FRONT VIEWS

Human Figure
(To Scale)

SIDE VIEWS

95

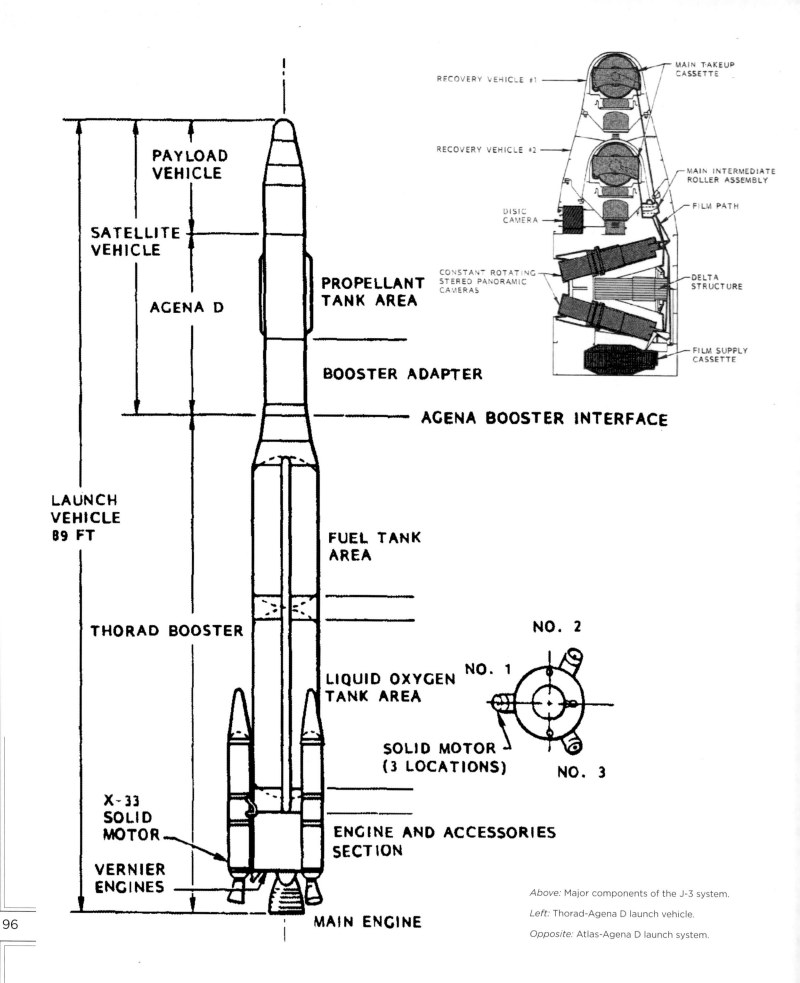

RECOVERY VEHICLE #1 — MAIN TAKEUP CASSETTE

RECOVERY VEHICLE #2

MAIN INTERMEDIATE ROLLER ASSEMBLY

FILM PATH

DISIC CAMERA

CONSTANT ROTATING STEREO PANORAMIC CAMERAS

DELTA STRUCTURE

FILM SUPPLY CASSETTE

PAYLOAD VEHICLE

SATELLITE VEHICLE

AGENA D

PROPELLANT TANK AREA

BOOSTER ADAPTER

AGENA BOOSTER INTERFACE

LAUNCH VEHICLE 89 FT

FUEL TANK AREA

THORAD BOOSTER

NO. 2

NO. 1

LIQUID OXYGEN TANK AREA

SOLID MOTOR (3 LOCATIONS)

NO. 3

X-33 SOLID MOTOR

ENGINE AND ACCESSORIES SECTION

VERNIER ENGINES

MAIN ENGINE

Above: Major components of the J-3 system.

Left: Thorad-Agena D launch vehicle.

Opposite: Atlas-Agena D launch system.

03 THE 1960s: ADVANCING THE STATE OF THE ART

"[I] went to Washington to discuss the A-12 as an air defense fighter to replace the F-108."

—KELLY JOHNSON, EXCERPT FROM HIS *A-12 LOG (ABRIDGED)*, MARCH 16–17, 1960

The 1960s brought nothing less than amazing—even mind-boggling—air vehicles that were created in the Skunk Works. The word *Classified* and the phrase *Top Secret* took on whole new meanings, for the Cold War was hot, and US national security was at the forefront of military planning. Except for those personnel with a need to know, nobody was privy to what was going on behind the closed doors in Burbank, California, and within a highly restricted place in Nevada called Area 51.

The Skunk Works changed what was borderline science fiction into clear-cut science fact during the 1960s by creating aircraft that were heretofore impossible to produce. Moreover, to build these futuristic aircraft, it had to use exotic ingredients and invent the means to process and assemble them from these materials.

It was a time for advanced creations, engineering, and inventions, and the Skunk Works triumphed.

Oxcart: The A-12

Project Gusto was established to find a replacement for the U-2. The ADP and the Convair Division of the General Dynamics Corporation were put to the task.

On August 20, 1959, two Project Gusto offerings from Lockheed and Convair were submitted to a joint CIA/DOD/USAF selection board. The Convair design as proposed—called Kingfish—featured a maximum speed of Mach 3.2 (about 2,370 miles per hour); 4,600-mile range (total unrefueled distance)/3,450-mile range (at maximum altitude); and a starting cruise altitude of 85,000 feet, a midrange altitude of 88,000 feet, and an end (maximum) altitude of 94,000 feet. It measured 79.5 feet long with a wingspan of 56.0 feet. Its gross weight was 101,700 pounds, of which 62,000 pounds was fuel.

The Lockheed design as proposed—called Archangel—featured a maximum speed of Mach 3.2 (about 2,370 miles per hour); 4,740-mile range (total unrefueled distance)/4,370-mile range (at maximum altitude); and a starting cruise altitude of 84,500 feet, a midrange altitude of 91,000 feet, and an end (maximum) altitude of 97,600 feet. It measured 102.0 feet long with a wingspan of 57.0 feet. Its gross weight was 110,000 pounds, of which 64,600 pounds was fuel.

Both firms promised first flight wenty-two months after receiving a contract: June 1961. Both firms had

Area 51

Area 51 is a secluded place in the truest sense of the word. But prying eyes are forever present. It's a place encompassing most of Groom Lake, a large dry lakebed in south central Nevada surrounded for the most part by foothills and mountains. It was used by the USAAF in World War II to train fighter pilots, but after the war it just faded away and was for the most part forgotten—until 1955, that is, when it was rediscovered.

Edwards AFB would have been perfect for the upcoming U-2 flight test program, but it was too conspicuous—even its secretive North Base facility. Thus a place had to be found where there would be no prying eyes.

In 1955, Kelly Johnson revealed the U-2 program to his preferred test pilot, Tony LeVier, and asked him to find an "off-the-planet" place to secretly conduct test flights of the new aircraft. LeVier and Dorsey G. Kammerer (a Skunk Works top mechanic) took the company Beechcraft Bonanza and searched southern Nevada for two weeks until they discovered Groom Lake, which Tony enthusiastically recommended for the program.

On April 12, 1955, Lockheed chief test pilot Tony LeVier, Kelly Johnson, CIA Director Richard M. Bissell Jr., and Col. (later Maj. Gen.) Osmund J. Ritland (senior USAF officer on the project) boarded that same company-owned Bonanza airplane and flew to the Edwards AFB–like place. LeVier landed and they all got out and investigated their surroundings. LeVier had landed adjacent to what appeared from the air to be a paved runway.

As the four men looked around, they discovered that the runway had been made from compacted dirt and that it had turned into some 4 inches of sand-like soil after over ten years of abandonment. But, with a new paved runway, it could be perfect. Thus the area, long uninhabited, was rediscovered.

On May 4, 1955, a survey crew laid out a 5,000-foot north/south runway on the southwest shore of the lake bed, farthest from the mountains to help avoid winter snow melt and rain water runoffs.

This expansive place, known only as Area 51 on a geological survey maps, was actually a dry lake named Groom Lake, but it was nicknamed "Watertown Strip," "The Ranch," "Site II," "Paradise Ranch," and "the new facility in the middle of nowhere." According to Johnson: "We flew over it and within thirty seconds, [we] knew that [it] was the place . . . it was right by a dry lake. Man alive, we looked at that lake, and we all looked at each other. It was another Edwards, so we wheeled around, landed on that lake, [and] taxied up to one end of it. It was a perfect natural landing field . . . as smooth as a billiard table without anything being done to it."

Thus the life and legacy of Area 51 was born.

This pair of SR-71As posed side by side in the fog at Beale AFB, circa early 1990s. *LMSW photo by Eric Schulzinger*

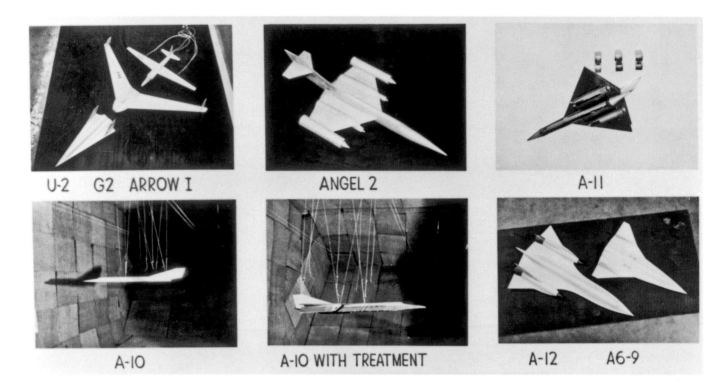

Evolution of A-12 showing: (upper left) Comparison of Arrow I, G2, and U-2; (upper center) Angel 2 (A-2); (upper right) Angel 11 (A-11); (lower left) Angel 10 (A-10); (lower center) A-10 with anti-radar (stealth) treatments; and (lower right) A-12 compared to A-6-9. *LM via Denny Lombard*

Two unidentified Skunk Works personnel discussing the Gusto 2 (G2) flying-wing design—temporarily known as the U-3—investigated under the Lockheed TDN CL-278 series of designs. *LMSW*

presented designs with similar characteristics, but the design from Lockheed won favor and the CIA/DOD/USAF chose the A-12 design of Lockheed over that of Convair. Project Gusto was terminated and replaced with Project Oxcart.

On September 3, 1959, the CIA authorized Lockheed to move forward with engineering designs, aerodynamic structural tests, and anti-radar studies. Then, on January 30, 1960, Lockheed was authorized to build twelve air vehicles. First flight was to occur on August 30, 1961, exactly nineteen calendar months after the production go-ahead.

Initial design studies included the U-3, Arrow I, and G2 (G2—*G* for "Gusto"—had TDN CL-278 assigned to it).

The design propulsive system for these twelve aircraft was the afterburning Pratt & Whitney J58 (Model JT11D) turbojet engine. By September 1960, however, Pratt & Whitney knew it wouldn't meet the required schedule. On September 11, 1959, it told Lockheed of continuing problems on its J58 program as far as its weight, delivery, and performance goals were concerned.

Lockheed had development problems as well, and the completion date for the first airplane slipped to December 22, 1961, and first flight to February 27, 1962, by which time, according to Pratt & Whitney, the J58 still wouldn't be available.

It was time for some agonizing reappraisals.

As an interim measure, it was decided, the afterburning Mach 2–rated Pratt & Whitney J75 turbojet engine—already propelling such notable aircraft as the

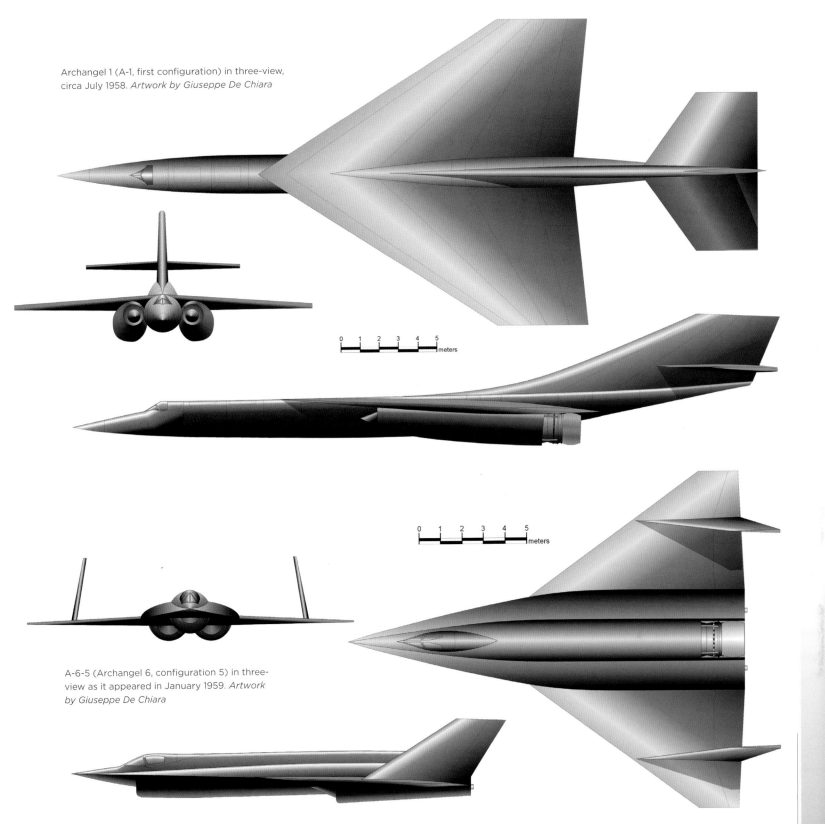

Archangel 1 (A-1, first configuration) in three-view, circa July 1958. *Artwork by Giuseppe De Chiara*

A-6-5 (Archangel 6, configuration 5) in three-view as it appeared in January 1959. *Artwork by Giuseppe De Chiara*

F-105, F-106, and even the latest versions of the U-2—would be used on a temporary basis to propel the aircraft. A-12 number one (with Lockheed factory serial number 121, USAF serial number 60-6924) was completed in Burbank in late December 1961. During January and February 1962 it underwent a series of checkouts and tests before it was partially disassembled and secretly transported by truck to Area 51. It departed Burbank on the night of February 26, 1962, and arrived late morning the next day.

After arrival, the airplane was reassembled and fitted with its two interim J75 engines. There were fuel

101

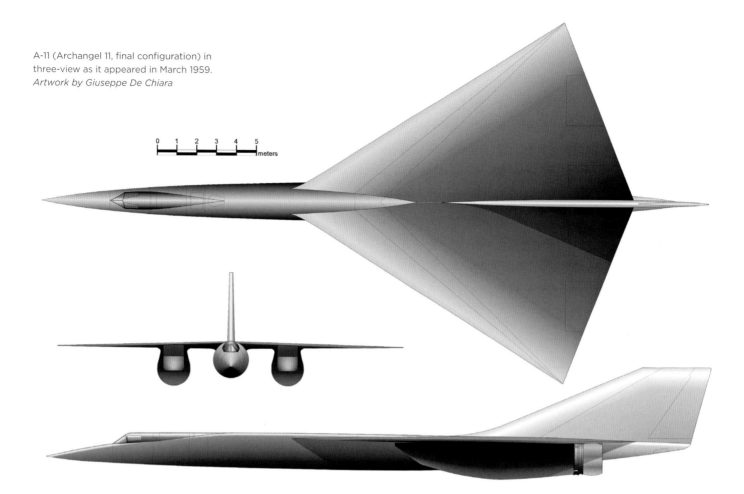

A-11 (Archangel 11, final configuration) in three-view as it appeared in March 1959.
Artwork by Giuseppe De Chiara

0 1 2 3 4 5 meters

tank sealing problems, and a cure had to be found and implemented. This was done, and a series of low-, medium-, and high-speed taxi runs were performed.

Finally, on April 25, 1962, the airplane was ready for flight. The official first flight was scheduled for April 30, 1962, but Johnson didn't want any surprises, so he decided to fly the airplane on April 25.

Skunk Works test pilot Louis Wellington "Lou" Schalk Jr. had joined Lockheed in 1957, and in 1959 Johnson selected him to serve as his chief engineering test pilot on the A-12 program. Schalk taxied A-12 number one out for its first unofficial flight and took off. It wasn't much of flight at all. Schalk flew Article 121 (as it was called) less than 2 miles around Groom Lake at an altitude of only 20 feet. He encountered flight control difficulties due to improper flight control hookups. These incorrect fittings were corrected, and the plane was ready for another attempt the following day.

On April 26 Schalk made the first flight on A-12 number one; it lasted forty minutes. During the flight the airplane shed some of the triangular fillets that covered the framework of the chines along the outer edge of the

aircraft body. These fillets, which had been attached to the airframe with epoxy resin, had to be recovered and reattached to the aircraft. This took the next four days.

Then on April 30, 1962, Schalk rotated at 195 miles per hour, retracted the landing gear, and climbed to 30,000 feet. He flew the airplane for fifty-nine minutes and reached a maximum speed of 390 miles per hour. This was considered to be the official first flight, as CIA and USAF officials were present. During the second test hop, on May 2, 1962, the airplane flew to a maximum speed of Mach 1.1 (815 miles per hour), thereby going supersonic for the first time.

Four more A-12 airplanes arrived at Area 51 before the end of the year, including the one-off two-seat trainer designated A-12T and named *Titanium Goose*.

Difficulties plagued Pratt & Whitney and its J58 engine program. By January 1963 the company had delivered ten J58 engines to the test site. Finally, on January 15, 1963, an A-12 powered by one J58 engine and one J75 engine made a test flight. The first A-12 flight with two J58s came about on January 19, 1963, some nine months after the first A-12 had flown.

Above: Two operational A-1s fly together in this conceptual illustration. *Artwork by Jozef Gatial*

Below: Single A-1 concept on wing. *Artwork by Jozef Gatial*

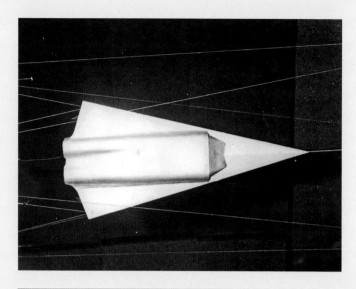

ARCHANGEL 1
JULY 1958

Length:	116.67 ft	Zero Fuel Weight:	41,000 lbs	Cruise Mach:	3.0
Span:	49.6 ft	Fuel Weight:	61,000 lbs	Cruise Alt:	83 - 93 kft
Height:	23.58 ft	Takeoff Gross:	102,000 lbs	Radius:	2,000 NM

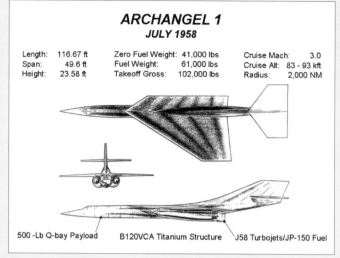

500 -Lb Q-bay Payload   B120VCA Titanium Structure   J58 Turbojets/JP-150 Fuel

ARCHANGEL 2
SEPTEMBER 1958

Length:	129.17 ft	Zero Fuel Weight:	54,000 lbs	Cruise Mach:	3.2
Span:	76.68 ft	Fuel Weight:	81,000 lbs	Cruise Alt:	94 -105 kft
Height:	27.92 ft	Takeoff Gross:	135,000 lbs	Radius:	2,000 NM

75" Dia Ramjets Burning HEF
(Lit @ Mach 0.95, 36,000 ft)

Reduced Wing Sweep
Compared to A-1

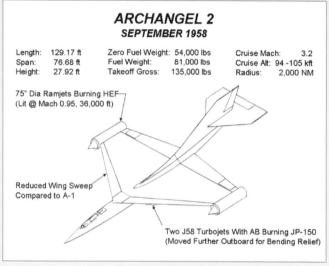

Two J58 Turbojets With AB Burning JP-150
(Moved Further Outboard for Bending Relief)

A-3
NOVEMBER 1958

Length:	62.3 ft	Zero Fuel Weight:	12,000 lbs	Cruise Mach:	3.2
Span:	33.8 ft	Fuel Weight:	22,600 lbs	Cruise Alt:	95 kft
Height:	14.6 ft	Takeoff Gross:	34,600 lbs	Radius:	2,000 NM

40" Dia. Ramjets for Cruise
(Burning ethyldecaborane)

250-lb Payload

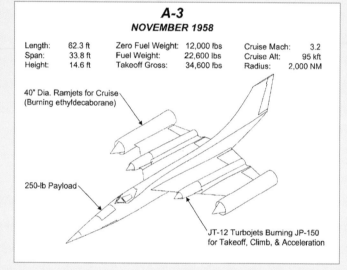

JT-12 Turbojets Burning JP-150
for Takeoff, Climb, & Acceleration

A-6-5
JANUARY 1959

Length:	64.0 ft	Zero Fuel Weight:	29,200 lbs	Cruise Mach:	3.2
Span:	47.2 ft	Fuel Weight:	33,750 lbs	Cruise Alt:	90 kft
Height:	22.85 ft	Takeoff Gross:	62,950 lbs	Radius:	1,287 NM

One J58 with afterburner

Two 34" dia ramjets

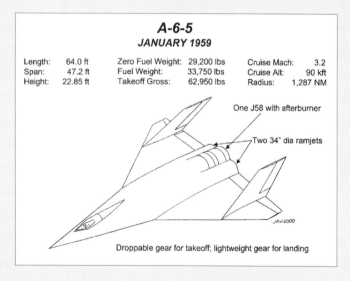

JRW 2000

Droppable gear for takeoff; lightweight gear for landing

A-7 THROUGH A-9 SERIES (A-7-3 SHOWN)
JANUARY 1959

Length:	93.75 ft	Zero Fuel Weight:	27,200 lbs	Cruise Mach:	3.2
Span:	47.5 ft	Fuel Weight:	43,700 lbs	Cruise Alt:	91.5kft
Height:	22.85 ft	Takeoff Gross:	70,900 lbs	Radius:	1,637 NM

Two 34" Dia Ramjets

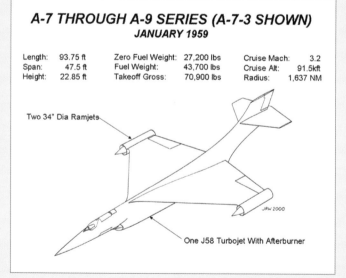

JRW 2000

One J58 Turbojet With Afterburner

A-10
FEBRUARY 1959

Length: 109.5 ft
Span: 46.0 ft
Height: 19.25 ft

Zero Fuel Weight: 33,300 lbs
Fuel Weight: 52,700 lbs
Takeoff Gross: 86,000 lbs

Cruise Mach: 3.2
Cruise Alt: 90.5 kft
Radius: 2,000 NM

Significant Improvement Over A-1;
- 18,000 Lb Reduction in TOGW
- 2,500 Ft Additional Altitude

Two General Electric
J93-3 Turbojets; 2-D
Under-wing Inlets

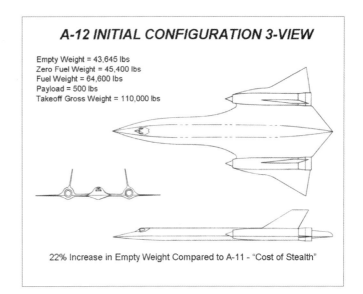

A-12 INITIAL CONFIGURATION 3-VIEW

Empty Weight = 43,645 lbs
Zero Fuel Weight = 45,400 lbs
Fuel Weight = 64,600 lbs
Payload = 500 lbs
Takeoff Gross Weight = 110,000 lbs

22% Increase in Empty Weight Compared to A-11 - "Cost of Stealth"

Above: February 1959 A-10 details. *LM* Code One

Above right: Initial A-12 details. *LM* Code One

Right: March 1959 A-11 details. *LM* Code One

Opposite top left: Bottom view of twin-engine Arrow I configuration with a ventral engine air inlet system. *LMSW*

Opposite top right: July 1958 A-1 details. *LM* Code One

Opposite middle left: September 1958 A-2 details. The acronym HEF means "high-energy fuel" (a borane-based chemical fuel). *LM* Code One

Opposite middle right: November 1958 A-3 details. *LM* Code One

Opposite bottom left: January 1959 A-6-5 details. This air vehicle was similar to the Arrow I design. *LM* Code One

Opposite bottom right: A-7 through A-9 details as of January 1959. The A-7-3 configuration is shown. *LM* Code One

Below: First A-12 (Article 123) in its early assembly phase in Burbank. *LMSW*

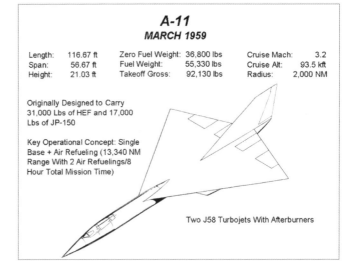

A-11
MARCH 1959

Length: 116.67 ft
Span: 56.67 ft
Height: 21.03 ft

Zero Fuel Weight: 36,800 lbs
Fuel Weight: 55,330 lbs
Takeoff Gross: 92,130 lbs

Cruise Mach: 3.2
Cruise Alt: 93.5 kft
Radius: 2,000 NM

Originally Designed to Carry 31,000 Lbs of HEF and 17,000 Lbs of JP-150

Key Operational Concept: Single Base + Air Refueling (13,340 NM Range With 2 Air Refuelings/8 Hour Total Mission Time)

Two J58 Turbojets With Afterburners

Top: Reassembled Article 123 (A-12 number one) at Area 51 undergoing preparations for its first flight. *LMSW*

Above: A-12 number one rotating for its first takeoff on April 26, 1962. *LMSW*

Above: First unofficial takeoff for A-12 number one on April 26, 1962, with Louis W. "Lou" Schalk Jr. at the controls. The official first flight followed four days later on April 30. *LMSW*

Below: Rare color view of A-12 number one on an early test hop. *LMSW*

Full-scale A-12 pole model for measuring RCS. *LMSW*

These "open-faced" J58s fed air via variable geometry doors and encountered numerous problems from Mach 2.4 to 2.8 speeds. A new engine air inlet system using "spikes" had to be developed and applied before these difficulties were eliminated. This new engine air inlet system was the brainchild of Skunk Works propulsive system engineer Benjamin Robert "Ben" Rich.

In 1962 the CIA and USAF ordered two new versions of the A-12 (in addition to the A-12 and AF-12; the AF-12 had been ordered by the USAF in early 1960 under the code name Kedlock, of which three examples were built). One of these new versions was the modification of two A-12s to carry and launch ramjet-powered, 43-foot-long Q-12 drones capable of reaching Mach 3.3 (2,512 miles per hour). This two-seat "mothership" received the designation M-12; the Q-12 drone was redesignated D-21. This program received the code name Tagboard, which created the M-12/D-21 combination.

TA-12

SPECIFICATIONS

CREW: One (pilot/reconnaissance system operator)

PROPULSIVE SYSTEM: Two axial-flow, afterburning, 31,500-lbf Pratt & Whitney J58 (Model JT11D-20A) turbojet engines

LENGTH: 102 ft 3 in

HEIGHT: 18 ft 6 in

WINGSPAN: 55 ft 7 in

WING AREA: 1,795 sq ft

GROSS TAKEOFF WEIGHT: 117,000 lbs

MAXIMUM SPEED: Mach 3.2 (2435.9 mph)

ARMAMENT: None

PAYLOAD: Photographic reconnaissance equipment

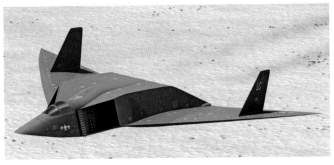

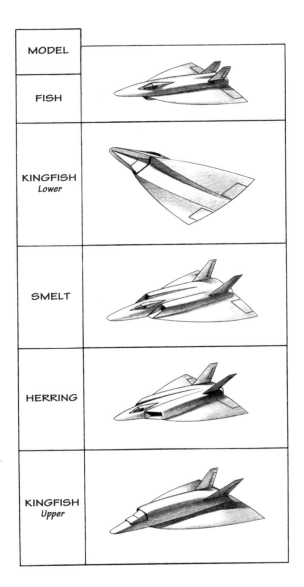

MODEL	
FISH	
KINGFISH *Lower*	
SMELT	
HERRING	
KINGFISH *Upper*	

Top left: Artist concept of proposed but never built B-58B launching its Super Hustler package. *LM Code One*

Above left: Conceptual illustration of a Kingfish air vehicle. *Artwork by Jozef Gatial*

Above right: In addition to Fish and Kingfish there were two lesser-known concepts called Smelt and Herring as shown here. *LM Code One*

The second new version of the A-12 was another reconnaissance aircraft. In December 1962 the USAF ordered six reconnaissance-strike aircraft designed for high-speed, high-altitude reconnaissance of enemy territory after a nuclear strike—to survey and give bomb damage assessment to restrike if necessary. In August 1963 the USAF upped the order to thirty-one total aircraft, adding twenty-five more to the original order. This aircraft was at first dubbed RS-12, then RS-71, then SR-12, and finally SR-71 under the Senior Crown program.

THE A-12T
The need for a pilot trainer and transition version of the A-12 became paramount, and the A-12T *Titanium Goose* was created. It never received the J58 propulsive system, however, retaining its J75 engines throughout its flying career.

Kelly Johnson himself took a ride on the *Titanium Goose* in mid-1963, a VIP like no other.

SUMMARY
The A-12 program was an unqualified success, and from it came several epic aircraft designs that remain significant in the chronicles of aviation history. The A-12 was flying at more than 2,000 miles per hour at nearly 100,000 feet (18.9 miles) at a time when other aircraft were struggling to reach two-thirds its speed and altitudes of 60,000 feet.

This program, closely followed by A-12 spinoff programs, earned the Skunk Works and its director the highest civilian praise of all, the Presidential Medal of Freedom, awarded to Kelly Johnson and his Skunk Works in 1964 by President Lyndon B. Johnson.

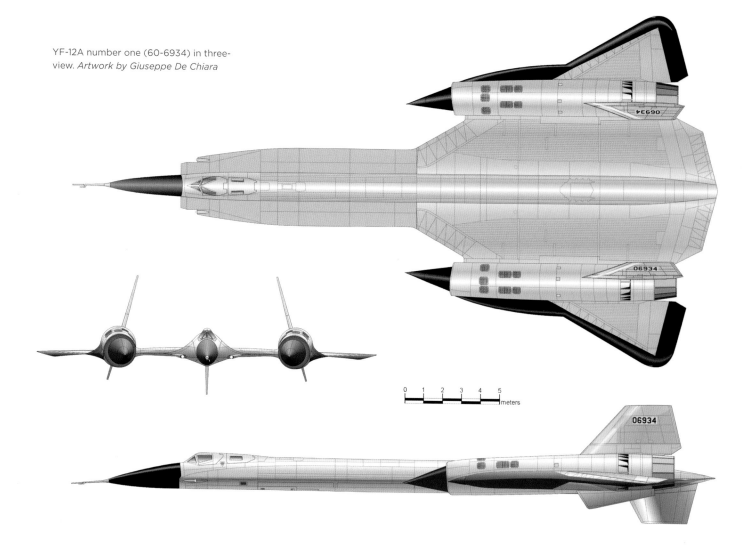

YF-12A number one (60-6934) in three-view. *Artwork by Giuseppe De Chiara*

Kedlock: The YF-12A

The AF-12 was proposed to the USAF as an air defense fighter version of the A-12 to take the place of the canceled F-108 Rapier.

The Lockheed YF-12A was, and remains, the fastest, heaviest, and highest-flying interceptor type of aircraft ever been built and flown. Its closest rival, the Russian Mikoyan-Gurevich MiG-25 Foxbat, could attain Mach 2.8 (2131.4 miles per hour) at 68,000 feet but had limited endurance.

The AF-12 program metamorphosed into the YF-12 program under the code name Kedlock. President Johnson announced, on February 29, 1964:

> The United States has successfully developed an advanced experimental jet aircraft, the A-11, which has been tested in sustained flight at more than 2,000 miles per hour and at altitudes in excess of 70,000 feet. The performance of the A-11 far exceeds that of any other aircraft in the world today. The development of this aircraft has been made possible by major advances in aircraft technology of great significance for both military and commercial applications. Several A-11 aircraft are now being flight tested at Edwards Air Force Base in California. The existence of this program is being disclosed today to permit the orderly exploitation of this advanced technology in our military and commercial programs.

On May 14, 1965, Lockheed received a USAF contract valued at $500,000 for engineering work on the F-12B. This was followed on November 10 with another $500,000 for continued F-12B work.

Based on the performance demonstrated by the three prototype YF-12As, the USAF ADC was profoundly interested in fielding a fleet of operational F-12 aircraft. So much so, in fact, that it ordered ninety-three production aircraft designated F-12B to fill two wings with three squadrons each.

On May 14, 1965, ninety-three F-12Bs were ordered and the US Congress voted $90 million US dollars to cover

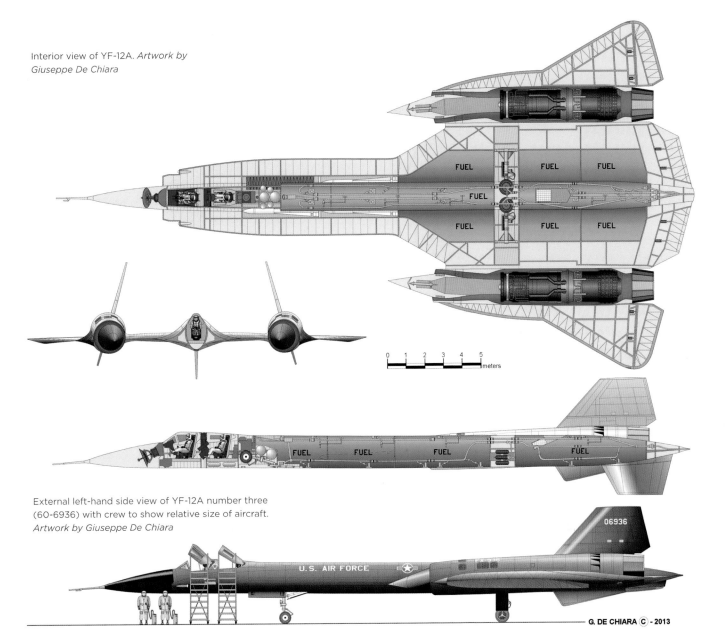

Interior view of YF-12A. *Artwork by Giuseppe De Chiara*

External left-hand side view of YF-12A number three (60-6936) with crew to show relative size of aircraft. *Artwork by Giuseppe De Chiara*

G. DE CHIARA Ⓒ - 2013

the cost of the Lockheed's starter fee for the project. But aerospace industry antagonist Robert S. McNamara, US secretary of defense, refused to release the appropriated funds to put the F-12B into production. His reasoning was that the growing cost of the Vietnam War wouldn't allow such an expenditure. He preferred the less expensive F-106X interceptor program, which, as it turned out, didn't come to fruition either.

The USAF, Congress, and the DOD teeter-tottered for several years over the Improved Manned Interceptor (IMI) program. Then the F-12B production program was abruptly canceled with little or no explanation. Lockheed management received an official F-12B program termination notice from the USAF on January 5, 1968. There would be no F-12B.

As an aside, one must remember that during this point in time in USAF history the ADC and TAC had three very capable interceptors—the F-101, F-106, and F-15—one capable of Mach 1.7 (1,294 miles per hour) speed and two capable of Mach 2.5 (1,903 miles per hour) speeds. The operational point- and area-defense McDonnell F-101B Voodoo was armed with two heat-seeking air-to-air missiles and two radar-guided rockets with nuclear warheads.

The Convair F-106A Delta Dart was fully operational. The F-106 was a point- and area-defense interceptor armed with four heat-seeking air-to-air guided missiles and a radar-guided rocket armed with a nuclear warhead. These radar-guided, nuclear-armed rockets were fully able to take out an entire flight of enemy bombers.

111

Above left: YF-12A being manufactured with F-12B nose section mockup to its right. *LM* Code One

Above right: Jim Eastham suited up in his astronaut gear for another YF-12A flight test. His secondary job was to write the pilot's YF-12A flight manual. *Author collection*

Below: YF-12A number one on the ramp at Area 51. *LMSW*

Bottom: YF-12A number one landing after its August 7, 1963, first flight with James D. "Jim" Eastham at the controls.

Above: YF-12A number one at Eglin AFB in Florida during its AIM-47A air-to-air missile firing tests. *LMSW*

Right above: Right-hand missile bay loading exercises. *USAF*

Right below: Left-hand missile bay loading exercises. *USAF*

YF-12A

SPECIFICATIONS

CREW: Two (pilot and fire control officer)

PROPULSIVE SYSTEM: Two axial-flow, afterburning, 34,000 lbf (with afterburning) Pratt & Whitney J58 (Model JT11D-20B) turbojet engines

LENGTH: 101 ft 7 in

HEIGHT: 18 ft 6 in

WINGSPAN: 55 ft 7 in

WING AREA: 1,795 sq ft

EMPTY WEIGHT: 60,730 lbs

GROSS TAKEOFF WEIGHT: 127,000 lbs

MAXIMUM SPEED: Mach 3.2 (2,110 mph)

MAXIMUM RANGE: 3,500 mi

COMBAT CEILING: 90,000 ft

ARMAMENT: Three Hughes AIM-47 infrared air-to-air missiles

113

YF-12A number three dropping away from KC-135 tanker after being refueled in flight. *LMSW photo by Denny Lombard*

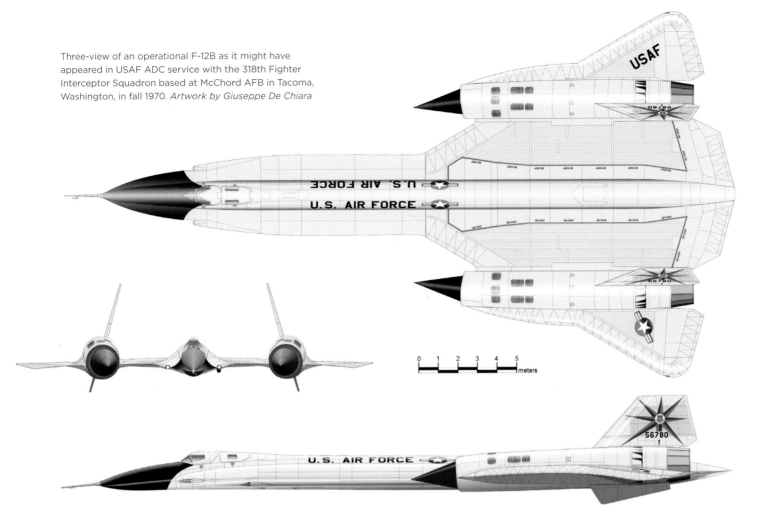

Three-view of an operational F-12B as it might have appeared in USAF ADC service with the 318th Fighter Interceptor Squadron based at McChord AFB in Tacoma, Washington, in fall 1970. *Artwork by Giuseppe De Chiara*

The McDonnell Douglas F-15A Eagle had just recently become operational. The F-15 was a dedicated air superiority fighter armed with eight air-to-air missiles—four heat-seeking and four radar-guided—and a 20mm cannon. And like the Delta Dart and Voodoo, the Eagle was capable of point- and area-defense missions.

Thus, while the decision to cancel the F-12B hurt Lockheed, it didn't hurt the USAF. But what a marvelous interceptor it could have been.

YF-12A AIM-47 Missile Firings at Eglin AFB, Florida, in Chronological Order

3/18/65, YF-12A 60-6935, fired at Ryan Q-2C drone; drone was at 40,000 ft, YF-12A was at 65,000 ft flying at Mach 2.2

5/19/65, YF-12A 60-6935, fired at Ryan Q-2C drone; drone was at 20,000 ft, YF-12A was at 65,000 ft flying at Mach 2.3

9/28/65, YF-12A 60-6934, fired at Ryan Q-2C drone; drone was at 20,000 ft, YF-12A was at 75,000 ft flying at Mach 3.2

3/22/66, YF-12A 60-6936, fired at Ryan Q-2C drone; drone was at 1,500 ft, YF-12A was at 74,500 flying at Mach 3.15

4/25/66, YF-12A 60-6934, fired at Boeing QB-47 drone; QB-47 was flying at 1,500 ft, YF-12A was at 75,000 flying at Mach 3.2

5/13/66, YF-12A 60-6936, fired at Ryan Q-2C drone; drone was flying at 20,000 ft, YF-12A was at 74,000 ft flying at Mach 3.17

9/21/66, YF-12A 60-6936, fired at Boeing QB-47 drone; QB-47 was flying at sea level, YF-12A was at 74,000 ft flying at Mach 3.20

SUMMARY

It was first publically known as the A-11, then the YF-12A, but it actually began life in total secrecy as the AF-12. We'll call it the YF-12A because that's what its buyer the USAF designated it, and it was just one of the many derivatives of the Lockheed-built, CIA-funded A-12 series of aircraft that ultimately led to the creation of the still amazing SR-71 Blackbird.

While Lockheed Skunk Works was manufacturing the fleet of CIA A-12s in Burbank, California, three of these A-12 airframes was completed as AF-12s instead—the *A* meaning Article and the *F* meaning Fighter. These three airframes (USAF serial numbers 60-6934 to 60-6936) had been ordered by the USAF using FY 1960 defense budget moneys for what was initially called the IMI program under the highly classified USAF Kedlock project.

115

Depiction of what a pair of 318FIS F-12Bs might have looked like in their pursuit of enemy bombers. *Artwork by Luca Landino*

In a number of successful Hughes AIM-47 FALCON air-to-air missile firings directed by the Hughes AN/ASG-eighteen fire control system the Mach 3 (2,000 miles per hour) YF-12A shined brightly and the USAF ADC ordered ninety-three production aircraft designated F-12B. However, then defense secretary Robert S. McNamara, refused to release the appropriated funds, and the F-12B program was canceled in early 1968. Thus the YF-12A aircraft were turned over to NASA for high speed research.

Recently celebrating its 50th anniversary of flight on August 7, 2013 the YF-12A still seems to be from the future.

Tagboard: The D-21 and M-21

The CIA/USAF project known as Tagboard created the unmanned, ramjet-powered D-21 (formerly Q-12) reconnaissance drone and the two-man M-21 carrier airplane. The two M-21 "mother" aircraft were new-build airplanes (not modified A-12s), while the 38 D-21 "daughter" drones were made of similar materials but wholly different in nature. When mated the M-21 and D-21 were known as M/D-21.

The first captive-carry flight of a mated M-21/D-21 was on December 22, 1964—the very same day the premier SR-71A made its first flight.

The first D-21 test launch was accomplished on March 5, 1966, from the back of M-21 number two.

During the second test launch, on April 27, the D-21 reached a speed greater than Mach 3.3 (2,512 miles per hour) and flew at 90,000 feet. This flight was cut short, however, because a hydraulic pump failed after the D-21 had flown a little over 1,400 miles, or about 90 percent of the intended distance.

The third test flight was on June 16, and the D-21 flew its entire 1,550-mile mission profile, although an electrical malfunction refused to release the camera housing panel.

The fourth test flight ended in tragedy. On July 30, 1966, Skunk Works test pilot Bill Park and flight test engineer/launch control officer Raymond Michael "Ray" Torick had attained launch altitude and speed while flying straight and level. The previous test launches were made

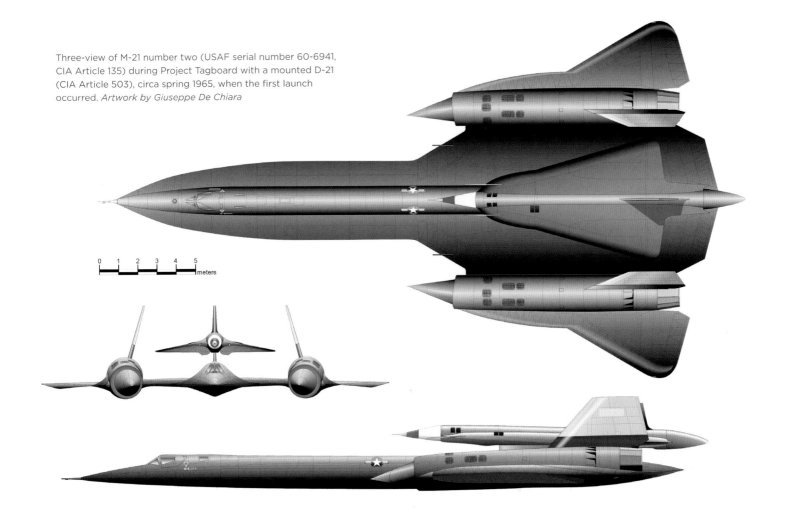

Three-view of M-21 number two (USAF serial number 60-6941, CIA Article 135) during Project Tagboard with a mounted D-21 (CIA Article 503), circa spring 1965, when the first launch occurred. *Artwork by Giuseppe De Chiara*

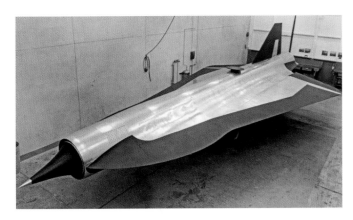

Above: Full-scale engineering mockup of a D-21. *LMSW*

Right: D-21 mounted atop M-21 number one (USAF serial number 60-6940, CIA Article 134). *LMSW*

with the M-21 in a slight nose-down attitude. Almost immediately after Torick released the D-21 drone its ramjet engine refused to gain full thrust, and the drone, went berserk, crashing into the vertical tails of the mothership. The M-21 went out of control and began to break up, so both men ejected from it and landed in the Pacific Ocean

off the coast of California. Park was rescued, but for some unknown reason Torick had prematurely opened the faceplate on his helmet. Water rushed in and dragged him under, and he drowned.

Ray Torick's body was recovered near NAS Point Magu. Since this program was highly classified, his August 2,

1966, obituary in the Los Angeles Times stated in part, "The engineer died Saturday after parachuting from an unknown aircraft."

At the behest of Kelly Johnson himself, the M-21/D-21 program was immediately terminated. The drone would have to find a new mother. That new mother came in the form of a subsonic carrier: the B-52H Stratofortress discussed below.

(Note: Most references refer to the D-21 mother plane as the M-21, others the M-12. But Kelly Johnson called it the M-21 in his performance reports, so M-21 it is.)

M/D-21 Launches in Chronological Order

3/5/66, D-21 Article 503, flew 172.6 mi; mission unsuccessful

4/27/66, D-21 Article 506, flew 1,288.8 mi; mission successful

6/16/66, D-21 Article 505, flew 1,323.3 mi; mission successful

7/30/66, D-21 Article 504, D-21 collided with M-21, destroying both aircraft

SUMMARY

The D-21/M-21 program didn't fare as well as had been hoped for. With the tragic loss of Ray Torick and two expensive air vehicles, the Tagboard program was terminated. It was replaced by the Senior Bowl program, which fared somewhat better but still left a lot to be desired.

Above: Beautiful in-flight study of M-21 mother and D-21 daughter. *LMSW*

Opposite top: First mated flight of M-21 number one and D-21 on December 22, 1964, as this "odd couple" come up for a drink of JP-7 from a KC-135 tanker. *LMSW*

Opposite bottom: M-21 number one with a mounted D-21 prepared for takeoff on December 22, 1964. *LMSW*

D-21/D-21B

SPECIFICATIONS

CREW: None

PROPULSIVE SYSTEM (D-21): One 1,500-lbf Marquardt RJ43-MA-20 ramjet engine

PROPULSIVE SYSTEM (D-21B): One 1,500-lbf Marquardt RJ43-MA-20S4 ramjet engine with a single ventral-mount 27,300-lbf solid-fuel booster rocket (the booster rocket was 44 ft 4 in long and weighed 13,286 lbs; 87-second burn time)

LENGTH: 42 ft 10 in

HEIGHT: 7 ft .25 in

WINGSPAN: 19 ft .25 in

GROSS LAUNCH WEIGHT (D-21): 11,000 lbs

GROSS LAUNCH WEIGHT (D-21B): 24,286 lbs

COMBAT CEILING: 80,000 to 95,000 ft

MAXIMUM SPEED: Mach 3.35 (2,210 mph)

MAXIMUM RANGE: 3,450 mi

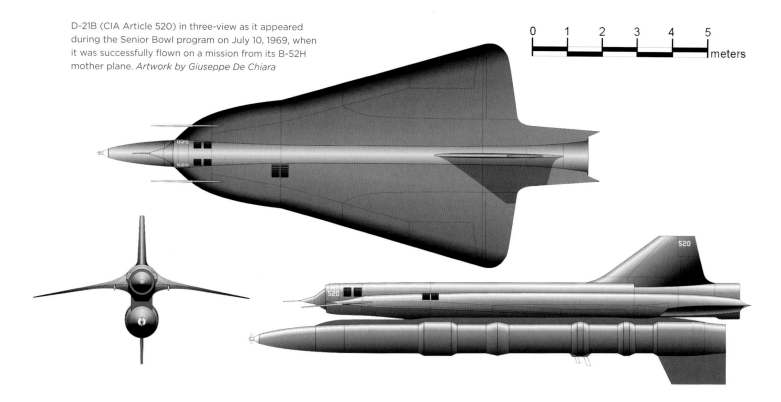

D-21B (CIA Article 520) in three-view as it appeared during the Senior Bowl program on July 10, 1969, when it was successfully flown on a mission from its B-52H mother plane. *Artwork by Giuseppe De Chiara*

Senior Bowl: The D-21B and B-52H

The B-52H became the new mother for the D-21 daughter, using a large solid-fuel booster rocket motor to take the place of the M-21 launch platform. This large booster—fitted underneath the drone—allowed the reconnaissance air vehicle to gather enough speed to light its ramjet engine. The D-21 drone was redesigned D-21B under the USAF Senior Bowl program.

The B-52H carried two D-21Bs—one under either inboard wing on a special pylon. There were a total of seventeen B-52H/D-21B launches, and just four of these were operational missions.

Two B-52H airplanes were used, *Tagboard Flyer* (60-0036), assigned to the 419th Flight Test Squadron at Edwards AFB, and *Iron Eagle* (61-0021), assigned to the 93rd Bomb Squadron at Barksdale AFB, Louisiana.

B-52H/D-21B Missions in Chronological Order
9/28/67, D-21B Article 501, drone dropped prematurely by accident; no mission flown

11/6/67, D-21B Article 507, drone flew 154.2 miles; mission unsuccessful

12/2/67, D-21B Article 509, drone flew 1,645.6 miles; mission successful

Test fitting of CIA Article 507 to a pylon that would be used by a B-52H mother plane. *LMSW*

1/19/68, D-21B Article 508, drone flew 322.2 miles; mission unsuccessful

4/30/68, D-21B Article 511, drone flew 172.6 miles; mission unsuccessful

6/16/68, D-21B Article 512, drone flew 3,279.7 miles; mission successful

7/1/68, D-21B Article 514, drone flew 92.06 miles; mission unsuccessful

8/28/68, D-21B Article 516, drone flew 89.7 miles; mission unsuccessful

12/15/68, D-21B Article 515, drone flew 3,398.2 miles; mission successful

Above: First mated flight of a B-52H and a D-21B. *LMSW*

Below: Good view of D-21B (CIA Article 501) mounted via pylon to a B-52H. *LMSW*

121

First test launch of a D-21B from a B-52H. *LMSW*

2/11/69, D-21B Article 518, drone flew 185.2 miles; mission unsuccessful

5/10/69, D-21B Article 519, drone flew 3,420.1 miles; mission successful

7/10/69, D-21B Article 520, drone flew 3,379.8 miles; mission successful

11/9/69, D-21B Article 517, drone flew the first Senior Bowl operational mission (classified results)

2/20/70, D-21B Article 521, drone flew 3,416.6 miles; mission successful

12/16/70, D-21B Article 523, drone flew second operational mission (classified results)

3/4/71, D-21B Article 526, drone flew third operational mission (classified results)

3/20/71, D-21B Article 527, drone flew fourth operational mission (classified results)

SUMMARY

The M-21/D-21 and B-52H/D-21B programs were fraught with unforeseen challenges and a tragic loss of life. But they did produce the world's first and still only operational air-launched triplesonic reconnaissance drone.

Senior Crown: The SR-71

Blackbird is accepted as the unofficial name of the SR-71. It was a direct spin-off of the A-12 airframe and power-plant combination. It was the end result of all that was learned from the Oxcart program.

The then Lockheed-California Company—specifically its Skunk Works division—produced twenty-nine SR-71As, two SR-71Bs, and the one-off SR-71C.

The Strategic Reconnaissance (SR) 71 was the unarmed version of the proposed but never built Reconnaissance Strike (RS) 71—offered to the USAF as an alternative to the North American RS-70 Valkyrie, which had been ordered into production but canceled before any examples were built.

Prior to the designations RS-71 and SR-71 the aircraft were known as the RS-12, R-12, and SR-12 respectively. But this all changed on July 24, 1964, when President Lyndon B. Johnson announced the existence of the SR-71

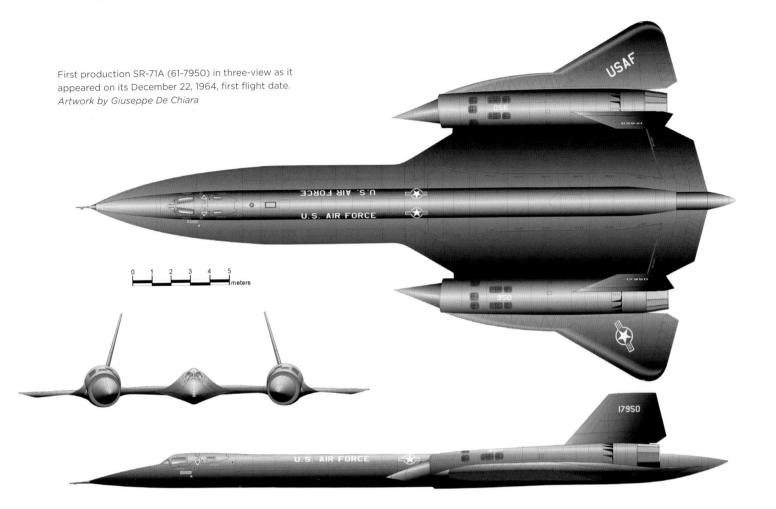

First production SR-71A (61-7950) in three-view as it appeared on its December 22, 1964, first flight date.
Artwork by Giuseppe De Chiara

0 1 2 3 4 5 meters

on a nationwide television program. In part Johnson said, "I would like to announce the successful development of a major new strategic manned aircraft system. This system employs the new SR-71 aircraft, and provides a long range advanced strategic reconnaissance plane for military use. The SR-71 will fly at more than three times the speed of sound . . . operate at altitudes in excess of 80,000 feet . . . [and it] will use the most advanced [ground] observation equipment in the world."

Kelly Johnson kept a log on the SR-71 program that he succinctly titled *SR-12 LOG.* In it he referred to the SR-12 as R-12. Johnson's first entry is dated January 5, 1962, and he wrote,

> Met with Dr. Charyk, Geary, and Lew Myer to discuss starting the bomber. We were given a verbal go-ahead, confirmed later, to do six months of engineering, to do a producibility study, and to move into Buildings 309 and 310 [in Burbank]. (We had started this previously.) I told them that Lockheed would build a million dollar engineering building on the strength of the proposed program, if they considered it a good bet. Dr. Charyk

The first three SR-71As under construction in Burbank. *LMSW*

agreed it was a good bet and that there would be some form of a fighter or bomber version produced.

Dr. Joseph V. "Joe" Charyk was chief scientist of the USAF; Col. Leo P. Geary was USAF A-12 program manager; and Lew Myer was a USAF financial officer.

A crated SR-71A being moved from Burbank to Palmdale. *LMSW*

First takeoff on SR-71A number one with F-104 chase plane in hot pursuit. *LM* Code One

During its career the SR-71 flew 3,551 operational sorties, totaling 17,294 hours, and 53,490 hours flying time, of which 11,675 hours were flown at 2,000-plus miles per hour. *LM* Code One

On January 19, 1962, Johnson wrote,

Colonel [H. A.] Templeton here in preparation for a visit by Dr. Joe Charyk. We discussed various means of getting started on the B-12 armament system. Prior to this, in a meeting with Major Hurley, from the B-70 project office, I told him that we would agree to go along with the sophisticated AF proposal on a missile with side-looking radar. This is done at a considerable added expense and reduction in airplane radius compared to our simpler glide -bomb concept but which, I did agree, would make the airplane more vulnerable in its attack phase. We are discussing pros and cons of how to set up the management for getting started on the armament, radar, and fire control systems. We are considering M-H [Minneapolis-Honeywell], Hughes, and Westinghouse and Goodyear.

SAC Commander Thomas S. "Tom" Power and some of his staff officers visited Burbank on August 7, 1964. They were shown R-12s coming down the production line. At this time the plan was to finish R-12 number one and send it to Palmdale on October 21, 1964. Johnson wrote, "Since the President's announcement, we have decided

to go there instead of [redacted] but we have to kick North American out, and they are dragging their feet."

The first SR-12 was delivered to Palmdale on October 29, 1964. Johnson recorded, "A large number of SAC people were here to see taxi tests of airplane number 2001. They were very much impressed with the smooth operation." Johnson delayed its first flight until the following day "due to unfavorable weather and to get it in better shape to fly."

In his log, Johnson later noted, "First flight of the SR-71. Bob Gilliland made it. Reached a speed of over 1,000 mph, which is some kind of record for a first flight. Colonel Geary and Col. Falk and others were highly pleased, particularly in that we went to [redacted] on the same day and flew the MD-21 [M-21 and D-21] mated, for the second first flight of a new type in one day."

On April 4, 1966 the first operational SR-71A (number 2009) was delivered to Beale AFB.

About January 19, 1967, Johnson wrote,

I called CIA Oxcart Program Manager John Parangosky to tell him of my discussions with Deputy Secretary of Defense Cyrus R. Vance and others regarding use of

Fine study of one of the two two-place SR-71Bs used for pilot training and transition flights as well as giving rides to VIPs. *NASA*

half the SR-71's as bombers to counter the ABM threat. Specifically, they would be adapted to taking out the hen-house radars. I suggested that the CIA re-open the problem of storing the Oxcart airplanes if the SR-71's should be so used, because then we would have only 25 reconnaissance airplanes, which is not too many to have. Of course, I would not deny that 40 reconnaissance airplanes are more than required under the present political situation, unless we have an actual war.

As of January 27, 1967, Johnson hadn't heard back on his suggestion.

In Johnson's *SR-12 Log* he states, "On December 4, 1967 Rus Daniell and I went with Dan Haughton to SAC in Omaha. We saw SAC commander General Joseph J. Nazzaro and his top echelon officers. We presented the FB-12, a common airframe for an air defense fighter or a bomber, making a strong case for high-altitude bombing. We had a very good reception." But as it turned out the FB-12 was not accepted.

Above: The SR-71 uses a drag chute to help slow it down after landing. *LMSW*

A family portrait of an SR-71A with a TR-1A (now U-2S), which is an advanced version of the U-2. *LM* Code One

SR-71A

SPECIFICATIONS

CREW: Two (pilot and reconnaissance System Officer)

PROPULSIVE SYSTEM: Two afterburning, axial-flow, 34,000-lbf (maximum) continuous-bleed Pratt & Whitney J58 turbojet engines; Model JT11D-20

On June 8, 1972, Johnson began to investigate the use of the SR-71 equipped with AIM-7 Sparrow air-to-air missiles and a Westinghouse AWG-10 radar for shooting down a MiG-23. He took the proposal to ADC (now Aerospace Defense Command) headquarters shortly thereafter to see if they were interested. But nothing ever came of this.

SUMMARY

The design and construction of the A-12 airframe was both ingenious and unique in that it offered itself up for the creation of no fewer than eight proposed derivatives and six production variants. These included the proposed B-12, R-12, RB-12, B-71, F-12B, FB-12, RS-12 (RS-71), SR-12, SR-71

Interceptor, and SR-71 Bomber derivatives and the A-12, A-12T, YF-12A, M-21, SR-71A, and SR-71B production variants. Even the design of the D-21 was based on the A-12.

Former 1st Strategic Reconnaissance Squadron commander Col. James L. "Jim" Watkins said, "I had six hundred hours piloting Blackbird, and my last flight was just as big a thrill as my first. At eighty-five thousand feet and Mach 3, it was almost a religious experience." He added, "Nothing had prepared me to fly that fast. . . . My God, even now, I get goosebumps remembering." Colonel Watkins commanded the 1st SRS from December 1969 to June 1971.

The crown jewel that came out of the A-12 program was none other than the still-incredible SR-71 Blackbird.

The Blackbird series of aircraft remains mystic. The Skunk Works produced twelve A-12s, one A-12T, two M-21s, thirty-eight D-21s and D-21Bs, three YF-12As, twenty-nine SR-71As, two SR-71Bs, and one1 SR-71C.

On January 1, 1965, the USAF SAC activated its first SR-71 unit—the 4200th Strategic Reconnaissance Wing

This SR-71A rotated and launched from Palmdale on May 23, 1995, as freeze-framed here by Skunk Works photographer Denny Lombard. Now retired, Lombard considered this photograph to be number four of his seven all-time favorites. He retired January 30, 2011, after forty-one years with Lockheed/Lockheed Martin. *LM* Code One

(4200 SRW)—at Beale AFB just outside of Sacramento, California. This came on the heels of a USAF announcement on December 7, 1964, that Beale AFB would be the home base for its fleet of SR-71s. Since the first SR-71 had only just flown on December 22, 1964, this action seemed immature, but it wasn't at all: an operational command structure had to be in place and prepared to operate the SR-71s as they arrived on base.

In 1965, the SR-71 entered into full rate production in Burbank, and the trio of prototype YF-12As continued to impress the USAF—especially its ADC. The best USAF/ADC fighter at this time was the Convair F-106, and the Skunk Works had offered up its optionally 20mm cannon-armed and/or all-missile-armed F-12B as its future replacement.

The proposed RS-71 and RB-71 and B-71 aircraft were to fill the gap left by the canceled B-70 Valkyrie.

SST:
Supersonic Transport

In 1961, President John F. Kennedy committed the US government to subsidize 75 percent of the cost to develop a supersonic transport (SST) to compete with the Anglo-French Concorde then in development. Russia too jumped on the SST bandwagon, but with disastrous results.

The North American F-108 and B-70

Did the Skunk-Works-designed-and-built Blackbird series of aircraft kill both the B-70 and F-108 production programs? There are those who think they did, and they just might be right.

Chronologically speaking, the F-108 Rapier and B-70 Valkyrie production programs were canceled on September 23, 1959, and March 28, 1961, respectively.

The first A-12 made its first flight on April 30, 1962; the first YF-12A on August 7, 1963; and the first SR-71A on December 22, 1964.

Editorially speaking, the Blackbird series of aircraft had two engines to propel craft beyond 2,000 miles per hour, whereas the XB-70A required six of them.

Finally, the two XB-70A airplanes totaled together just one hour forty-eight minutes of Mach 3 flight during their respective flight test programs.

In just one flight an SR-71 exceeded that total time by several hours.

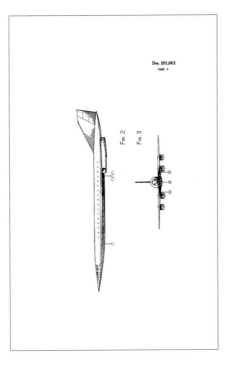

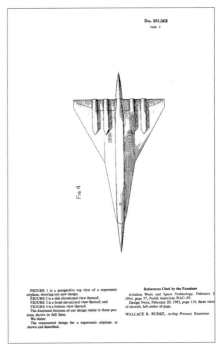

Above: This patent application was filed on May 15, 1964, by co-inventors Kelly Johnson and William H. Statler. They were awarded a fourteen-year patent on May 4, 1965. *United States Patent Office*

Right: Page 2 of patent.

Far right: Page 3 of patent.

Full-scale engineering and marketing mockup of the Lockheed L-1000 SST. *LM* Code One

L-2000-7A

SPECIFICATIONS

CREW: Three (pilot, copilot, flight engineer/ navigator); unknown number of food service and flight attendant workers

PROPULSIVE SYSTEM: Four afterburning, 30,000 lbf–class General Electric GE4/J5M turbofan engines or four afterburning Pratt and Whiney JTF17A-21L turbofan engines

LENGTH: 273 ft 2 in

WINGSPAN: 116 ft 0 in

WING AREA: 9,424 sq ft

EMPTY WEIGHT: 238,000 lbs

GROSS TAKEOFF WEIGHT: 590,000 lbs

ACCOMMODATIONS: 273 passengers

CRUISE SPEED: Mach 2.7 to 3 (1,780 to 2,225 mph)

RANGE: 4,600 mi

SERVICE CEILING: 76,500 ft

On June 5, 1963, the American SST program was launched by the US Federal Aviation Administration (FAA). A number of US airframe contractors responded, including the Boeing Airplane Company, Convair Division of General Dynamics, Douglas Aircraft Company, Glenn L. Martin Company, North American Aviation, and the Lockheed Aircraft Corporation.

It was not a Skunk Works program per se, but using its criterion, Kelly Johnson and William H. "Bill" Statler designed the Lockheed entry: the Model L-2000-7A and L-2000-7B. They filed for patent on May 15, 1964, and received a fourteen-year patent on May 4, 1965. As proposed, the L-2000-7A was to be an intercontinental model for up to 266 passengers, while the slightly larger L-2000-7B was to carry 308 passengers domestically.

In June 1964, Lockheed was one of two competitors chosen to continue work on the SST program. The other was Boeing, with its Model 2707.

The Lockheed Model L-2000-7A would have had a 4,000-mile range and Mach 3 cruise speed. It featured a double delta wing design for swift transonic acceleration and excellent low-speed handling qualities. The L-2000 lost out to the Boeing 2707 on December 31, 1966, for the chance to build a competitor to the Concorde of Great Britain and France and Russia's Tupolev Tu-144.

On May 20, 1971, the American SST program was canceled outright after Congress stopped funding on March 24. This was due in part to cost overruns, delays, technical problems, and economic and environmental questions.

SUMMARY

The late Gordon S. "Gordy" Williams—a distinguished photojournalist who worked in the public relations department of Boeing, summed up the American SST program best when he told this writer in 1984, "It cost more to cancel the SST program than it would have cost to proceed with it." As the legacy of the Concorde SST proved, flights across populated areas were forbidden throughout its tenure.

F-X: Fighter-Experimental

The F-X program got its start in April 1965, and on December 8, 1965, the USAF issued its F-X RFP to thirteen airframe contractors. Eight bids came forth, and on March 18, 1966, the USAF awarded study contracts to the

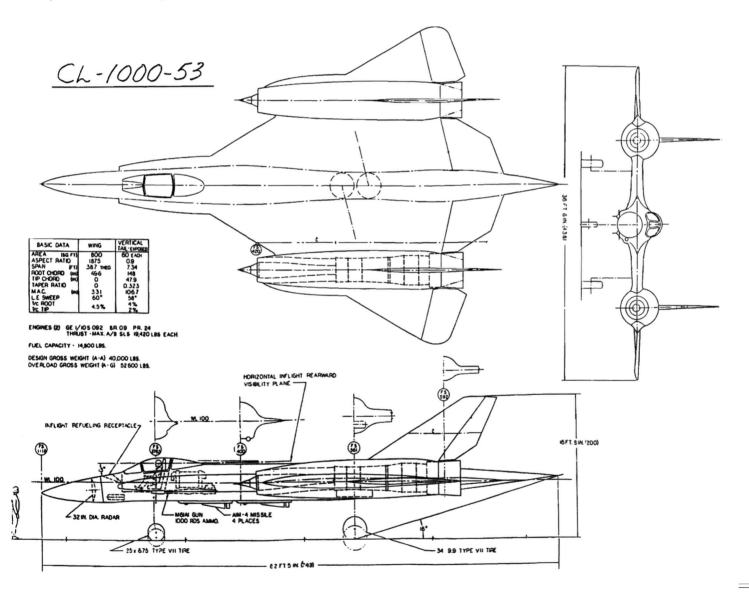

CL-1000-53 configuration was of a mini YF-12 with a single seat. *LM Code One*

Boeing Airplane Company, North American Aviation, and the Lockheed-California Company. Grumman Aerospace participated in the study but without a contract—that is, without government funds.

Lockheed initiated F-X studies under CL-979 early on and then finally under CL-1000. Under CL-1000 the Skunk Works investigated numerous concepts running

from CL-1000-01 through at least CL-1000-67. Among these were fixed- and swing-wing designs, several of which, especially the CL-1000-53, looked like smaller and lighter variations of the YF-12.

The USAF established its F-X (now designated F-15) contract definition phase on September 30, 1968, soliciting bids from eight airframe contractors. Fairchild-Hiller,

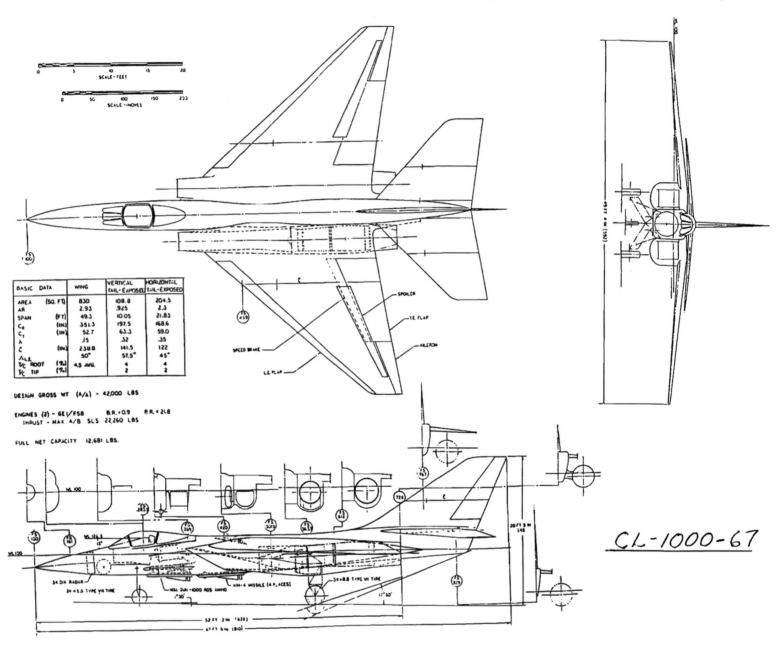

CL-1000-67 configuration showing cheek-type engine air inlets and single seat. *LM Code One*

Conceptual drawing of two CL-1000-47 aircraft on the prowl. *Artwork by Jozef Gatial*

General Dynamics, McDonnell Douglas, and North American responded. Boeing, Northrop, Grumman, and Lockheed did not submit F-X proposals. Lockheed-California—which had planned to team up with Ling-Temco-Vought Aerospace—withdrew from the F-X competition in early October 1968.

As an aside, the McDonnell Douglas Corporation won the F-X competition on December 23, 1969, and moved on to manufacture a fleet of F-15s for the USAF. The F-15 proved to be the best air superiority fighter in the world. Its reign lasted until the advent of the Lockheed Martin F-22 Raptor, which is now the King of Fighters.

SUMMARY

Doublesonic aircraft speeds were relatively new when the 1960s began. But by the end of the decade, triple-sonic aircraft speeds were commonplace—and it was the Skunk Works that made this possible.

The Skunk Works was solely responsible for the creation of not one but two aircraft—the A-12 and SR-71—that could routinely fly at speeds exceeding 2,000 miles per hour during their daily operations. It created two more triplesonic aircraft as well, the proposed F-12B and SST, but these were canceled. Yet another triplesonic airplane emerged from Lockheed ADP: the service test YF-12A, which served as the prototype for the F-12B and flew for several years before it was retired.

THE 1970s:
ERA OF WIZARDRY

> "We follow the golden rule. Whoever has the gold makes the rules. If the air force wanted them painted pink we would have painted them pink."

—BEN RICH, IN REFERENCE TO THE BLACK PAINT LIVERY ON THE FLEET OF F-117S

Secrets are just that—secrets. Or are they?

Since day one, secrecy has been and continues to be the paramount policy within the walls of the Skunk Works. Of late it wants to be more transparent, but openness was unheard of in the 1970s. In fact, the 1970s were every bit as secretive—if not more so—than the preceding decades.

There were several reasons for this ultra-hush-hush attitude: 1) The fleet of SR-71s and their ongoing worldwide operations; 2) keeping any knowledge of its method of operations away from its competitors, the general public, and especially enemy nations; and 3) the advent of very low observables to create aircraft that were actually undetectable.

Thus, the 1970s became the era of wizardry.

CL-1200/X-27 Lancer

In the late 1960s, Lockheed California offered its proposed Model CL-1200 Lancer, an improved version of the F-104 Starfighter which was offered for export to US allies and friends. It was a Skunk Works design funded solely by Lockheed, and it was offered as an unsolicited alternative to the Dassault Mirage F1, McDonnell F-4 Phantom II, and the Northrop F-5E Tiger II. Lockheed built a full-scale engineering mockup to show potential customers with deliveries to begin in 1972.

Lockheed offered two versions of its proposed Lancer in the International Fighter Aircraft (IFA) competition: 1) The Model CL-1200-1, to be powered by an improved version of the General Electric J79 turbojet engine; and 2) The Model CL-1200-2, to be powered by a single Pratt & Whiney TF30 turbofan engine.

The CL-1200-1/-2 Lancer configuration featured an F-104 style fuselage with improved internal systems, a single vertical stabilizer, a high shoulder-mounted wing with increased span, and low-mounted all-moving horizontal tail planes.

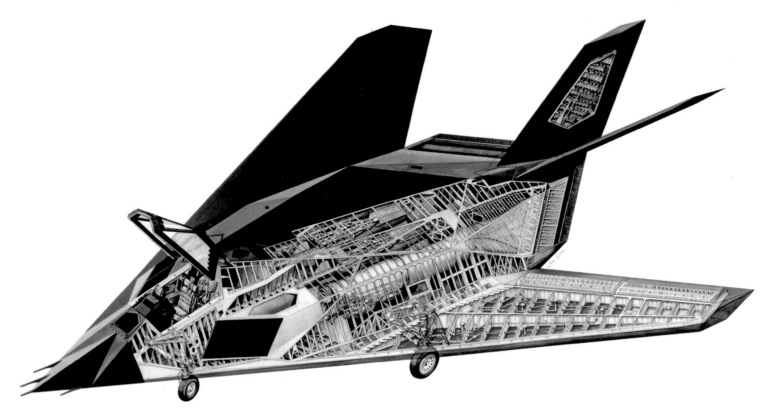

Phantom view of F-117A. *LMSW photo by Denny Lombard*

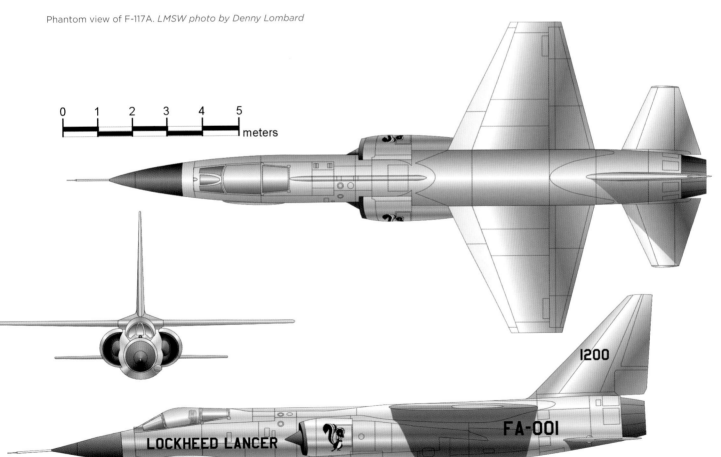

0 1 2 3 4 5 meters

LOCKHEED LANCER

1200

FA-001

Original California Lockheed Lancer mockup in three-view. *Artwork by Giuseppe De Chiara*

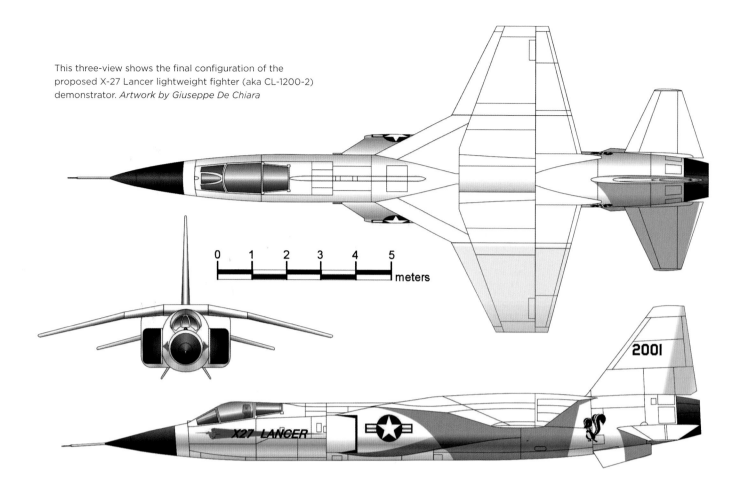

This three-view shows the final configuration of the proposed X-27 Lancer lightweight fighter (aka CL-1200-2) demonstrator. *Artwork by Giuseppe De Chiara*

0 1 2 3 4 5 meters

2001

X27 LANCER

CL-1200/X-27

SPECIFICATIONS

PROPULSIVE SYSTEM: One axial-flow, afterburning, 25,000-lbf (with afterburning) Pratt & Whitney TF30-P-100 turbofan engine

LENGTH: 57 ft 3 in / 53 ft 2 in

HEIGHT: 17 ft 2 in / 16 ft 2 in

WINGSPAN: 29 ft 2 in / 28 ft 7 in

EMPTY WEIGHT: 17,885 lbs / 17,250 lbs

GROSS WEIGHT: 35,000 lbs

MAXIMUM SPEED: Mach 2.57 (1,956.3 mph / Mach 2.19 (1,667.0 mph)

SERVICE CEILING: 60,000-plus ft

TF30-P-100 ENGINE

RELOCATED WING AND TAIL

WING AREA INCREASED 59%

INTERNAL FUEL INCREASED 56%

IMPROVED AIR INTAKE TRANSLATING SPIKE

IMPROVED HIGH LIFT DEVICES

INCREASED PAYLOAD

ADDED STORE STATIONS

RESULT

IMPROVED
• TAKE-OFF/LANDING PERFORMANCE
• COMBAT MANEUVERABILITY
• MISSION PERFORMANCE
• SAFETY

Lancer design features. *LM Code One*

The F-104 was out of production in Burbank at this time, but Lockheed still had all of its resources on tap including jigs, tooling, and factory floor space. Thus production could be accelerated if Lancer orders were forthcoming. There were no orders, though, because in November 1970 the IFA competition was won by the Northrop F-5E Tiger II.

Undeterred, Lockheed continued to refine its Lancer design, which had been noticed by the USAF. The USAF opted to procure several of these refined Lancers to be used as joint USAF/NASA aerodynamic and propulsive system testbeds capable of speeds approaching Mach

2.6 or about 1,930 miles per hour. For this purpose the refined Lancer was designated X-27 by the USAF.

Similar to the overall design of the Cl-1200-/-2 Lancer the X-27 (sometimes referred to as the Model CL-1600) featured large area rectangular engine air inlets. Several versions of the X-27 were proposed, and one version became an unsolicited offering to the USAF in 1972 as a proposed competitor in the Lightweight Fighter (LWF). Another version—the Model CL-1400—was offered to the navy as an aircraft carrier-based area- and point-interceptor.

The LWF competition was won by the General Dynamics YF-16 in 1974, and by that time, interest from all parties had all but disappeared. Worse, the USAF cancelled the X-27 program and not a single Lancer was built and flown.

F-X Program

On December 8, 1965, the USAF released its F-X RFP to thirteen airframe and powerplant contractors: Bell, Boeing, Douglas, Fairchild, General Electric, General Dynamics, Grumman, Martin, McDonnell, North American, Pratt & Whitney, Republic, and Vought. Eight airframe contractors responded with their proposals.

The Fighter-Experimental (F-X) program competition that led to the production of the McDonnell Douglas F-15 Eagle was lengthy and hard-fought. The Lockheed-California Company entered the fray with a number of Skunk Works designs based on its Model CL-1000 F-X design studies. On October 24, 1968, the F-X was designated F-15.

On December 23, 1969, the entry from McDonnell Douglas was selected.

In the end it was the Model 199 offering from McDonnell Douglas that won the F-X competition. To give credit where credit is due, its F-15 Eagle proved to be the best choice.

Above: Original CL-1200 Lancer mockup with its intended test pilot, Skunk Works test pilot William C. "Bill" Park Jr. *LMSW*

Below: Final X-27 Lancer (CL-1200-2) mockup. *LMSW*

Advanced Day Fighter/Lightweight Fighter Program

On January 6, 1972, the USAF released its RFP calling for a 20,000-pound-class fighter with an exceptional turn rate, acceleration, and range, optimized for combat at speeds of Mach 0.60 to 1.60 (456.7 to 1,217.9 miles per hour) and altitudes of 30,000 to 40,000 feet.

Five airframe contractors submitted proposals: Boeing's Model 908-909; General Dynamics' Model 401-16B; Northrop's P-600 Cobra; Vought's Model V-1100; and Lockheed's Model CL-1200 Lancer.

The preliminary design department in the Skunk Works worked hard to generate an offering suitable for the USAF Advanced Day Fighter (ADF) program of the late 1960s. The ADF program soon gave way to the Lightweight Fighter (LWF) program. Lockheed ADP came up with numerous LWF designs under its CL-1200-1 Lancer series of concepts. But these were rejected.

Project Harvey

In 1974 the Defense Advanced Research Projects Agency (DARPA), an arm of the DOD, created a confidential project codenamed Harvey (after the invisible white rabbit from the movie of the same name starring James M. "Jimmy" Stewart). Project Harvey was created to find a way to build air vehicles with very low observability so that they could not be detected by radar and thus be invisible to an adversary.

DARPA awarded $1 million contracts to Boeing, Fairchild Republic, Northrop, General Dynamics, and Grumman. Their job was to come up with the least observable air vehicle they could bring about. The winner would be given a contract to build and flight test two demonstrator aircraft.

But a leader in the making of air vehicles with low radar signatures had been passed over. Lockheed, under the direction of then new Skunk Works president Ben Rich, lobbied hard to get one of the $1 million contracts, but to no avail. So Rich pushed Lockheed management to fund the program in-house, and up to $10 million was approved. Rich and the brains within his Skunk Works set about to create the winning air vehicle.

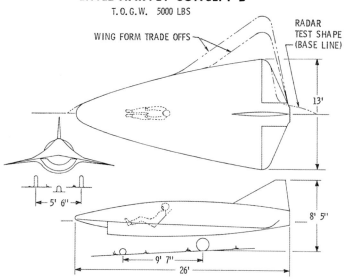

This Skunk Works three-view shows what was dubbed "Little Harvey Concept B" with several wing configurations.

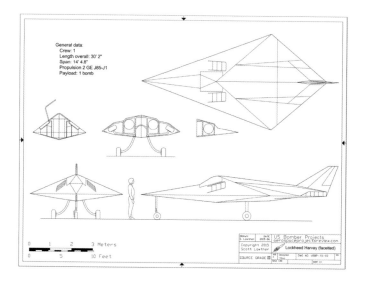

Lockheed "Harvey (faceted)" additional views. *Artwork by Scott Lowther/Aerospace Projects Review.com*

Have Blue XST

The Have Blue Experimental Survivable Testbed (XST) program was begun in November 1975 under a joint USAF and DARPA contract with Lockheed and its Skunk Works to build and fly two XST air vehicles. The first example (Have Blue number one, or HB-1), the aerodynamic testbed, was initially flight-tested at Area 51 by Lockheed test pilot Bill Park on December 1, 1977. The second example (HB-2) was first flown on July 20, 1978, at Area 51 by USAF Lt. Col. Norman Kenneth "Ken" Dyson.

The pair of XST aircraft were assembled in Building 82 at Lockheed's Burbank, California, facility before they were transferred to Groom Lake, Nevada, within the Area 51 complex, for their respective flight test activities. The highly classified Have Blue program ended in November 1978, when Lockheed got the go-ahead on the Senior Trend program. Flight testing on HB-2 continued however. Both air vehicles were lost in separate crashes. Have Blue number one crashed to destruction on May 4, 1978, on its thirty-sixth test flight; HB-2 was lost on July 11, 1979, on its fifty-second test flight. Both Park and Dyson survived these crashes, and the remains of the aircraft were buried somewhere within Area 51. Lockheed applied factory serial numbers 1001 and 1002 to their two Have Blue XST air vehicles.

The Have Blue XST aircraft were the inventions of Richard Scherrer, Denys D. Overholser, and Kenneth E. Watson. They filed for patent on February 13, 1979, and were granted a fourteen-year patent on October 5, 1993.

Have Blue Experimental Survivable (read stealth) Testbed (XST) demonstrator number two (HB-1002) in Burbank just prior to being shipped to Area 51. *LMSW*

Have Blue XST demonstrator number one (HB-1001) in three-view after its camouflage paint scheme was replaced by a light gray livery. *Artwork by Giuseppe De Chiara*

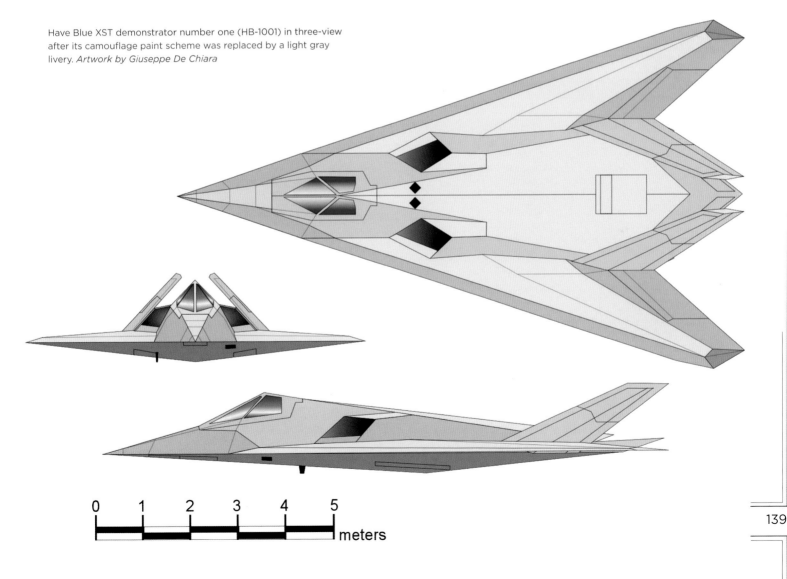

0 1 2 3 4 5
meters

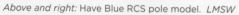

Above and right: Have Blue RCS pole model. *LMSW*

Rear view of Have Blue number one, still in its camouflage livery. *LMSW*

Above: Close-up bottom view of Have Blue number one. *LMSW*

Below: Have Blue number two in flight with USAF Col. Ken Dyson at the controls. *LMSW*

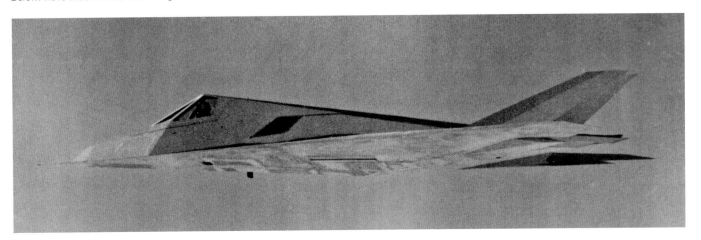

HAVE BLUE XST

SPECIFICATIONS

CREW: One (pilot)

PROPULSIVE SYSTEM: Two non-afterburning, axial-flow, 2,950 lbf-class General Electric J85-GE-4A turbojet engines

LENGTH: 38 ft 0 in

HEIGHT: 7 ft 6 in

WINGSPAN: 22 ft 6 in

EMPTY WEIGHT: 8,950 lbs

GROSS WEIGHT: 12,000 lbs

MAXIMUM SPEED: Mach 0.80 (600 mph)

PAYLOAD: None

The unique engine exhaust system used by the Have Blue XST air vehicles, as well as the F-117s, was designed by Stephen G. Justice, who applied for his patent on October 2, 1995. He received a fourteen-year patent on December 14, 1999.

As a matter of interest, the Northrop entry featured triangular wings, a single vertical tail and rudder, and no horizontal tail planes. Its propulsive system—most likely a pair of aft-mounted J85s—were to be fed air via a single dorsal inlet and duct system mounted just after of the cockpit.

SUMMARY

The pair of Have Blue XST prototypes played a significant role in the creation and success of the F-117 stealth fighter. Although both were lost in crashes, the eighty-eight test

USAF/NASA X-24C (TDN L-301) Hypersonic Research Airplane (HRA) air vehicle configuration in three-view, circa August 1976.
Artwork by Giuseppe De Chiara

flights between them demonstrated that near-invisible aircraft could be put into service and operate without detection. The success of the F-117 Nighthawk program proved this.

X-24C: Hypersonic Research Airplane

The joint USAF-NASA X-24 program, dubbed PILOT, was created to research various lifting body types of aircraft. The Martin Marietta Corporation of Bethesda, Maryland built a single X-24A and created the one off X-24B by rebuilding the X-24A. The X-24A made its first unpowered glide flight on April 17, 1969, with USAF test pilot Maj. Jerauld R. Gentry at the controls, the X-24B made its first unpowered glide flight on August 1, 1973, with NASA test pilot John A. Manke at its controls. The former had a maximum speed of 1,036 miles per hour or Mach 1.56, the latter 1,164 miles per hour or 1.76 Mach number.

In the meantime a cornucopia of hypersonic (Mach 6 to 8) X-24C proposals emerged from several airframe contractors during the 1972 to 1978 time period. And USAF/NASA selected Lockheed with it Model L-301

series which evolved into the X-24C-12I lifting body design from out of the Skunk Works with James A. "Jim" Penland as project engineer. Two examples were to be built and flown as a follow-on to the X-15 program and the X-24C air vehicles would be air-launched via B-52 mother plane much like the X-15s were.

The joint USAF-NASA Lockheed X-24C-12I Hypersonic Research Aircraft (HRA) was a dedicated lifting body design with short, stubby wings with upturned wingtips and three short vertical tail fins—the center one being higher than the two outboard ones. And to help reduce cost and speed up its manufacturing process, it was to use off-the-shelf government-furnished equipment such as its emergency ejection seat, landing gear, and avionics.

Unlike the previous lifting body air vehicles programs, the X-24C program was classified. And in the end no X-24C air vehicles were ever built as the entire program was cancelled in 1978.

Since the Space Shuttle program had been launched at this time, the need for the X-24C was over. This was because the Space Shuttle during its ascent into orbit, its reentry, and its descent for landing could provide the exact same hypersonic speed science that were to be gleaned from the X-24C.

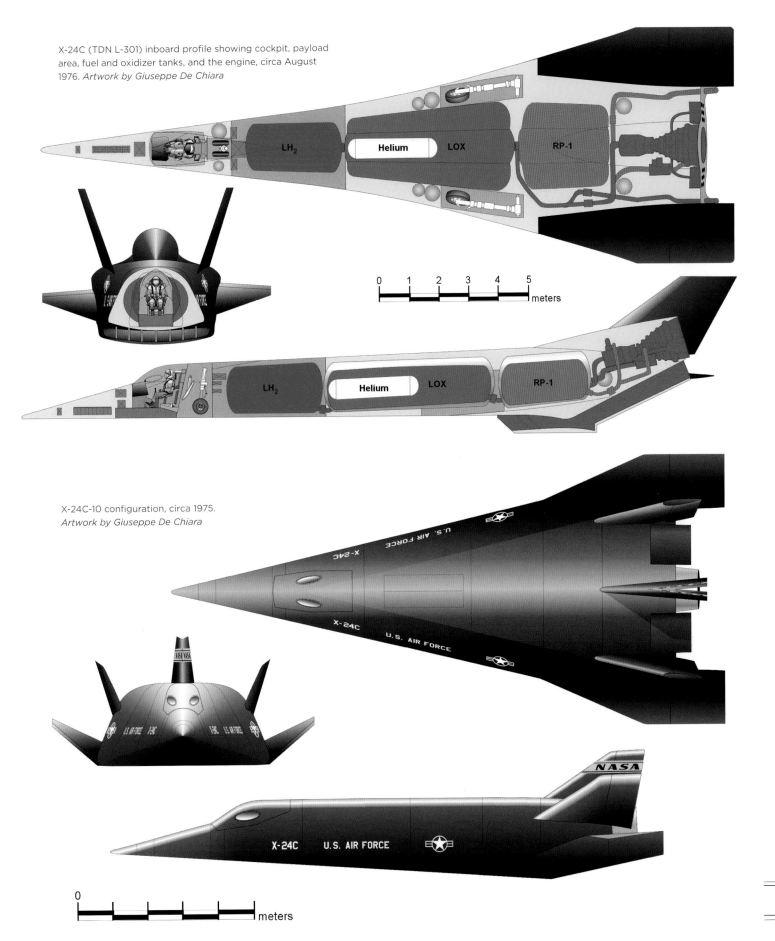

X-24C (TDN L-301) inboard profile showing cockpit, payload area, fuel and oxidizer tanks, and the engine, circa August 1976. *Artwork by Giuseppe De Chiara*

LH₂

Helium   LOX

RP-1

0 1 2 3 4 5
meters

LH₂

Helium   LOX

RP-1

X-24C-10 configuration, circa 1975.
Artwork by Giuseppe De Chiara

U.S. AIR FORCE

X-24C

X-24C

U.S. AIR FORCE

NASA

X-24C   U.S. AIR FORCE

0
meters

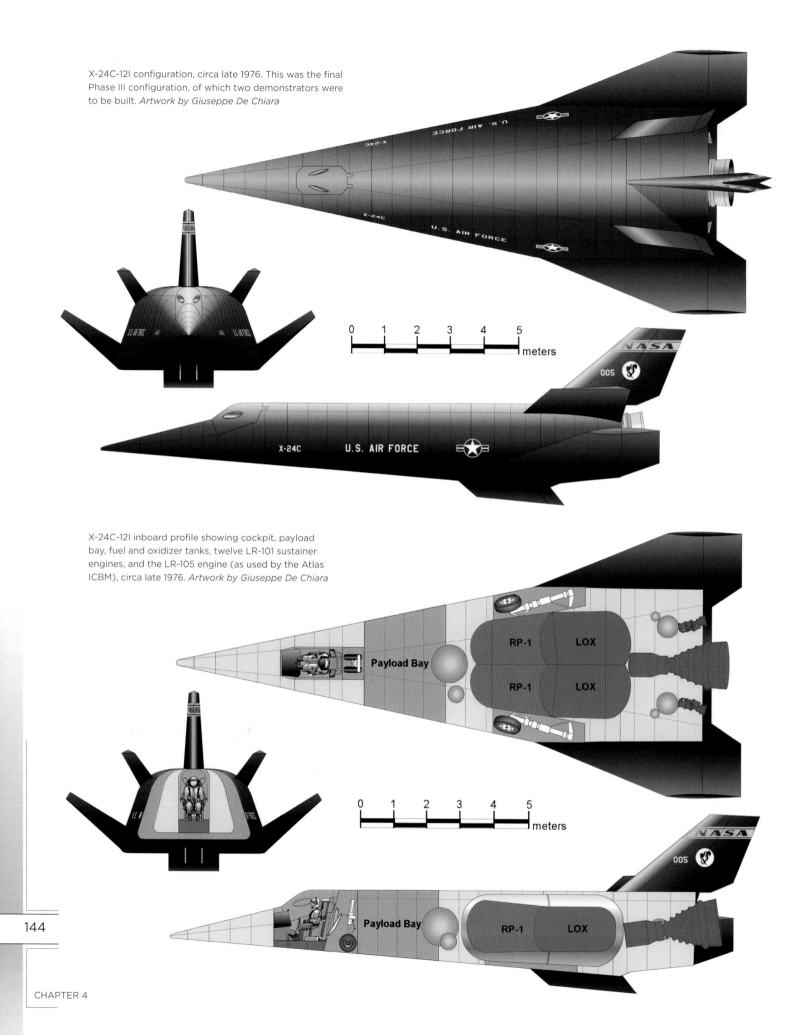

X-24C-12I configuration, circa late 1976. This was the final Phase III configuration, of which two demonstrators were to be built. *Artwork by Giuseppe De Chiara*

X-24C-12I inboard profile showing cockpit, payload bay, fuel and oxidizer tanks, twelve LR-101 sustainer engines, and the LR-105 engine (as used by the Atlas ICBM), circa late 1976. *Artwork by Giuseppe De Chiara*

Payload Bay

RP-1   LOX

RP-1   LOX

Payload Bay   RP-1   LOX

X-24C

SPECIFICATIONS

CREW: One (pilot)

PROPULSIVE SYSTEM: One LR-105 liquid-fueled rocket engine for boost, 12 LR-101 liquid-fueled sustainer engines for cruise (when not on scramjets), and an 8-scramjet module mounted ventrally for cruise (when not on sustainer engines) (All engines would have used Rocket Propellant-1 or RP-1 for fuel and liquid oxygen for oxidizer; helium would have pressurized the fuel tanks.)

LENGTH: 74 ft 10 in

HEIGHT: 20 ft 7 in

WINGSPAN: 24 ft 2 in

EMPTY WEIGHT (NO FUEL): 12,000 lbs

GROSS WEIGHT (LAUNCH WEIGHT): 19,500 lbs

MAXIMUM CRUISE SPEED: Mach 6.78 (5,161.0 mph) cruise speed on scramjets (40 seconds); Mach 6.00 cruise speed on sustainer engines (70 seconds)

MAXIMUM SPEED: Mach 8.00 (6,089.7 mph)

ARMAMENT: None

PAYLOAD: 1,000 lbs

SUMMARY

The X-24C Hypersonic Research Airplane program never left the ground, as the information gathered from the X-15A-2 flight test program provided the data the X-24C had been designed for. But if the X-15A-2 had failed, the X-24C was on tap. It would have been most interesting to have seen the X-24C fly.

Senior Prom: Stealth Cruise Missile

With the success of the two Have Blue XST air vehicles—especially their anti-radar characteristics—the Skunk Works offered up its design of a stealthy cruise missile loosely based on the configuration of its XST aircraft for the Advanced Cruise Missile (ACM) competition.

So promising was the Skunk Works' stealth cruise missile offering, the USAF ordered an unknown quantity of these missiles under a highly classified program dubbed Senior Prom.

X-24C12I (Phase III) wind tunnel model. *NASA*

To evaluate these missiles in flight, a USAF C-130 Hercules was modified to carry and launch them. A special attachment point was installed under the outer left-hand wing of this C-130, and the first test launch was made on October 1978.

The results of this or subsequent flights are not known to the public, for this program remains classified and no further Senior Prom details are available. It is known, however, that no full-scale production orders for Senior Prom air vehicles were forthcoming and that it was the General Dynamics Corporation that produced the ACM that became known as the AGM-129A.

145

Senior Prom details remain scarce. This C-130 is carrying a black-colored prototype low-observable (stealth) cruise missile under its outer left-hand (port) wing. *Jim Goodall Collection via LMSW*

Senior Trend: The F-117A

The F-117A Nighthawk was the first operational stealth airplane in the world. And until the advent of the B-2 stealth bomber, it was the world's only stealth aircraft.

Although the existence of such a warplane had been rumored for several years as the "F-19," the existence of the F-117A wasn't made public until November 10, 1988, when Pentagon spokesman James Daniel "Dan" Howard announced the Lockheed F-117A during a press briefing.

Along with his announcement came a release of a very poor quality photograph of the F-117A that largely distorted its actual appearance. It didn't even have an official name at the time, as it was only known as the "Black Jet" to those associated with it.

Developed and produced for the USAF TAC by the Skunk Works, the F-117A Nighthawk was classified as a strike fighter and designed from the outset to advantageously utilize very low observables (VLO), or stealth, technologies.

No X or Y versions of the F-117A were built. Rather, two XST aircraft under the Have Blue program and five

Above: Best in-flight view of an orange-colored Senior Prom shape carried by its C-130 test launch airplane. *Jim Goodall Collection via LMSW*

Left: Closer view of a black-colored Senior Prom shape. *Jim Goodall Collection via LMSW*

YF-117A number one (LM factory serial number 780/USAF serial number 79-10780) during its assembly process in Burbank. *LMSW*

full-scale development (FSD) F-117A aircraft were built under the Senior Trend program. These aircraft were used in part for aerodynamics, stealth, and airborne tactical warfare evaluations. The five FSD F-117A airplanes ordered for service test duties (Lockheed factory serial numbers 780 to 784) were later redesignated YF-117A to better describe their prototype status. These five aircraft were called Scorpion 1 through Scorpion 5 by those closely associated with them and known collectively as the Baja Scorpions. Their respective first flights are as follows:

SCORPION 1 (780) 18 June 1981 Harold C. "Hal" Farley Jr. (Bandit 117)

SCORPION 2 (781) 24 September 1981 David L. "Dave" Ferguson (Bandit 105)

SCORPION 3 (782) 18 December 1981 Thomas A. "Tom" Morgenfeld (Bandit 101)

SCORPION 4 (783) 7 June 1982 (flew after Scorpion 5) Tom Morgenfeld (Bandit 101)

SCORPION 5 (784) 10 April 1982 (flew before Scorpion 4) Robert L. "Bob" Riedenauer (Bandit 103)

Lockheed Martin F-117A artwork for the USAF. *LM Code One*

YF-117A number one being prepared for its first flight on June 18, 1981, at Area 51. *LMSW*

Subscale RCS F-117 pole model. *LMSW*

149

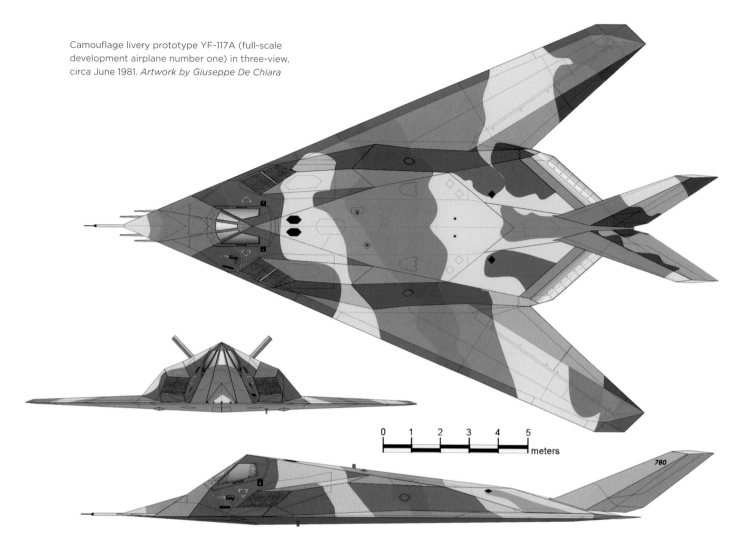

Camouflage livery prototype YF-117A (full-scale development airplane number one) in three-view, circa June 1981. *Artwork by Giuseppe De Chiara*

0 1 2 3 4 5 meters

(When pilots made their first flight on an F-117A and/or other classified aircraft, they earned Bandit status and were issued a Bandit number.)

The first production F-117A (785) attempted its first flight on April 20, 1982, out of Area 51 with Skunk Works test pilot Bob Riedenauer at the controls. Unfortunately, its computerized fly-by-wire flight control system had somehow been connected up wrong, and when Riedenauer rotated for takeoff, the airplane immediately went out of control, flipped over onto its back, and crashed inverted onto the ground. Riedenauer survived but was severely injured during the ordeal; he would never fly again. This airplane therefore was not accepted by the USAF, and it wasn't counted in the total of fifty-nine production F-117As built and delivered.

On August 23, 1982, the third production F-117A (787) became the first production F-117A to be accepted by the USAF. Its first flight date was July 20, 1982. The first flight date of the second production F-117A (786)—the

Above: Weapon loading tests at Eglin AFB in Florida. *LMSW photo by Denny Lombard*

Opposite: The F-117A is of a semi-flying-wing design with highly sweptback flying surfaces. *LMSW photo by Denny Lombard*

F-117A

SPECIFICATIONS

CREW: One (pilot)

PROPULSIVE SYSTEM: Two axial-flow, non-afterburning, 10,600-lbf General Electric F404-GE-F1D2 turbofan engines

LENGTH: 65 ft 11 in

HEIGHT: 12 ft 9.5 in

WINGSPAN: 43 ft 4 in

EMPTY WEIGHT: 29,500 lbs

GROSS WEIGHT: 52,500 lbs

MAXIMUM SPEED: Mach 0.92 (617 mph)

MAXIMUM RANGE: 1,070 miles

SERVICE CEILING: 45,000 ft

ARMAMENT: None

PAYLOAD: Two 2,000-pound precision guided bombs carried internally

F-117A number one, aka Scorpion 1, in its light gray livery, with its three Skunk Works test pilots: Hal Farley, Tom Morgenfeld, and Skip Anderson. *LMSW*

first F-117A to fly—was July 15, 1982. Hal Farley—chief engineering test pilot, made both of these first flights.

As F-117A production increased the fleet was assigned to a specifically built air base complete with individual hangers for each airplane. This once top-secret facility is called Tonopah Test Range (also known as Area 10) and is located about 70 miles northwest of Area 51, some 30 miles southeast of Tonopah, Nevada.

SUMMARY

With the advent of the operational F-117A Nighthawk in October 1983, the USAF—its TAC in particular—had a dedicated stealth combat aircraft that could carry and deliver two 2,000-pound laser-guided (later satellite-guided) Joint Direct Attack Munitions (JDAM) bombs and then escape enemy territory without detection.

Every single aviation history historian in the world was astonished at the surprising configuration of the precision strike stealth fighter. Expected to be of a curvaceous and sleek design to achieve its anti-radar characteristics, it was instead angular and jutted. It looked more like a flying iron than an airplane. Moreover, since the F/A-18 Hornet and F-20 Tigershark had already flown (in 1978 and 1982 respectively), everybody wondered what happened to the F-19 and assumed it would be designated as such. Instead it was designated F-117A, which was a

perfect cover, because after the F-111 there were no more century-numbered designations.

The F-117A Nighthawk was a very successful warfighter and has served in numerous combat situations. It flew combat missions over Panama, Iraq, and Yugoslavia. Just one was shot down, and that loss was considered by many to have been nothing more than a lucky shot.

The 49th Fighter Wing at Holloman AFB, New Mexico, has been the sole operator of the F-117A Nighthawk since July 8, 1992. Prior to that it was operated by the 4450th Tactical Group (absorbed by the 37th Tactical Fighter Wing on October 5, 1989) at Tonopah Test Range.

The F-117A was replaced by the F-22A Raptor at Holloman AFB. Ten were retired in December 2006 followed by another twenty-seven between January and March 2008. A retirement ceremony honoring the contributions made by the F-117A, the world's first operational stealth warplane, took place at Wright-Patterson AFB in Dayton, Ohio, on March 11, 2008. The last F-117As that flew into retirement left Holloman AFB on April 21, 2008, stopped in Palmdale, California, for another retirement ceremony, and arrived at their final destination on April 22. The entire remaining fleet of Nighthawks will be mothballed at their original home, Tonopah Test Range. All in all, the F-117A Nighthawk had been operational for less than twenty-two years. Its

Above: Proposed USN F-117N for carrier-based operations at sea. *LMSW*

Left: Another view of the proposed F-117N "Seahawk." *LMSW*

153

Benjamin Rich, President of Lockheed Advanced Programs (1975–1991)

Benjamin Robert "Ben" Rich joined the Lockheed Aircraft Corporation in 1950 as a thermodynamicist. By request of Kelly Johnson, he joined the Skunk Works in mid-1953 to work on the design engine air inlets for the experimental and prototype F-104s.

On January 17, 1975, Vice President Ben Rich—Johnson's handpicked candidate—became the second president of the Skunk Works. In this capacity he pushed corporate management into the very low observables world and found great success in the Have Blue–cum–Senior Trend programs. So much so, in fact, that he earned the title "Father of Stealth."

Rich was born on June 18, 1925, in Manila in the Philippines. He passed away on January 5, 1995. He was sixty-nine.

earlier-than-expected retirement is regarded as saving money for application to other programs, such as the F-35 Lightning II. The government has no plans to bring F-117s out of retirement but could do so if need be.

The F-117A program demonstrated that a stealth aircraft can be designed for reliability and maintainability and revolutionized military warfare by incorporating VLO technologies into operational aircraft. Now that it has been replaced by the F-22A—a fifth-generation stealth airplane and the USAF's stealth fighter of choice—one can say that the F-117A has been overtaken by the stealth technologies it in itself had created.

Finally, the official name of the F-117A is "Night Hawk," but the word "Nighthawk" is used most often.

SUMMARY

The 1970s forbade curiosity seekers from learning anything about the programs within the Skunk Works. Rumors of hypersonic and invisible aircraft were widespread but went unsubstantiated. A number of magical aircraft appeared, but they were not seen by the public for some eight years to come. It must have been a glorious time in aviation history for those associated with the products that came forth from the Skunk Works and a proud time indeed for the Skunks themselves.

Above: Two GBU-10s falling away from an F-117A during a bombardment test at Eglin AFB. *LM* Code One

Opposite: F-117A adorned with the American flag for its retirement ceremony. *LMSW*

05 THE 1980s: BEWILDERING VENTURES

"Be quick, be quiet, [and] be on time."

—KELLY JOHNSON

The 1980s were pretty lean years for the Skunk Works, with little business generated from all of its hard work. It nevertheless produced a number of interesting concepts, albeit carryovers from the 1960s and 1970s. These remnants from the past included a highly evolved U-2R, which was successfully sold and produced as the TR-1, and of course the F-117 stealth fighter.

Skunk Works programs in the 1980s also laid the foundation for what became the F-22 Raptor of the 1990s and, eventually, the F-35 Lightning II of the 2000s. Both are considered to be fifth-generation fighters built by the Lockheed Martin Corporation.

Other Skunk Works programs from the 1980s remain classified. Who knows how many creations from these secret projects could be out there? To paraphrase the popular Fox Network television show *The X-Files*, the truth is out there—somewhere.

Senior Peg: The Advanced Technology Bomber

On August 22, 1980, President James E. "Jimmy" Carter Jr. announced in part that "the US Department of Defense is working to develop stealth aircraft, including a bomber. That this had been going on since 1979 as the Advanced Technology Bomber (ATB) program."

The Lockheed Aircraft Corporation was first to join forces with another airframe contractor on the low-observables bomber program, selecting the Rockwell International Corporation, which had built the four prototype B-1A Advanced Manned Strategic Aircraft. The Lockheed/Rockwell offering was issued the codename Senior Peg. The Northrop Corporation and the Boeing Airplane Company followed suit, and their entry was issued the codename Senior Ice. In retrospect, at this particular time in aviation history the only dedicated stealth aircraft that had flown were the two Have Blue XST aircraft. Their success had made additional stealth aircraft possible.

The Lockheed/Rockwell and Northrop/Boeing teams submitted their respective ATB offerings. On October 20, 1981, the Northrop/Boeing ATB design was selected. The

B-2 Spirit was the result. Unfortunately, at this writing some twenty-five years later, Skunk Works public affairs refuses to release any pertinent information or photographs in reference to its ATB proposal. Thus, no further details on the Senior Peg program are available.

ATA: Advanced Tactical Aircraft

Although the Lockheed Skunk Works participated in the USN's Advanced Tactical Aircraft (ATA) program, which began in 1983, only a few details were released on its participation. The ATA was to be a long-range, very-low-observable, high-payload, medium-attack aircraft to replace the Vietnam War–era Grumman A-6 Intruder in the carrier-based, medium-attack role.

On January 13, 1988, the team of McDonnell Douglas and General Dynamics was selected over a Northrop-led team (Northrop/ Grumman/Vought) to build the ATA. McDonnell Douglas and General Dynamics were contracted to

Above: The stealthy Lockheed Sea Shadow was created for the USN Naval Sea Systems Command. *USN photo via Naval Sea Systems Command*

Next pages: U-2S (formerly U-2) in Senior Span configuration. *LM*

Lockheed/Rockwell Senior Peg in three-view as it appeared in September 1980. *Artwork by Giuseppe De Chiara*

157

SR-71(I)

On November 11, 1982, at the request of USAF Lt. Col. Donald "Don" Emmons, Lockheed ADP presented a solicited proposal entitled *Interceptor Aircraft Proposal*. The five-part proposal was submitted in response to Emmons's inquiry for the development of an interceptor variant of the SR-71 dubbed SR-71(I) (*I* suffix in parenthesis meaning "interceptor"). It was planned to use modified SR-71A airplanes for this program. The actual designation of this proposal was SR-71 I, but for clarity purposes it has been changed to SR-71(I).

The SR-71(I) was to carry and fire four advanced medium-range air-to-air missiles or up to six Hughes AIM-54C Phoenix air-to-air missiles—four internally with folding fins, two externally.

build five full-scale static test articles and eight flight test aircraft. By contract the first flight was to take place on June 17, 1990.

Designated A-12 and named Avenger II, this all-flying-wing design was to be a two-place, long-range, subsonic aircraft with a large internal weapons load including air-to-ground and air-to-air weapons.

Following the disclosure of severe cost and schedule overruns and technical problems in late 1990, the A-12 Avenger II program was canceled outright on January 7, 1991.

ASTOVL: Advanced Short Takeoff and Vertical Landing

DARPA began a program in 1983 to look at the technologies available to design and manufacture a follow-on supersonic replacement for the AV-8 Harrier. The program, known as Advanced Short Takeoff and Vertical Landing (ASTOVL), eventually became a joint US-UK collaboration. In 1987 the results of the ASTOVL program made clear that the technologies available were not yet advanced enough to generate a replacement that would satisfy both countries. At this time, DARPA secretly approached the Skunk Works in the hopes that they would be able to develop an aircraft like that they had hoped would appear from the first phase of ASTOVL. Lockheed told DARPA that they had some ideas that could be matured and that, if successful, would meet the goals that DARPA was trying to achieve. At the same time, DARPA continued with ASTOVL Phase II as a cover for the covert work being done at the Skunk Works.

Above: May 1988
ASTOVL concept. *LM*

Left: Early Lockheed
ASTOVL concept. *LM*

Opposite: Lockheed
ASTOVL mockup.
LMSW

Sea Shadow: Stealth upon the Waves

The ADP division of Lockheed was renowned for creating aircraft and spacecraft, not seacraft. Nevertheless, on October 22, 1982, the Skunk Works joined the USN by getting a contract to design and produce a single stealth ship demonstrator, designated IX-529, for the USN.

The one-off *Sea Shadow* was completed in 1984 to investigate the application of stealth technology on seagoing naval vessels. It was used in secret until its public debut in 1993. In addition, the ship was designed to test the use of automation to enable the reduction of crew size. The ship was created by the DARPA, the USN, and Lockheed. The *Sea Shadow* was manufactured at Lockheed's Redwood City, California, facility inside Hughes Mining Barge-1 (HMB-1), which functioned as a floating dry dock during its construction and testing.

It was acquired by the USN on March 1, 1985.

SUMMARY

The USN took the *Sea Shadow* out of service and struck it off its register simultaneously in September 2006. At that same time the USN tried to sell it to the highest bidder, to no avail. In 2012 Bay Ship procured it for scrap and totally dismantled it.

161

Above: The *Sea Shadow* wasn't made public until 1993, almost a decade after it was built. *USN*

Left: The *Sea Shadow* heads on its first sailing. *USN*

Below: The *Sea Shadow* made plenty of waves during its 1984 sea trials. *LM Code One*

Above: Sea Shadow docking in its covered mooring area next to a pier shared by an identified aircraft carrier. *LMSW photo by Eric Schulzinger*

Below: Sea Shadow in its special berth. *LMSW photo by Eric Schulzinger*

SEA SHADOW

SPECIFICATIONS

CREW: Four

PROPULSIVE SYSTEM: Diesel-electric

DISPLACEMENT: 563 long tons (1,261,120 lbs)

LENGTH: 164 ft 0 in

BEAM: 68 ft 0 in

DRAFT: 15 ft 0 in

MAXIMUM SPEED: 14.2 knots (16.3 mph)

ARMAMENT: None

SSF: The STOVL Strike Fighter

In the late 1980s the Lockheed Skunk Works was involved in a classified, non-acknowledged program with NASA Ames that looked into the feasibility of designing a stealthy supersonic Short Takeoff and Vertical Landing (STOVL) strike fighter, or SSF. This was a cooperative program that utilized the assets of NASA (wind tunnels, personnel, supercomputers, etc.) along with the expertise of the Skunk Works in designing stealthy air vehicles. The results from this highly classified program proved that a SSF could be successfully flown. Management at the Skunk Works was convinced that the SSF design could be sold to both the USAF and the USN. (The US Naval Air Systems Command [NAVAIR] is the procuring office for Marine Corps aircraft.) The Skunk Works proposed a teaming between the USAF and the USN. The services agreed, a Memorandum of Understanding (MOU) was signed between the services, and the SSF program began to come out of the black.

Finally, FY 1995 budget legislation passed in October 1994 by Congress directed that ASTOVL be merged into the Joint Advanced Strike Technology (JAST) program immediately.

RIVET

Little is known about the so-called RIVET program other than the fact that the Skunk Works investigated an invention patented by Daniel P. "Dan" Raymer, a noted aerospace design engineer. This particular invention is called "Reverse Engine VSTOL" and had something to do with the RIVET program. He applied for patent on February 27, 1989, and received a fourteen-year patent on February 20, 1990.

An abstract from his patent says in part that the invention is "a vertical/short takeoff and landing (VSTOL) aircraft." It was most likely part of Lockheed's pre-JAST design efforts to develop a suitable VSTOL combat aircraft.

Raymer was director–advanced design in the Skunk Works from 1987 to 1990. He later joined the Conceptual Research Corporation—a design and consulting firm—and serves as its president as of this writing.

SUMMARY

In the 1980s the Skunk Works generated the world's first operational VLO (stealth) precision strike aircraft—the F-117A—and laid the groundwork for what became the F-22A Raptor stealth fighter. It also created an advanced U-2R derivative, the TR-1A, and participated in numerous programs leading to the creation of the multi-service JSF, which in turn became the F-35A/B/C series of stealth strike fighters.

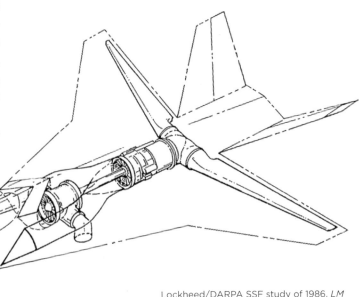

Lockheed/DARPA SSF study of 1986. *LM*

Above: Artist rendition of a RIVET aircraft. *LM*

Above right: RIVET conceptual illustration. *LM*

Below: Internal view of RIVET showing 1) the propulsive system; 2) the reverse flow exhaust system; and 3) the weapons area. *Steve Pace Collection*

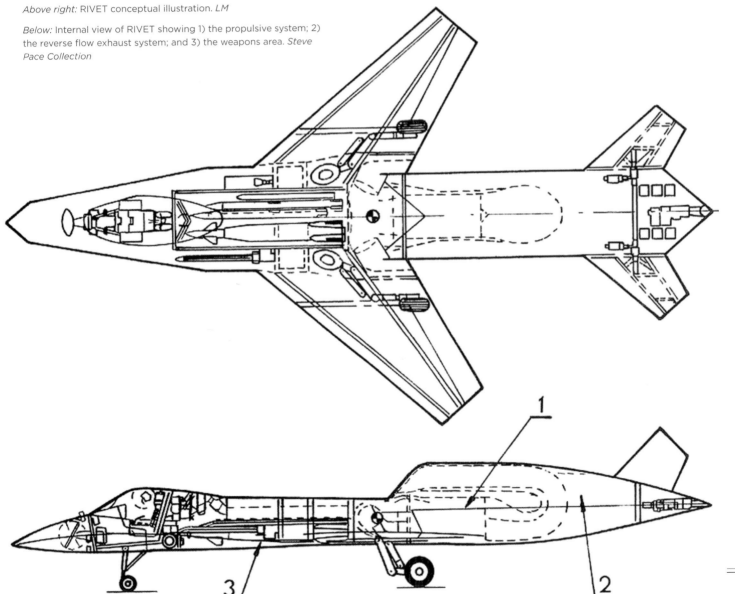

06 THE 1990s: MANNED VERSUS UNMANNED

"Although I expect few in the media to believe me, there is no code name for the hypersonic plane because it simply does not exist."

—BEN RICH, IN HIS 1994 BOOK *SKUNK WORKS*

The 1990s got off to a rousing start. In 1990 the Skunk Works–designed YF-22 entered into a winner-take-all competition against the YF-23 to see which air vehicle would be the USAF's ATF. In April 1991 the YF-22 won the ATF competition, which resulted in the F-22A Raptor of today.

During the years 1990 to 1999 a number of unique aircraft came from the Skunk Works' three-dimensional computer-aided-design and computer-aided-manufacturing programs. Some were stillborn, but a number of others took flight. These included the YF-22, the Naval Advanced Tactical Fighter (NATF), the proposed multi-role fighter aircraft, the X-33 VentureStar, the proposed Attack-Experimental (A-X) aircraft, the RQ-3A DarkStar, the proposed Attack/Fighter-Experimental (A/F-X) aircraft, the Common Affordable Lightweight Fighter aircraft, the proposed Joint Advanced Strike Technology program, the P-420 LightStar, the Joint Air-to-Surface Standoff Missile, and finally the X-35 series of JSF Concept Demonstration Aircraft, to be discussed in the next chapter.

It was during these very same years that the Lockheed Aircraft Corporation purchased General Dynamics Fort Worth Division and merged with Martin Marietta to form the Lockheed Martin Corporation. The Skunk Works became a part of the Lockheed Martin Aeronautics Company at that time.

Lockheed Martin Aeronautics is headquartered in Fort Worth, Texas, with additional production and operations facilities in Clarksburg, West Virginia; Greenville, South Carolina; Johnstown, Pennsylvania; Marietta, Georgia; Meridian, Mississippi; Palmdale, California (home to the Skunk Works); and Pinellas Park, Florida. It also has offices and personnel in various countries throughout the world.

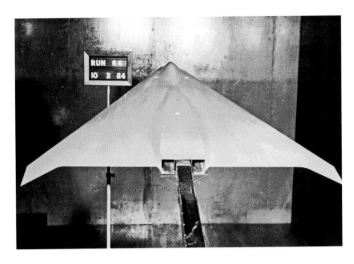

Early wind tunnel test model of an all-flying-wing ATF concept dated October 3, 1984. *LM* Code One

Another ATF wind tunnel test ATF configuration with ventral engine air inlet, dated February 12, 1985. *LM* Code One

ATF configuration 614 study. *LM* Code One

ATF configuration 631 study. *LM* Code One

ATF: Advanced Tactical Fighter

It is the now the day after tomorrow, and two flights of eight F-22 Raptors flying out of an undisclosed air base in Germany are over eastern Europe and fast approaching the northwestern border of Ukraine. All sixteen are carrying a full complement of ammunition for their 20mm cannon, and they are fully armed with infrared- and radar-guided air-to-air guided missiles. The F-22s are flying escort for a flight of six B-2 Spirits, which they had just rendezvoused with, each B-2 carrying sixtten weapons of an undisclosed nature, and all twenty-two of these aircraft are in full stealth mode . . .

Above: ATF configuration 1095. *LM* Code One

Next pages: F-22A Raptor makes a high-speed pass with its two Pratt & Whitney F119 turbofan engines in afterburn. Close-coupled stabilators/ wings are noteworthy. *LMSW*

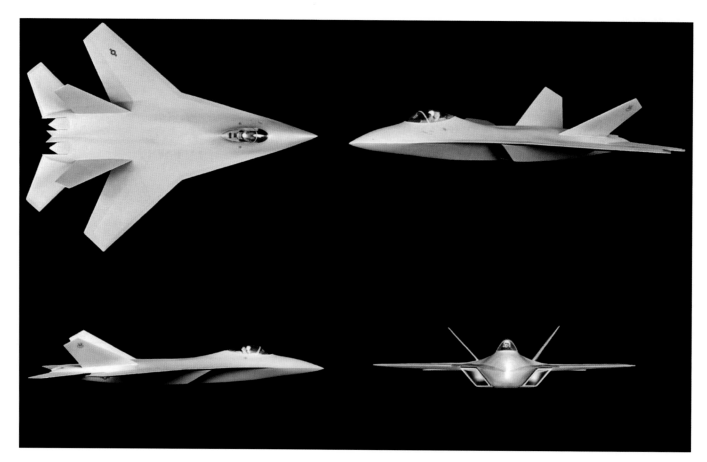

Above: ATF configuration study 090P. *LM* Code One

Opposite top: Early Lockheed ATF concept. *LM* Code One

Opposite bottom: First look at the Lockheed YF-22 design as released by the USAF in 1989. *USAF*

This is just one of several scenarios that could occur in the early twenty-first century as civil unrest and international war continually threatens the Ukraine, Iraq, and Syria, and also as tensions mount between Russia, ISIS, and the United States. The time may come when the F-22 Raptor takes to the skies.

The F-22 Raptor is classified as an air dominance fighter—that is, it is a superior fighter that can gain and maintain control of the air arena by outperforming its enemies because of its advantages in speed, firepower, thrust, range, avionics, agility, and maneuverability. The existing fleet of F-22s is relatively small when compared to other USAF fighter fleets, and yet it is a very healthy fleet of fighters capable of carrying and delivering a wide variety of air-to-air and air-to-ground ordnance without detection by enemy forces. It is a Very Low Observable fighter in the truest sense of this phrase. Moreover, it is a somewhat new fleet of fighters that has not yet been

baptized under fire. When and if the F-22 earns its spurs, it will no doubt do it with vigor.

The F-22 was born from the ATF program first envisaged during the very early 1980s to supplement and then replace the F-15 Eagle. The initial requirement for this was a total buy of 750 ATFs, but this amount dwindled several times: first to 648, then to 448, then to 339, then to 277, then to 181, finally settling at 187 (adding four due to several aircraft losses).

Out of seven contenders Headquarters USAF selected two primary airframe contractors: Lockheed and Northrop. These firms joined forces with principal contractors Boeing and General Dynamics (Lockheed) and principal contractor McDonnell Douglas (Northrop). Each team was contracted to produce two service test aircraft each, respectively designated YF-22 and YF-23. Since two powerplant contractors—Pratt & Whitney and General Electric—were contending to produce the propulsive system for the winning ATF design, each firm was contracted to produce service test examples of their engines, respectively designated YF119 and YF120. One YF-22 and one YF-23 would be powered by the YF119 while one YF-22 and one YF-23 would be powered by the YF120. Thus, the USAF would have

Top: YF-22 number one on an early test flight. *LMSW photo by Denny Lombard*

Above: YF-22 number one is shown here while it was being manufactured at the Skunk Works facility in Palmdale. *LMSW*

Opposite: YF-22 number two in its element. *LMSW photo by Denny Lombard*

four choices, and since it was a winner-take-all competition, the winner would be the preferred airframe and power-plant combination, and the loser would go home.

From this intense competition came the Pratt & Whitney YF119-powered Lockheed-Boeing-General Dynamics YF-22 winner, considered to have "clearly better capability with lower cost, thereby providing the Air Force with a true best value," according to Secretary of the Air Force Dr. Donald B. Rice, who announced the winning combination on April 23, 1991.

Lockheed subsequently received an Engineering, Manufacturing, and Development (EMD) contract to produce seven single-seat F-22As and a pair of two-seat F-22B pilot training and transition airplanes. This contract was later amended, and the two tandem-seat F-22Bs were canceled and replaced by an additional two single-seat F-22As for a total of nine F-22A EMD airplanes.

Pratt & Whitney Aircraft Engines were also given the green light to produce the F119 EMD engines for the nine

EMD F-22As plus spares. The F119 axial-flow turbofan engine is 16 feet 11 inches long, has a diameter of 46 inches, and weighs 3,900 pounds. It is a twin-spool, counter-rotating, low-aspect-ratio engine with three-stage low pressure/six-stage high pressure compressor; it has an annular combustor. It has a 7.95 to 1 thrust-to-weight ratio.

In his words to this writer, the late Lt. Gen. David J. "Dave" McCloud (call sign *Marshall*) said, "All fighter pilots must have a killer mentality. With the F-22 they'll be very well armed." McCloud was a part of the ATF selection board that found the YF119-powered entry from Lockheed superior to either one of the two Northrop contenders.

(Note: McCloud was a former member of the Joint Chiefs of Staff as director of force structure, resources, and assessment. When he passed away, on July 26, 1998, he was the commander of Alaska Command, 11th Air Force, overseeing all military forces in Alaska. A Vietnam War combat veteran, he had flown a wide range of

Comparison view of Lockheed/Boeing/General Dynamics YF-22 (bottom) and Northrop/McDonnell Douglas YF-23. *USAF*

classified, experimental, foreign [Red Eagles, as Bandit 6], and numerous other combat aircraft, primarily fighters, including the F-117A Nighthawk as Bandit 201.)

The Northrop-McDonnell Douglas YF-23 runner-up was to many the contender that should have won the ATF competition, for it appears to be stealthier than the YF-22 and much sleeker as well. The YF-23 featured twin wide-spaced, outward-canted tail plane assemblies that

tripled as horizontal stabilizers, vertical stabilizers, and rudders—they are dubbed ruddervators. Appearance-wise, instead of its wings being attached to its fuselage, it looks like its nose section is attached to its wings. Performance-wise, the YF120-powered YF-23—the first of the two to fly—hit Mach 1.6 (1,217.9 miles per hour) in supercruise on only its second flight. The YF-23 is a very eye-pleasing and interesting design, to be sure.

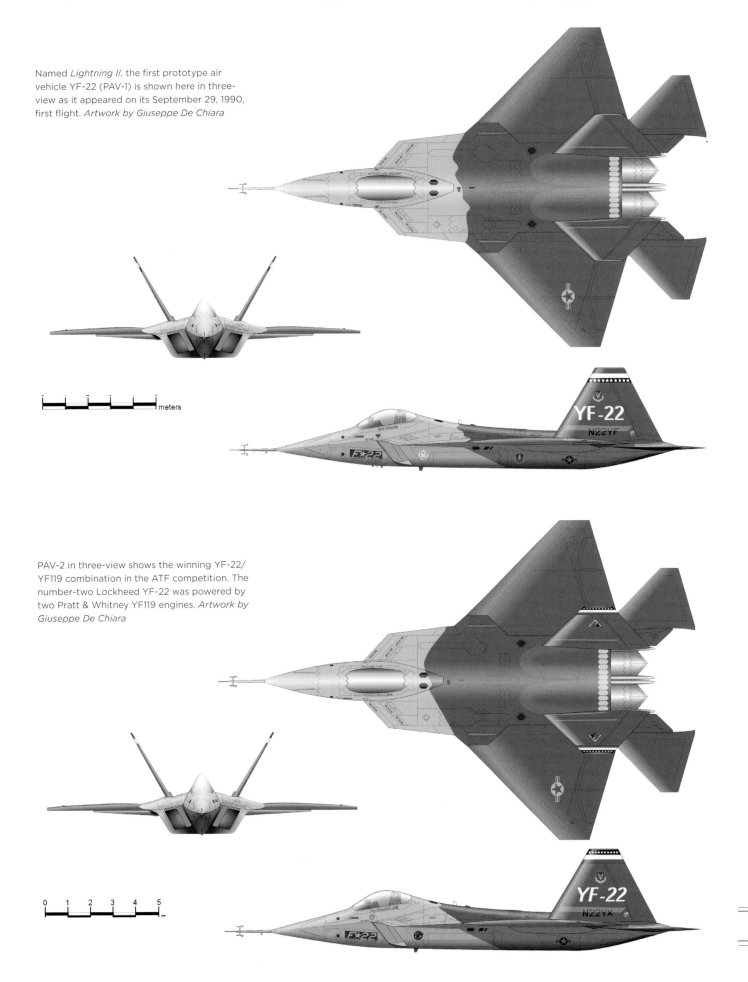

Named *Lightning II*, the first prototype air vehicle YF-22 (PAV-1) is shown here in three-view as it appeared on its September 29, 1990, first flight. *Artwork by Giuseppe De Chiara*

PAV-2 in three-view shows the winning YF-22/ YF119 combination in the ATF competition. The number-two Lockheed YF-22 was powered by two Pratt & Whitney YF119 engines. *Artwork by Giuseppe De Chiara*

YF-22 and F-22A comparison shows the differences between the prototype (right) and the first EMD airplane. *LM* Code One

It took a number of years from EMD contract award—six, to be exact—to finalize design issues and complete the first EMD airplane, which was ceremoniously rolled out on April 9, 1997, as the *Spirit of America*. It took another five months to get it airborne. Nevertheless, Raptor 01, as the first EMD F-22A (USAF serial number 91-001) was called, successfully entered into flight test on September 27, 1997, with USAF and test pilot veteran and F-22 chief test pilot Alfred P. "Paul" Metz at its controls. (Metz also made the first flight of the premier Northrop-McDonnell Douglas YF-23 as Northrop ATF chief test pilot, thereby becoming the only pilot to fly both ATF types of aircraft.)

In the meantime, the Lockheed Aircraft Corporation had purchased the aircraft manufacturing division of the General Dynamics Corporation in Fort Worth, Texas, in 1993 and then merged with the Martin Marietta Aerospace Corporation in Marietta, Georgia, to become the Lockheed Martin Corporation in 1995. This eliminated ATF principle contractor General Dynamics and left only the Boeing Airplane Company as an ATF principle contractor. With the Lockheed Martin–Marietta merger,

Nicknamed "Spirit of America," *Raptor 01* appears during its roll-out ceremony. *LMSW*

Lockheed subsequently moved its corporate headquarters from Burbank, California to Bethesda, Maryland.

By December 30, 2002, the eight other EMD F-22s had all flown. Subsequent testing of these aircraft found the design to be exceptional, and additional production contracts were forthcoming through FY 2010.

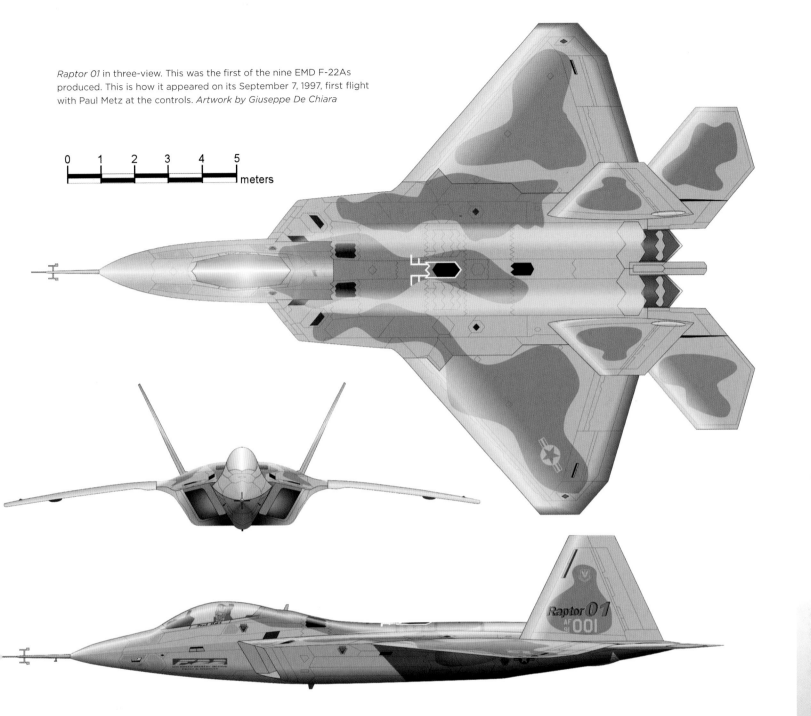

Raptor 01 in three-view. This was the first of the nine EMD F-22As produced. This is how it appeared on its September 7, 1997, first flight with Paul Metz at the controls. *Artwork by Giuseppe De Chiara*

The EMD phase continued on through December 27, 2005, by which time twelve combat-ready F-22As had been delivered. During the EMD phase the nine EMD F-22As flew 3,496 flights totaling more than 7,600 flight hours. More than 26,000 flight envelope expansion test points and 3,500 avionics mission test points were met during these flight tests. The EMD F-22 test fleet continued to fly from the Air Force Flight Test Center at Edwards AFB, California, after the EMD phase ended.

The USAF Air Combat Command procured its fleet of F-22A Raptor air dominance fighters from the Lockheed Martin Corporation in Marietta, Georgia. The first combat-ready F-22A was delivered May 12, 2005, and the last May 2, 2012. Fully operational since December 12, 2007—more than nine years—no Raptor has seen combat action against an enemy airplane as of this writing. It has, however, bombed ISIS targets.

For over three years, the F-22A had a different designation. As it happened, on September 17, 2002, Headquarters USAF ordered that the F-22A would from that date forward be designated F/A-22A to better describe its multi-role fighter-attack (read

YF-22 PAV

SPECIFICATIONS

CREW: One (pilot)

PROPULSIVE SYSTEM (PAV-1): Two axial-flow, afterburning, 35,000-lbf General Electric YF120-GE-100 turbofan engines

PROPULSIVE SYSTEM (PAV-2): Two axial-flow, afterburning, 35,000-lbf Pratt & Whitney YF119-PW-100 turbofan engines

LENGTH: 64 ft 2 in

HEIGHT: 12 ft 8.25 in

WINGSPAN: 43 ft

EMPTY WEIGHT: 34,000 lbs

GROSS TAKEOFF WEIGHT: 60,000 lbs

MAXIMUM SPEED: Mach 2 class

SERVICE CEILING: 60,000 ft

MAXIMUM RANGE: 1,250 mi

F-22 EMD/F-22A

SPECIFICATIONS

CREW: One (pilot)

PROPULSIVE SYSTEM: Two axial-flow, afterburning, 35,000-lbf Pratt & Whitney F119-PW-100 turbofan engines

LENGTH: 62.08 ft

HEIGHT: 16.67 ft

WINGSPAN: 44.5 ft

WING AREA: 840 sq ft

EMPTY EIGHT: 43,340 lbs

GROSS TAKEOFF WEIGHT: 83,500 lbs

MAXIMUM SPEED: Mach 2-plus class

SERVICE CEILING: 60,000 ft

MAXIMUM RANGE: 1,840 mi (with two external tanks)

Raptor 01 on an early test flight out of Edwards AFB. *LMSW*

fighter-bomber) capabilities. But then, on December 15, 2005—the very same day the airplane achieved Initial Operational Capability (IOC) with 27FS—it was ordered that the somewhat unpopular F/A-22A designation was no longer pertinent and that the preferential F-22A designation had been reinstated several days earlier.

Raptors have been dispersed to several key air bases on both coasts of the continental United States, Hawaii, and in the southwest in New Mexico. These units often rotate to temporary-duty air bases in Guam, Japan, and elsewhere. They also operate from test bases at which their systems are constantly evaluated, updated, and repaired as needed. Moreover, their current armament capabilities are hardened while possible new armaments for them are developed at these facilities.

Except for Japan and South Korea, as of this writing, no allied or friendly air bases abroad have been used by Raptor units, although they remain an option for any future war foothold requirements. And because the F-22 is the top-of-line fighter in the Air Combat Command of the USAF, any and all export sales of it have been banned to any foreign nation whether it be a staunch ally or a true friend.

F-22 FLIGHT TEST AND EVALUATION UNITS

EDWARDS AFB, California
　411TH Flight Test Squadron

NELLIS AFB, Nevada
　422ND Test & Evaluation Center
　433RD Fighter Weapons School
　AIR Warfare Center

TYNDALL AFB, Florida
　325TH Fighter Wing
　43RD Fighter Squadron
　F-22 Combat Units

JOINT Base Langley-Ustis, Virginia
　27TH Fighter Squadron
　94TH Fighter Squadron
　192ND Fighter Wing Virginia Air National Guard

JOINT Base Elmendorf-Richardson, Alaska
　302ND Fighter Squadron
　525TH Fighter Squadron
　90TH Fighter Squadron

HICKAM AFB, Hawaii
　199TH Fighter Squadron

EGLIN AFB, Florida
　95TH Fighter Squadron
　301ST Fighter Squadron

Lockheed Naval ATF (NATF) concept based upon F-22 design with variable *Sweep* wings, circa 1990. *Lockheed Martin*

NATF: Naval Advanced Tactical Fighter

Congress ordered the USN to evaluate a navalized version of the USAF's ATF as a possible replacement for their fleet of F-14 Tomcats. In return, the USAF would evaluate a derivative of the ATA as a replacement for its fleet of F-111s.

Earlier, in late 1988, a NATF program office had been set up at Wright-Patterson AFB, and the existing ATF Demonstration/Validation (Dem/Val) contracts were modified to include studies of potential NATF variants.

The Major Aircraft Review reduced the peak production rates of both the ATF and NATF. This substantially increased the program cost. In August 1990, Adm. Richard M. Dunleavy, who was in charge of USN aircraft requirements, stated that he did not see how the NATF could fit into any affordable plan for naval aviation.

In early 1991, before the final contractor for the ATF was even selected, the consideration of the NATF was dropped. This was mainly due to the fact that the navy realized that a series of upgrades to their existing F-14s could meet its air superiority needs through the year 2015. Thus, on January 7, 1991, all work on the Skunk Works–designed NATF-22 came to a halt.

179

The FB-22 Interim Bomber

In 2002 Lockheed Martin began investigating the potential of producing a stealthy medium-range bombardment platform based on the F-22A. Among other alterations, it would have a larger primary weapons bay, wing weapons bays, and a larger wing. It was to retain the supercruise feature of the Raptor and carry up to thirty small-diameter bombs (SDBs). These 250 pound–class SDBs are satellite-guided glide bombs designated GBU-39 and manufactured by Boeing.

In 2003 Secretary of the Air Force James Roche envisioned the procurement of 150 FB-22s. On April 29, 2004, the USAF issued a Request for Information (RFI) to the industry for what it called an "Interim Bomber," the idea being to field a medium-range bomber to fill the gap between the current fleets of bombers and the so-called 2037 Bomber of the future.

By this time Lockheed Martin had a pretty good flock of FB-22 offerings to present to the USAF, and

Above: Three-view of the proposed FB-22-4 version of the Interim/Regional Bomber. *Artwork by Giuseppe De Chiara*

Opposite: FB-22. *Artwork by Luca Landino*

Below: Competing Northrop Grumman FB-23 design. *Artwork by Jozef Gatial*

several FB-22 configurations were offered, including the FB-22-1 through FB-22-4. The FB-22-1 was to have a stretched and widened fuselage, carry one 5,000-pound plus two 2,000-pound bombs in main bay, and retain the F-22A wing and tails. The FB-22-2 was to have a stretched fuselage, carry four 2,000-pound bombs in main bay, use a different wing size and sweep for range and speed, beside bay small-diameter bomb (SBD) capable, and have low observable axisymmetric engine exhaust nozzles. The FB-22-3 was to have a standard fuselage, larger wing and more fuel, increased capacity in weapons bays plus wing weapons bays, and the capability of carrying SBDs in side bays. The FB-22-4 was to have a standard fuselage, larger wing, more fuel, increased capacity main weapons bay, and wing weapons bays, and be side-bay SBD capable.

Above: Another view of FB-23. *Artwork by Jozef Gatial*

Opposite top: FB-22-4 concept by aviation artist Eddie Moore. *LM* Code One

Opposite bottom: FB-22 concept. *Artwork by Jozef Gatial*

The USAF wanted its temporary bomber to be available by 2018, and this led to the 2018 Bomber program, which superseded the Interim Bomber program. The USAF wanted a bomber with much greater unrefueled range than the proposed FB-22 could provide. Thus, on February 6, 2006, when the *2006 Quadrennial Defense Review* was released, it became clear that the FB-22 wasn't the answer; the program did not move forward.

THE 1990S: MANNED VERSUS UNMANNED

Lockheed Procures the Aircraft Division of General Dynamics

On December 9, 1992, the Lockheed Aircraft Corporation announced that it would acquire the aircraft production facilities of the General Dynamics Corporation in Fort Worth, Texas. On March 1, 1993, the acquisition of General Dynamics Fort Worth Division was completed.

With this $1.5 billion purchase, Lockheed's share of the F-22 program rose from 35 percent to 67.5 percent; Boeing's percentage remained unchanged at 32.5 percent.

Moreover, in part with this purchase, Lockheed took over the production of the F-16 Fighting Falcon series of aircraft and became responsible for the existing fleet of F-111 and FB-111 aircraft.

MRF: Multi-Role Fighter

In 1991 the USAF—its Aeronautical Systems Center (ASC) specifically—created its Multi-Role Fighter (MRF) program in hope of finding a low cost supplement and ultimate replacement for its fleet of F-16s. With a flyaway cost of 35 to $50 million US dollars (USD) each the single seat MRF, like F-16, was to have a single engine for its propulsive system.

USAF/ASC held a meeting with avionics, airframe, and powerplant contractors in October 1991 simultaneously issuing its Request for Information (RFI). Their responses were due in January 1992. In the meantime, using their own funds, these contractors, including Lockheed's Skunk Works, created concepts and designs in hope of meeting the specific MRF demands.

As projected by mid-1992 the MRF program was to become an official venture by late 1993 or early 1994. The MRF, designed to replace not only high-time F-16s but ageing A-10s and F/A-18s that were nearing the end of their service lifes, gained speed.

Then, suddenly, defense budget cuts became rife and there were a number of aircraft program drawdowns.

Especially new aircraft programs. Moreover, in mid-1992, the B-2 stealth bomber program and Lockheed's own F-22 air dominance fighter program had top priority and were eating up most of the funding. As the result of this, the MRF program was shoved to the proverbial back burner in August 1992. And in mid-1993 the MRF program was cancelled outright.

A-X and A/F-X: The Advanced Attack and Advanced/Fighter-Attack Programs

The US Navy Advanced-Attack (A-X)–cum–Advanced Fighter/Attack (A/FX) programs began in January 1991. This was due in part to the cancellations of both the Advanced Tactical Aircraft (ATA) and Naval Advanced Tactical Fighter (NATF) programs.

On December 30, 1991, five airframe contracting teams received $20 million USD contracts to Concept Evaluation/Demonstration (CE/D) contracts to come up with an advanced, aircraft carrier-based, all-weather capable, two-man, two-engine, stealthy, long-range aircraft with advanced avionics and countermeasures to ultimately replace the US Navy A-6 and the US Air Force F-111, F-15E, and the F-117. These contracting teams included: Grumman/Lockheed/Boeing, Lockheed/Boeing/General Dynamics, McDonnell Douglas/Vought, Rockwell/Lockheed, and General Dynamics/McDonnell Douglas/Northrop.

The CE/D phase was to be finished in September 1992. The Demonstration/Validation (Dem/Val) proposals were to be offered in late 1992. Dem/Val was to begin in 1994 with Engineering Manufacturing Demonstration (EMD) in 1996. In late 1992 the US Congress demanded that the A-X Dem/Val phase must also include prototype aircraft to be evaluated in a fly-off competition. This move increased the initially scheduled Dem/Val phase from two to five years. Moreover, since the NATF program had been cancelled, the need for improved air-to-air combat was attached to the A-X program. This necessitated the change from A-X to A/F-X. This caused the existing A-X CE/D contracts to be extended, causing the projected Initial Operational Capability (IOC) to be delayed from

50th Anniversary

The Lockheed Aircraft Corporation celebrated the 50th anniversary of its Skunk Works on June 17, 1993.

2006 to 2008. A Milestone 1 Review of the A/F-X program was to be held by the Defense Acquisition Board (DAB) in spring 1993, but the government placed a stop on the program to see the result of the DAB report. For some yet unexplained reason the DAB Milestone 1 Report never materialized. And on September 1, 1993, the A/F-X program was cancelled and no further A/F-X work was done after December 31, 1993.

The pre-JAST Common Affordable Lightweight Fighter program generated a Skunk Works concept called configuration 100. Configuration 140—shown here as a powered 92-percent-scale model, was thoroughly evaluated through 1993. This design ultimately led to the design of the X-35B STOVL. *LM* Code One

CALF: Common Affordable Lightweight Fighter

The short-lived Common Affordable Lightweight Fighter (CALF) aka Joint Attack Fighter (JAF) program began in 1993 and was over by the end of 1994.

The Defense Advanced Research Projects Agency (DARPA) was responsible for the CALF program as the aircraft to evolve from it was to be a highly advanced experimental vertical takeoff and landing (VTOL) aircraft to eventually replace the US Marine Corps AV-8 Harrier "Jump-Jet."

The Lockheed Skunk Works and McDonnell Douglas had provided DARPA with unsolicited proposals that seemed feasible, but the government wanted more than just these two airframe contractors to provide concepts. Boeing tried to get on the band wagon later but to no avail.

The Joint Advanced Strike Technology (JAST) program was gaining favor, and the CALF and/or JAF programs quietly disappeared.

JAST: Joint Advanced Strike Technology

The Joint Advanced Strike Technology (JAST) program was the immediate precursor to what became the Joint Strike Fighter (JSF) program.

When the JAST program appeared it called for the merging of known and forthcoming technologies into a formula whereby a common airframe could be used for several different types of tactical aircraft.

It came time to mix the SSF, ATA, NATF, A-X, A/F-X, MRF, CALF/JAF, and the ASTOVL concepts into a strike fighter to do it all. And when the ASTOVL program was integrated with the JAST program in October 1994, the Joint Strike Fighter (JSF) program was born.

Lockheed, primarily its Skunk Works, had a good handle on all of these programs and with its clever designs and inventions, came up with what became the X-35 series of JSF concept demonstration aircraft, earned a contract to produce them in November 1996, and won the right to produce three versions of the JSF—the F-35A, F-35B, and F-35C in October 2001.

185

"A Merger of Equals"

On March 15, 1995, the Lockheed Aircraft Corporation merged with Martin Marietta to form the Lockheed Martin Corporation. It was called "A Merger of Equals," and it created one of the largest aerospace corporations in the world.

Above: Artist rendition of JAST coming aboard an aircraft carrier. *LMSW*

Left: Full-scale Joint Advanced Strike Technology wind tunnel model. *LMSW*

Below: Artist concept of JAST onboard a carrier at sea. *LMSW*

X-33 VentureStar on orbit. *LMSW*

VentureStar: The X-33

On July 2. 1996, NASA selected Lockheed Martin to produce a Reusable Launch Vehicle (RLV) designated X-33. The X-33 was to be a half-scale prototype to demonstrate the attributes of a future RLV twice its size. Lockheed Martin dubbed the prototype X-33 VentureStar, which was designed and managed in the Skunk Works.

The ultimate goal of a full-sized RLV was to reduce the cost of putting payloads into Earth orbit—from $10,000 to $1,000 USD per pound. Moreover, the full-scale RLV was to demonstrate improved launch, orbit, re-entry, and landing safety while advancing the state-of-the-art of space flight. That is, to generate the possibilities of private rather than government operations.

Much like the existing Space Shuttle, the X-33 was of a lifting body design with improved thermal protection, powered by two linear aerospike rocket motors of an innovative design.

The half-scale X-33 VentureStar demonstrator was to be an autonomously flown air vehicle by pilots on the ground. Suborbital, the X-33 prototype was to be launched vertically and land horizontally like the Space Shuttle. It was to reach an altitude of 60 miles and a maximum speed of more than 9,600 miles per hour or about 13.0 Mach number. It was to have a seven-day turnaround which is standard, a two-day emergency turnaround.

Fifteen test flights were scheduled to begin in the year 2000, the first of these covering the distance of 450 miles between Edwards AFB and the Dugway Proving Ground in Utah. Later flights were to cover the 950 miles between Edwards AFB and Malmstrom AFB in Montana.

A number of program setbacks including the failure of a liquid hydrogen fuel tank during a test and the air vehicle instability demonstrated by a wind tunnel model forced NASA to cancel the entire X-33 VentureStar program in 2001.

Another view of X-33. *NASA*

X-33

SPECIFICATIONS

LENGTH: 69 ft 0 in

WIDTH: 77 ft 0 in

GROSS TAKEOFF WEIGHT: 285,000 lbs

FUEL: LH2/LO2

FUEL WEIGHT: 210,000 lbs

MAIN PROPULSION: Two J-2S Linear Aerospikes

TAKEOFF THRUST: 410,000 lbf

MAXIMUM SPEED: Mach 13-plus

PAYLOAD TO LOW EARTH ORBIT: N/A

DarkStar: The RQ-3

The Lockheed RQ-3 DarkStar was a UAV to be used in the Tier III scheme of ISR planning for US warfighters.

The results of that study led to a three-tier approach to acquiring endurance UAVs for the critical need for near-real-time reconnaissance, surveillance and target acquisition, command and control, signals intelligence, and similar missions. Tier I was to be a quick reaction capability to address an urgent need in Bosnia; Tier II was medium-altitude endurance system, and Tier III was a high-altitude endurance capability. It was expected that the first two could be satisfied by the General Atomics Gnat 750 and Predator, respectively. Tier III was intended

Above: The Lockheed RQ-3 DarkStar lifting off from the main runway at Edwards AFB for the first time on March 29, 1996. *LMSW*

Below: The first of two DarkStar UAVs is shown here during its first flight. *LMSW*

Above: DarkStar was to be a Tier III- (or Tier III Minus) high-altitude long-endurance UAV with a very high aspect ratio. *LMSW*

Opposite: DarkStar number two—with improved aerodynamics and redesignated RQ-3A—posed on the ramp at Armstrong Flight Research Center, Edwards AFB, on September 14, 1997. *NASA photo by Tony Landis*

RQ-3/-3A

SPECIFICATIONS

CREW: None

PROPULSIVE SYSTEM: One axial-flow, non-afterburning, 1,900-lbf Williams F-129 turbofan engine

LENGTH: 15 ft 0 in

HEIGHT: 3 ft 6 in

WINGSPAN: 69 ft 0 in

EMPTY WEIGHT: 4,360 lbs

GROSS TAKEOFF WEIGHT: 8,500 lbs

CRUISE SPEED: 288 mph

MAXIMUM RANGE: 575 mi

ENDURANCE: 8 hr

SERVICE CEILING: 45,000 ft

PAYLOAD: 1,000 lbs

to be a large, stealthy, highly sophisticated solution; however, due to cost concerns, the effort was terminated.

It was eventually recognized that the Predator did not address all of the Tier II requirements, while the objective Tier III system was unaffordable. A new strategy was soon put forth to develop so-called Tier II+ and Tier III- systems. Both systems were to have unit flyaway costs of $10 million. Tier II+ was to be highly capable and moderately survivable, while Tier III- was to be highly survivable and moderately capable. This mix of systems was envisioned to address the full spectrum of warfighter requirements.

DARPA was asked to undertake the development of the high-altitude endurance aircraft such as Tier II+ and Tier III in a joint office with the air force. Based on their previous work, Lockheed and Boeing submitted an unsolicited proposal to address the Tier III- requirements with a smaller, less capable, but still stealthy, high-altitude endurance concept. The aircraft was to carry either an electro-optical/infrared (EO/IR) or synthetic aperture radar with moving target indication, allowing day/night, all-weather reconnaissance over hostile terrain. It was expected to reach an altitude of 50,000 feet, have a range of 500 nautical miles, and fly with an endurance of eight hours.

Lockheed and Boeing were awarded a contract in June 1994 for their concept; the UAV was rolled out less than a year later and made its first flight on March 29, 1996. Unfortunately, the next month the demonstrator crashed on takeoff for its second flight. Due to the fast pace of designing and building, the demonstrator and the landing gear configuration, as well as the general aerodynamic design, were found to have been compromised. A modified, more stable design (the RQ-3A) first flew on June 29, 1998, and made a total of five flights. The additional redesign necessary for an operational concept was deemed to be too expensive, and the unit cost had now exceeded the $10 million requirement. The aircraft did, however, successfully demonstrate the ability to execute a fully autonomous flight from takeoff to landing utilizing differential GPS. Two additional RQ-3As were built but never flew.

LightStar UAV: The P-420

On May 28, 1996, Skunk Works personnel Eric D. Knutson, Joseph M. Wurts, and Michael H. Pohlig filed for a patent for what they called an "Unmanned Aircraft." A fourteen-year patent for this unmanned aircraft was issued to them on August 26, 1997. It is believed to be related to the P-420 LightStar UAV.

UCAV: Unmanned Combat Aerial Vehicle

The UCAV or Unmanned Combat Aerial Vehicle programs of 1990s were filled with numerous concepts, and the Skunk Works offered up many UCAV designs. Among these were several "stealthy" single- and twin-engine concepts with very low radar cross-sections and internal weapons carriage. In the end none of the known UCAV concepts from the Skunk Works were procured for service—or were they?

JASSM: Joint Air-to-Surface Standoff Missile

The Joint Air-to-Surface Standoff Missile (JASSM) program began in 1995. Lockheed Martin won the EMD contract phase of the JASSM program in April 1998 for its design. Its inventors—Grant E. Carichner, Stephen P. Ericson, Stephen G. Justice, Joseph M. Wurts, and Scott D. Van Weelden applied for the "JASSM" patent, as they called it, on August 3, 1998, and on December 14, 1999, they received a fourteen-year patent.

Earlier, Skunk Works personnel Paul H. Nicholas, Larry Lipera, Stephen G. Justice, and Joseph M. Wurts applied for a patent on February 26, 1996, for a missile-like air vehicle they called an "Airborne Vehicle with Wing Extension and Roll Control." They received a fourteen-year patent for it on September 30, 1997. This air vehicle is believed to be related to the JASSM design.

SUMMARY

As the 1990s came to a close and the new millennium was about to start, the Skunk Works set its sights on the coming prospects in the new century—to continue its unique ways of expanding the envelope of flight.

New vernaculars, such as autonomous, remotely piloted, unmanned, and unoccupied, came out of the 1990s. This new lingo of course referred to the growing number of unmanned air vehicles. The Skunk Works was a major player in the design and development of drones in that era, as it continued to be in the 2000s and continues to be in the 2010s.

The F-117A made its combat debut—albeit with limited success—as a part of Operation Just Cause in late 1989. Six F-117As launched from the base in Tonopah, Nevada, on December 19, 1989. They were used in the effort to help remove dictator Gen. Manuel Antonio Noriega Moreno from his post of Panamanian leader.

Beginning on January 17, 1991—during Operation Desert Storm, which opened the Gulf War—a much larger contingent of F-117As were used for several months to destroy strategic targets in Iraq. The allied forces captured Baghdad, the capitol of Iraq, but not its ousted leader Saddam Hussein, as he had gone into hiding. Even though Iraq's former leader and dictator had not been captured, he was no longer in power. Thus the Gulf War ended on February 28, 1991. During the conflict forty F-117As were used, and they flew some 1,300 sorties, scored direct hits on 1,600 high-value targets, and dropped 30 percent of all the guided munitions used in the war. The stealth fighter's second combat deployment was hailed a great success, and no F-117As were lost. And on April 1, 1991, the first eight of the forty deployed F-117As arrived back in United States from their base in Saudi Arabia.

Opposite top: Unmanned Combat Air Vehicle (UCAV) concept one. *LMSW*

Opposite bottom: UCAV concept two. *LMSW*

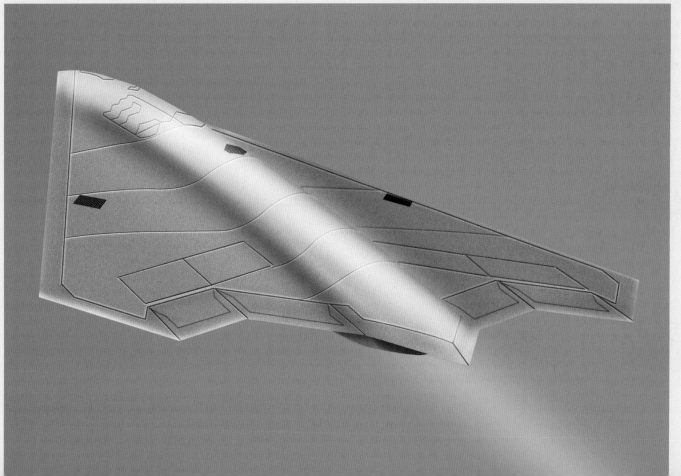

Above: UCAV concept three. *LMSW*

Below: UCAV concept four. *LMSW*

UCAV concept five. *LMSW*

E. MOORE

07 THE 2000s: OUT WITH THE OLD, IN WITH THE NEW

> "About eighty percent of the group's work is classified, the other twenty percent we can talk about."
>
> —ROB WEISS, VICE PRESIDENT AND GENERAL MANAGER, SKUNK WORKS, FEBRUARY 18, 2015

The twenty-first century—the new millennium—began without any truth to the so-called Y2K problem, which was to begin at one millisecond past midnight on January 1, 2000. Computers throughout the world continued to operate, as did those within the Skunk Works.

Much as the 1990s began with the winning of the ATF competition, the 2000s opened as Skunk Works created yet another winning fighter design—the JSF.

Other known Skunk Works programs in the 2000s included the Quiet Supersonic Transport, RATTLRS, the Polecat UAV demonstrator, a hybrid airship, the X-55A Advanced Composite Cargo Aircraft, an airship called ISIS, the still classified RQ-170, Desert Hawk, and a series of NASA N-plus demonstrator concepts.

QSST: Quiet Supersonic Transport

The Quiet Supersonic Transport (QSST) program was the brainchild of Supersonic Aerospace International (SAI), which planned to develop a supersonic and "virtually boomless" commercial business jet. To do this in part, putting up $25 million in May 2001, SAI contracted with the Skunk Works to begin the development of such an aircraft.

SAI was begun in early 2001 by Michael Paulson, son of Gulfstream Aerospace founder Allen Paulson. The proposed QSST business jet was its first venture.

As hoped for, the QSST was to cruise at 60,000 feet at speeds of Mach 1.6 to 1.8 (1,217.9 to 1,370.2 miles per hour) for 4,600 miles. It was of a gull-wing design, with two engines, and its sonic boom was to be just 1 percent (or $\frac{1}{100}$) as strong as that generated by the Concorde SST.

General Electric, Pratt & Whitney, and Rolls-Royce were invited to provide engine proposals. SAI wanted two 33,000-pound-foot engines for its QSST. SAI wanted to create an international consortium to build its QSST; once that was put into place it planned to choose the QSST's propulsive system. The first flight was planned for 2017, with the first delivery to a customer in 2018. The estimated cost per airplane was in the $80 million range.

To help reduce its sonic boom level by such a large margin, the QSST's fuselage length to wingspan ratio was increased, with the use of canard foreplanes, to help

Above: Northrop Grumman X-47B full-scale pole model at Lockheed Martin Skunk Works' Helendale, California, RCS Range in the Mojave Desert, 2005. Lockheed Martin partnered with Northrop Grumman to further reduce the already low RCS of the X-47B. *LMSW photo by Denny Lombard*

Below: The Quiet Supersonic Transport program produced many concepts, including this one. *SAI/LM*

QSST

SPECIFICATIONS

PROPULSIVE SYSTEM: Two 33,000-lbf turbofan
engines

LENGTH: 132 ft 3 in

HEIGHT: 21 ft 3 in

WINGSPAN: 63 ft 0 in

EMPTY WEIGHT: 70,000 lbs

MAXIMUM WEIGHT: 153,000 lbs (takeoff)

MAXIMUM SPEED: Mach 1.6 to 1.8 (1,217.9 to
1,370.2 mph)

MAXIMUM RANGE: 4,600-plus mi

NOISE (SONIC BOOM): 0.3 lbs/sq ft

NOISE (AIRPORT): Stage IV noise level

insure that the individual pressure waves generated by each part of the aircraft structure reinforce each other less significantly, producing a light rumble on the ground without the objectionable sonic boom like conventional supersonic aircraft.

A larger business jet/commercial transport version, dubbed QSST-X, was touted as late as March 2014. But there has been no news of the QSST/QSST-X projects on the company's website since March 2014.

JSF: Joint Strike Fighter

It is 5:30 a.m. local time in the early fall of 2018, and a four-ship flight of stealthy USMC F-35B aircraft have just departed vertically from their secluded base to attack a heavily defended surface-to-air radar and missile facility in "Operation Police Force."

For this particular mission, each one of these recently deployed Lockheed Martin joint strike fighters is armed with two high-explosive, satellite-guided SDBs carried within their weapons bays. Upon approach in two two-ship formations, now in conventional level-attitude flight, while they are still some 10 miles away from their respective targets, the four multi-role strike fighters release their eight 250-pound bombs and immediately turn back toward home base.

Simultaneously several reconnaissance UAVs loitering high overhead record the event and immediately return in real-time the bomb damage assessment to the field commander in charge of the operation. Even before the F-35Bs return to home base and land vertically, the result of the coordinated effort is in: all targets destroyed!

The foregoing scenario is but one of many that might someday be realized with the introduction of the Joint

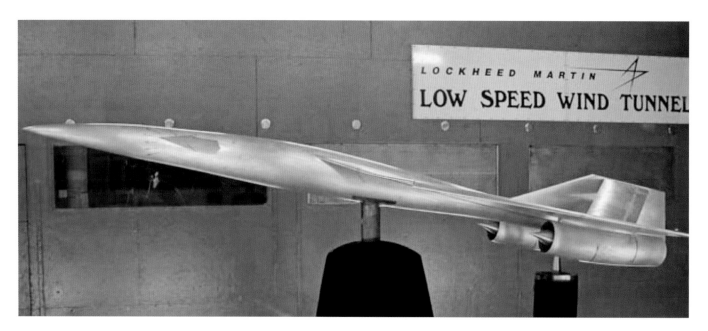

QSST low speed wind tunnel test model. *LM Code One*

A pair of Joint Strike Fighters split the sky.

Strike Fighter (JSF) to the air forces of the United States and a growing number allies and friends. With its STOVL capability, the F-35B is just one of the three JSF versions, which have a more than 80 percent commonality factor. The other two are the Conventional Takeoff and Landing (CTOL) variant—the F-35A—and the aircraft Carrier Variant (CV), the F-35C.

In the late 1980s, an RFP was led by the DOD—specifically, DARPA—to the US airframe and powerplant industries. The RFP called for the creation of what was then called the JAST fighter aircraft, discussed in the previous chapter. But the JAST acronym was soon superseded by the JSF. So after some ten years of design and development, including a large number of flight test

Illustration of a USN/USMC STOVL X-35B. *LMSW*

evaluations, the JSF proposals from Boeing and Lockheed Martin were thoroughly examined by Pentagon officers and officials. Both Boeing and Lockheed Martin had met all of the JSF specifications and flight test requirements, but it was the latter JSF offering that had won favor.

One very important reason the X-35 was judged superior to the X-32 was the overall design configuration of the Lockheed Martin entry, which featured cheek-type engine air inlets on either side of the fuselage rather than the large sugar scoop–type of air inlet featured on the X-32 entry from Boeing. In fact, the forward-mounted maw on the Boeing entry was so large that almost the whole face of the turbofan engine could be seen by eye when viewed straight-on, and even worse, by radar as it approached a danger zone. For this a special anti-radar screen was engineered by Boeing to scatter radar beams. And since stealth (VLO, radar cross-section, etc.) was one of the primary prerequisites, and because the engine "face" was better hidden within the airframe of the X-35, it was preferred over the X-32.

On October 26, 2001, the DOD announced that Lockheed Martin and its team members had won the competition to build the JSF, a stealthy, supersonic, multi-role, multi-service fighter for the USAF, USN, and USMC, and the UK RAF and RN.

As the result, the team of Lockheed Martin, Northrop Grumman, and BAE Systems was to produce an initial batch of twenty-two (fourteen flyable) F-35 airplanes in the $25 billion System Development and Demonstration (SDD) phase of the JSF program.

At the time of the announcement, the first flight of the first SDD airplane—an F-35A CTOL airplane—was scheduled for late 2005 with a projected first delivery of an operational JSF scheduled for 2008. Final assembly was to be in Fort Worth, Texas, at the Lockheed Martin Aeronautical Company facility, while major components would be supplied by Northrop Grumman and BAE Systems.

Three versions of the fourteen "flyable" SDD JSF aircraft will be built. These include the USAF F-35A CTOL, USMC F-35B STOVL, and USN F-35C CV. The F-35B

USN X-35C Carrier Variant. *LMSW*

STOVL version will also be evaluated by the USMC and both the RAF and RN. The twenty-two F-35 SDD phase airplanes will be built as one radar signature test airframe, seven static-test airframes, and fourteen F-35A/B/C flying examples.

At the same time that Lockheed Martin won the right to produce the F-35 JSF aircraft, Pratt & Whitney was awarded a contract to produce three versions of its F135, the initial propulsive system for the F-35A, F-35B, and F-35C; for the F-35C, the F135-PW-100; F-35B, the F135-PW-600; the F-35C, the F135-PW-400. In the Alternative Engine Program, begun in 1997, General Electric received a contract to produce three versions of its F136 for later evaluations.

Some three years after the SDD phase was initiated, Lockheed Martin and its team members were busy creating a common strike fighter for an ever increasing number of land- and sea-based air forces, which now include those of Australia, Canada, Denmark, Italy, Netherlands, Norway, Turkey, and the United Kingdom.

It has been tried before. That is, the creation a multi-mission, multi-service fighter with a similar airframe, powerplant, and weapon system that would meet the demands of all US land- and sea-based air forces. It was called the TFX (Tactical Fighter, Experimental) multi-service program, which generated the General Dynamics F-111A and Grumman F-111B and subsequent F-111 derivative aircraft beginning in the mid-1960s. While the USAF version went on to become one of the stars of the air war in Southeast Asia, with several follow-on versions being built—including the FB-111A for the USAF SAC—the carrier-based USN version never met its user requirements. Among a number of discrepancies, the F-111B version was simply too heavy for aircraft carrier operations, its maximum takeoff weight being about 86,500 pounds or some 14,500 pounds more than a fully loaded F-14A Tomcat. Worse, the F-111B did not possess some of the most important USN requirements: agility and maneuverability. (Note: When the F-111B program was canceled, to the delight of the USN, Grumman was

201

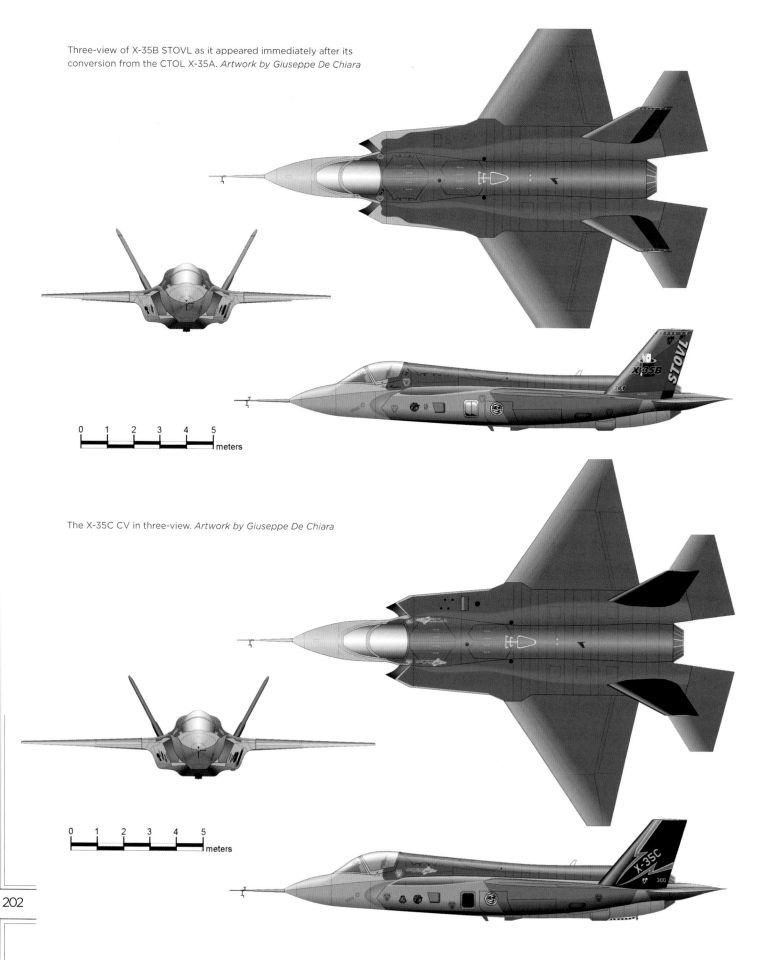

Three-view of X-35B STOVL as it appeared immediately after its conversion from the CTOL X-35A. *Artwork by Giuseppe De Chiara*

meters

The X-35C CV in three-view. *Artwork by Giuseppe De Chiara*

meters

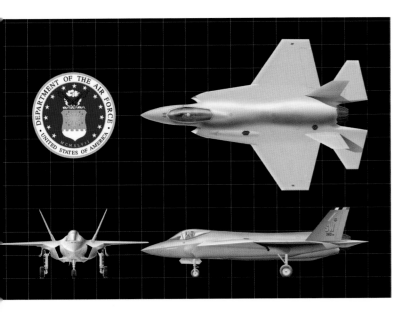

USAF CTOL X-35A. *LMSW*

UK STOVL X-35B. *LMSW*

USN CV X-35C. *LMSW*

awarded a USN contract to design and develop what became the F-14A Tomcat. The first example made its first flight on December 21, 1970, and to this day, it and subsequent versions have been the best carrier-based area- and point-defense fighter-interceptors ever produced. Only recently, with the advent of the Boeing F/A-18E Super Hornet, has talk of imminent F-14 retirement been heard.)

But, with its reported 80-plus percent commonality, the Lockheed Martin F-35 satisfies completely the needs of all parties.

To win the JSF competition, Lockheed Martin had to first prove that its JSF Concept Demonstration Aircraft (CDA) designated X-35 was superior to the JSF/CDA put forth by Boeing—the X-32. Both firms produced two airplanes to demonstrate their respective CTOL, CV, and STOVL performance capabilities.

The Boeing X-32A was used for both CTOL and CV performance tests, while its X-32B was the STOVL demonstrator. Boeing demonstrated CTOL and CV operations without any structural modifications to its X-32A.

The Lockheed Martin X-35A demonstrated CTOL, and after its structural modifications to X-35B, it showed its STOVL characteristics. The one-off X-35C was the dedicated CV test bed.

X-32 AND X-35 FLIGHT TEST DATA

First Flight	Designation	Number of Flights	Flight Hours	Comment
9/18/00	X-32A CTOL	33	25.2	approximate
10/24/00	X-35A CTOL	27	27.4	actual
11/15/00	X-32A CV	33	25.2	approximate
12/16/00	X-35C CV	73	58	actual
3/29/01	X-32B STOVL	78	56.6	approximate
6/23/01	X-35B STOVL	39	21.5	actual

TOTALS:

X-32A/B—144 flights and 107 flight hours

X-35A/B/C—139 flights and 106.9 flight hours

Above: X-35A full-scale engineering mockup. *LMSW*

Opposite: X-35Bs coming aboard ship. *LMSW*

Both firms energetically met their respective JSF/CDA commitments, even surpassed them. But in the end it was the X-35A, X-35B, and X-35C entries that convinced the DOD. Thus, Lockheed Martin and its team members will build the F-35 JSF. At this writing the USAF wants to procure 1,763 F-35As, the USMC and USN need 480 F-35B and F-35Cs each, and the RAF and RN respectively desire the service of about 60 to 80 F-35Bs. It remains to be seen just how many F-35s will actually be produced for the US Armed Forces and foreign air forces.

When the three versions of the F-35 begin to enter service at home and abroad, they will at first supplement and ultimately replace a wide range of existing warfighters. In the United States the F-35A will supersede the USAF A-10A Thunderbolt II and F-16C Fighting Falcon; the F-35B the USMC AV-8B Harrier II; and the F-35C the F/A-18C Hornet. In the United Kingdom the F-35B will replace the RAF GR7 Harrier and the RN AF2 Harrier. It remains to be seen what specific aircraft the F-35 will replace in the air forces of Australia, Canada, Denmark, Italy, Netherlands, Norway, Turkey, and subsequent others.

PROPULSIVE SYSTEM

The F-35 series of operational JSF aircraft will be powered by either the Pratt & Whitney F135 or General Electric/Rolls-Royce (GE/R-R) F136. Both are augmented (afterburning) turbofan engines in the 40,000-pound thrust class and will propel the F-35 aircraft to speeds in excess of Mach 1.6 (1,217.9 miles per hour).

Pratt & Whitney F135

The augmented 43,000-pound-foot–class Pratt & Whitney F135 turbofan engine is a close relative of the F119 used by the Lockheed Martin F/A-22 Raptor, but it is specifically optimized for the F-35 series of aircraft.

The F135 turbofan engine integrates the proven F119 core, a high-performance six-stage compressor, and single-stage turbine unit with a new low-pressure spool. The first production F135 propulsive system for operational service was delivered in 2007.

The CTOL F-35A employs the F135-PW-100, the STOVL F-35B depends on the F135-PW-600, and the CV F-35C uses the F135-PW-400. While the USAF -100 and

F-35A/B/C

SPECIFICATIONS

F-35A

MISSION: CTOL multi-role stealth fighter

LENGTH: 51.1 ft

WINGSPAN: 35 ft

WING AREA: 460 sq ft

HEIGHT: 15 ft

EMPTY WEIGHT (APPROXIMATE): 26,500 lbs

GROSS WEIGHT (APPROXIMATE): 60,000 lbs

POWERPLANT: One Pratt & Whitney F135-PW-100 or General Electric F136

ENGINE THRUST (WITHOUT AFTERBURNER): 25,000 lbs

ENGINE THRUST (WITH AFTERBURNER): 40,000 lbs

MAX SPEED: Mach 1.6+ (1,217.9+ mph)

MAXIMUM RANGE (18,000+ LB INTERNAL FUEL): 1,200nm

ARMAMENT (INTERNAL): One 25mm cannon; 2 air-to-air missiles; two precision air-to-ground weapons

ARMAMENT (EXTERNAL): 15,000+ lb varied ordnance on four hard points; two missiles

F-35B

MISSION: STOVL multi-role stealth fighter

LENGTH: 51 ft

WINGSPAN: 35 ft

WING AREA: 460 sq ft

HEIGHT: 15 ft

EMPTY WEIGHT (APPROXIMATE): 30,000 lbs

GROSS WEIGHT (APPROXIMATE): 60,000 lbs

POWERPLANT: Pratt & Whitney F135-PW-600 or General Electric F136

ENGINE THRUST (WITHOUT AFTERBURNER): 25,000 lbs

ENGINE THRUST (WITH AFTERBURNER): 40,000 lbs

VERTICAL ENGINE THRUST: 39,700 lbs

MAXIMUM SPEED: Mach 1.6+ (1,217.9+ mph)

MAXIMUM RANGE (13,000+ LB INTERNAL FUEL): 900nm

ARMAMENT (INTERNAL: two air-to-air missiles; two precision air-to-ground weapons

ARMAMENT (EXTERNAL): One 25mm cannon in stealth pod; 15,000+ lb varied ordnance on four hard points; two missiles

F-35C

MISSION: Aircraft carrier-based multi-role stealth fighter

LENGTH: 51.4 ft

WINGSPAN: 43 ft

WING AREA: 620 sq ft

HEIGHT: 15.5 ft

EMPTY WEIGHT (APPROXIMATE): 30,000 lbs

GROSS WEIGHT (APPROXIMATE): 60,000 lbs

POWER PLANT: One Pratt & Whitney F135-PW-400 or General Electric F136

ENGINE THRUST (WITHOUT AFTERBURNER): 25,000 lbs

ENGINE THRUST (WITH AFTERBURNER): 40,000 lbs

MAXIMUM SPEED: Mach 1.6+ (1,217.9+ mph)

MAXIMUM RANGE (19,000+ LB INTERNAL FUEL): 1,400nm

ARMAMENT (INTERNAL): Two air-to-air missiles; two precision air-to-ground weapons

ARMAMENT (EXTERNAL): One 25 mm cannon in stealth pod; 15,000+ lb varied ordnance on four hard points; two missiles

---

USN -400 versions on the F135 are relatively similar, the USMC/RAF/RN -600 derivative is exclusive to the series.

In particular, the F135-PW-600 is optimized for the USMC/RAF/RN F-35B STOVL version of the JSF and features a Lockheed Martin-designed, shaft-driven counter-rotating lift fan assembly that produces cool air lifting force during STOVL operations. The Rolls-Royce fan, actuated by a clutch that can be engaged at any power setting, works in concert with an articulating rear duct and underwing lateral-control nozzles to lift the airplane with 43,000 pounds of vertical force. Because the fan amplifies the engine's power, the engine is able to run cooler and with less strain, increasing reliability and extending service life. The lift fan provides the propulsive system with about 15,000 pounds more thrust than the base F135 engine alone could generate.

Proposed General Electric/Rolls-Royce F136

Later high-rate production Lot 4 F-35A/B/C aircraft might have been powered by the General Electric/Rolls-Royce (GE/R-R) F136—an alternative propulsive system that had been proposed.

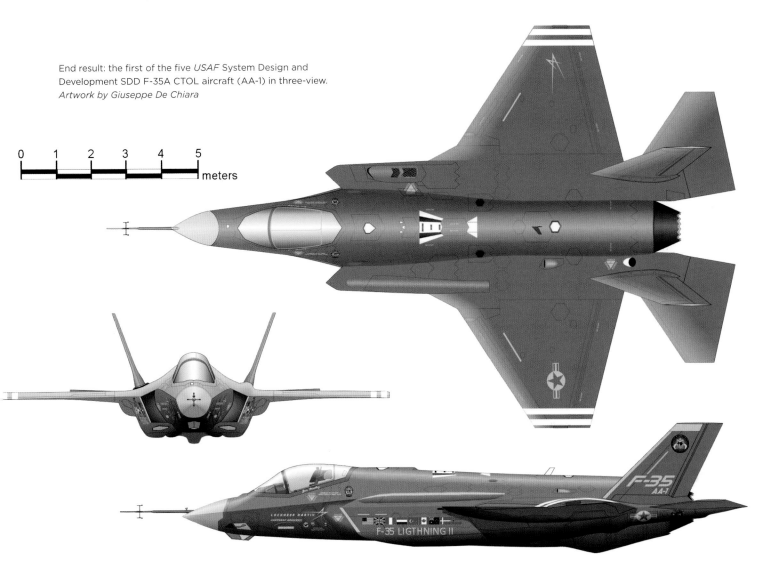

End result: the first of the five *USAF* System Design and Development SDD F-35A CTOL aircraft (AA-1) in three-view.
Artwork by Giuseppe De Chiara

0 1 2 3 4 5
meters

The GE/R-R F136 turbofan was an augmented 40,000-pound-foot–class engine. It is derived from the 35,000-pound-foot–class General Electric YF120-GE-100 engine used by both the Lockheed/Boeing/General Dynamics YF-22 and Northrop/McDonnell Douglas YF-23 in the ATF competition in the early 1990s. As it happened, two YF-22s and two YF-23s were built. One of each was powered by two Pratt & Whitney YF119-PW-100 engines, and the other by two General Electric (GE) YF120-GE-100 engines. The YF119-powered YF-22 was selected as the winner of the ATF competition, and as a result, the YF-23 was shelved and further development of the YF120 went into limbo. Or did it?

The GE YF120 engine had proved its worth as well, for in its non-augmented super cruise mode it actually pushed one of the YF-23s to a still classified top speed near Mach 1.8 (1,370.2 miles per hour). Moreover, it proved to be easy to maintain and reliable. So by the time the JSF program matured in the late 1990s, it was decided to resuscitate the F120 as an alternative propulsive system for the F-35.

In its new life, the F120 became the F136. But since its development for the JSF program began later than the Pratt & Whitney F135, the GE/R-R F136 will not power any of the F-35 SDD or low rate initial production (LRIP) aircraft. It was, however, to propel fourth production lot F-35s during 2011 (after some ninety aircraft have been built). But this never came about, as the F-135 was ruled adequate and the F136 program was canceled.

Almost from the outset of its JAST-cum-JSF program, the Lockheed Martin Corporation chose to partner up with two significant team members. These are the Northrop Grumman Corporation and BAE Systems.

The Northrop Grumman Corporation—its Baltimore, Maryland–based Northrop Grumman Electronic Systems division specifically—is responsible for the F-35 fire control radar, the AN/APG-81, which features an active electronically scanned array (AESA) that enables near-simultaneous performance of multiple radar functions.

207

X-32A and X-32B JSF Concept Demonstration Aircraft

The Boeing Airplane Company, its Phantom Works in particular, designed and produced two JSF CDA designated X-32A and X-32B. These were shown simultaneously to the public during their official unveiling ceremony in Palmdale, California, on December 14, 1999.

Flight Data

Date, Aircraft, Pilot, Comment

9/18/00, X-32A, Fred Davey Knox Jr., Palmdale to Edwards; sixty-six total flights

11/15/00, the X-32A initiated field carrier landing practice tests with USN Cmdr. Phillip "Rowdy" Yates serving as its test pilot; no X-32C CV aircraft was created, thus the X-32A was used to demonstrate Boeing's Carrier Variant performance

3/29/01, X-32B, Dennis O'Donoghue, Palmdale to Edwards; seventy-eight total flights

---

Because the radar's beam is moved electronically, it can find targets much more quickly than older radars that move the antenna mechanically.

BAE Systems' Information and Electronic Warfare Systems division, which is headquartered in Nashua, New Hampshire, is responsible for F-35 Electronic Warfare system integration for the SDD and LRIP phases of the JSF program.

SUMMARY

When the stealthy F-35A, F-35B, and F-35C JSF threesome meet their respective operational capabilities at home and abroad, the United States, as well as its allies and friends, will have a very capable multi-role tactical strike warfighter—a future-day warfighter with the abilities to supplement and replace a growing number of tried-and-true victors from the past.

For example, the USAF F-35A will be as agile and capable of the high-g maneuvering qualities of the Block 50 and later versions of the F-16C Fighting Falcon, which according to one high-ranking USAF pilot is a "hot rod from hell." The F-35A will also complement the F-15C Eagle and F/A-22 Raptor. The F-35B will give USMC, RAF and RN pilots something they will never have with their current AV-8B Harrier II aircraft: supersonic performance. And with the F-35C, USN pilots will enjoy a carrier-based warfighter that is more capable than the F/A-18C Hornet.

Finally, according to the DOD, the multi-mission, multi-service Lockheed Martin F-35A, F-35B, and F-35C birds of a feather will serve the nation until at least the 2040s and possibly far beyond that decade. It is a cutting-edge fighter on the fringe.

RATTLRS: Revolutionary Approach to Time Critical Long Range Strike

The Revolutionary Approach to Time Critical Long Range Strike (RATTLRS) supersonic cruise missile concept program was initiated in early 2004 by the Skunk Works. Operational RATTLRS were to be air-launched, ground-launched, and ship-launched.

The Office of Naval Research awarded Lockheed Martin a phase-two contract for its continued RATTLRS work on July 20, 2004. At the behest of the Office of Naval Research (ONR) early 2004, the Skunk Works was tasked with the creation of a supersonic cruise missile that could be air-, ground-, and ship-launched. The program was called RATTLRS or Revolutionary Approach to Time Critical Long Range Strike. The ONR awarded a five-year $175 million USD RATTLRS Phase II contract to Lockheed Martin on July 20, 2004.

For RATTLRS Lockheed Martin teammate, the Allison Advanced Development Company (AADC), was to develop a maximum Mach 4–rated propulsive system known as the YJ102R, which was also to provide supersonic cruise speed without the high fuel burn associated with afterburner-equipped engines.

"Our team's RATTLRS approach will contribute landmark technologies toward Long Range Strike," said Neil Kacena of the Skunk Works.

Above: The RATTLRS demonstrator never received a designation. This missile was to be air-, sea-, and ground-launched and used by all branches of the US Armed Forces. One such is being air-launched here from a B-52H. *LMSW*

Below: The F-35 could have carried two RATTLRS externally. One is launched from a Lightning II in the artist concept. *LMSW*

Artist rendition of a RATTLRS sea launch. *LMSW*

"The Lockheed Martin–led team builds on years of demonstrated success in high speed, hypersonic technology development, and weapon system performance in support of the Office of Naval Research's RATTLRS program goals," Kacena said.

Lockheed Martin announced on August 18, 2005, that it had successfully tested the warhead dispenser system it was developing for the RATTLRS supersonic cruise missile. Then on September 28, 2007, it announced that it had completed structural testing of its 1,760-pound RATTLRS missile.

During the late-2007–2009 time period prototype RATTLRS air vehicles were to undergo flight test evaluations. The Lockheed Martin BGM-178, as RATTLRS was designated, had been slated to replace the BGM-109 Tomahawk cruise missile, but this never came to fruition. No new information on the RATTLRS program has been released by Lockheed Martin or the ONR.

On August 18, 2005, Lockheed Martin announced that it had successfully tested the warhead dispenser system it was developing for the RATTLRS supersonic cruise missile. A potential warhead housing six light kinetic-energy penetrating submunitions guided by semi-active laser/millimeter-wave dual-mode seekers was successfully driven by sled into a concrete barrier that simulated a hardened bunker. This test was accomplished in October 2006, and the rail-riding sled was traveling at over Mach 2 or about 1,480 miles per hour. RATTLRS was initially designed to attack fleeting and stationary targets with a combat range of 345 to 460 miles. A longer-range version was to be developed later.

On September 28, 2007, Lockheed Martin announced that it had completed structural testing of its 1,760-pound RATTLRS missile. A flight demonstrator prototype with a dry thrust baseline and a technology demonstrator prototype with augmented, ram-burner air vehicles were to be flight tested in the 2008–2009 time period. However, the RATTLRS program fell out of favor soon after and was canceled.

Polecat: The P-175 Unmanned Aerial System Demonstrator

On July 19, 2006, the Lockheed Martin Aeronautics Company unveiled to the world its P-175 Polecat unmanned aerial system (UAS) at the Farnborough International Airshow at the Farnborough Airport in Hampshire, England.

The Skunk Works began its design work on the Polecat in March 2003, and it was scheduled to fly eighteen months later in September 2004. Its autonomous first flight was accomplished five months behind schedule in February 2005 at the Nevada Test and Training Range or NTTR, which is part of the Nellis AFB complex. While its first flights were flown at 15,000-foot altitudes, the Polecat was expected to fly later to heights above 60,000 feet.

During one of its scheduled flight tests on December 18, 2006, the P-175 crashed to destruction at the NTTR. Few

Above: It's not clear why the phrase "Howard is my co-pilot" was applied to the nose landing gear door, but there was a Three Stooges movie entitled *Beer Barrel Polecats* in 1946, and Curly (whose last name was Howard)—considered to be the funniest of the Stooges—was the Polecat adopted by the Skunk Works. *LMSW photo by Denny Lombard*

Below: The one-off P-175 Polecat posed for this freeze-frame in front of Old Glory on June 23, 2006. *LMSW photo by Denny Lombard*

POLECAT

SPECIFICATIONS

CREW: None (ground-based operators)

PROPULSIVE SYSTEM: Two axial-flow, non-afterburning, 3,000 lbf–class Williams International FJ44-3E turbofan engines

LENGTH: NA

HEIGHT: NA

WINGSPAN: 90.0 ft

MAXIMUM SPEED: NA

EMPTY WEIGHT: NA

GROSS TAKEOFF WEIGHT: 9,000 lbs

MAXIMUM RANGE: (Four hours loiter)

MAXIMUM CEILING: 65,000 ft

PAYLOAD: 1,000 lbs

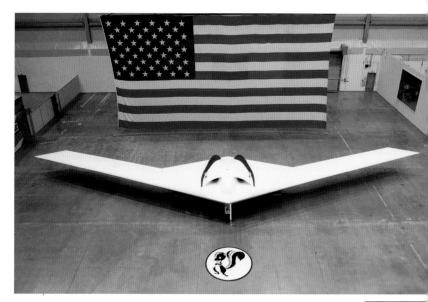

Above: The Polecat is shown here during what is believed to be its first flight. *LMSW via Heather Kelso*

Below: Right-hand side view of Polecat UAV demonstrator. *LMSW*

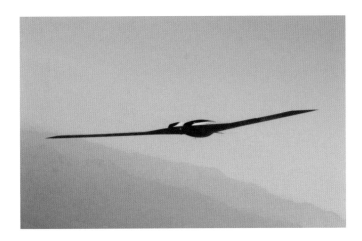

In-flight view of Skunk Works P-number 175 from a camera ship, circa mid-2006. *LMSW*

details were released on the cause of the crash except that it was due to "irreversible unintentional failure in the flight termination ground equipment, which caused the aircraft's automatic fail-safe flight termination mode to activate."

Only the one example was built using in-house funding, and its technology was shared with other Lockheed Martin UAVs such as the RQ-170 Sentinel.

SUMMARY

The P-175 Polecat UAS demonstrator was a relatively large, tailless, all-flying-wing air vehicle. It was propelled by two hidden turbofan engines buried deep within its structure to assist with its low observability.

It's not definite just how many times the Polecat flew or exactly which flight it was on when it crashed. But it did fly successfully several times—unoccupied, takeoff to landing.

Hybrid Air Vehicle: The P-791

On June 16, 2015, Hybrid Enterprises, in association with the Lockheed Martin Corporation—who will manufacture the hybrid air vehicles—announced it would be taking orders for hybrid airships with deliveries planned as early as 2018.

A Lockheed Martin press release stated,

More than two-thirds of the world's land area and more than half the world's population have no direct access to paved roads. As you move farther away from infrastructure, cost, time and the safety of transport becomes more of a challenge.

Hybrid Airships enable affordable and safe delivery of heavy cargo and personnel to virtually anywhere—water or land, in normal flying weather conditions—with little to no infrastructure.

Skunk Works P-number 791 was issued to this experimental aerostatic/aerodynamic hybrid airship, shown here during its first flight on January 31, 2006. *LMSW*

213

Another view of the P-791 hybrid airship to show its finer details. *LMSW* –

"Lockheed Martin's Hybrid Airships will significantly reduce the cost and environmental impact of remote operations, making it possible to reach locations previously thought inaccessible," said Rob Binns, chief executive officer of Hybrid Enterprises.

Customers will feel confident that with more than a century of proven experience, Lockheed Martin has repeatedly solved seemingly impossible challenges through its products and technologies.

The technologies required for Hybrid Airships are already mature and have been demonstrated in-flight by Lockheed Martin's P-791, a fully functional, manned flight demonstrator.

"We've invested more than twenty years to develop the technology, prove the performance, and ensure there are compelling economics for the Hybrid Airship," said Orlando Carvalho, executive vice president of Lockheed Martin Aeronautics.

"We have completed all required FAA certification planning steps for a new class of aircraft and are ready to begin construction of the first commercial model and the completion of the FAA Type certification process."

Work is currently underway on the twenty-ton variant at the Lockheed Martin Aeronautics facility in Palmdale, California.

The aforementioned Skunk-Works-designed-and-built P-175 Hybrid Air Vehicle made its first flight out of Palmdale, California, on January 31, 2006.

The subscale two-crew P-791 has a tri-hull shape with disk-shaped cushions on the bottom for landing. As a hybrid airship, part of the weight of the craft and its payload are supported by aerostatic (buoyant) lift and the remainder is supported by aerodynamic lift. The combination of aerodynamic and aerostatic lift is an attempt to benefit from both the high speed of aerodynamic craft and the lifting capacity of aerostatic-type air vehicles.

The Advanced Composite Cargo Aircraft known as the X-55A made its first flight on June 2, 2009. Its first liftoff is shown here. *LMSW*

ACCA: The X-55A Advanced Composite Cargo Aircraft

The USAF X-55A Advanced Composite Cargo Aircraft (ACCA)—nicknamed the "Carbon Comet"—is a modified Dornier 328J twin-jet airplane that served as a technology demonstrator for the design and manufacture of future aircraft using advanced composite materials. It is yet another creation of the Skunk Works.

Its fuselage aft of the cockpit and the vertical stabilizer was removed from a 328J and replaced with completely new structural designs made of advanced composite materials fabricated with the use of out-of-autoclave curing. The X-55A was developed by Lockheed Martin ADP and the Air Force Research Laboratory (AFRL), and it was fabricated at Air Force Plant 42 in Palmdale, California. Lockheed Martin officials said the ACCA took off to the east from Air Force Plant 42 at 6:55 a.m. Pacific Time. The aircraft then banked west and climbed to an altitude of approximately 10,000 feet where the two-pilot crew took the vehicle through a series of airspeed and stability and control tests. Officials said the tests are important to understand how the composite cargo aircraft performs at varying speeds, attitudes, and altitudes. This data will be used as a baseline for future tests.

"Today is one of those perfect days where I get to be the first to fly a new aircraft and everything goes exactly as planned. The aircraft was a real pleasure to fly and we experienced absolutely no issues," said Robert A. "Rob" aka "Skid" Rowe, the Lockheed Martin lead ACCA test pilot. Duration for the first flight was about eighty-seven minutes. Its first flight was from that facility on June 2, 2009.

The X-55A ACCA was designed in five months; then, after go-ahead, it was built and flown in twenty months.

215

Close-up details of the X-55A during its first flight with landing gear extended (civil registration number N807LM). *LMSW*

X-55A

SPECIFICATIONS

CREW: Three (pilot, copilot, and flight test engineer)

PROPULSIVE SYSTEM: Two axial-flow, non-afterburning, 6,050-lbf Pratt & Whitney Canada PW306B turbofan engines

LENGTH: 69 ft 10 in

HEIGHT: 23 ft 9 in

WINGSPAN: 68 ft 10 in

MAXIMUM SPEED: 467 mph

The fuselage was built in two large half-sections (upper and lower) featuring sandwich with MTM-45 skins and Nomex core, bonded together with adhesive and ply overlays along the longitudinal seam rather than numerous frames, stiffeners, and metal fasteners used commonly in conventional aircraft. The vertical tail was designed using tailored stiffness technology. These were joined with an existing Dornier 328J crew cabin, wing, horizontal tail, and engines. The suffix *J* means "jet," and it is a turbofan-powered derivative of the Dornier 328-300.

Compared to the original metallic components, the composite structure used approximately three hundred structural parts versus three thousand metallic parts and approximately four thousand mechanical fasteners compared to forty thousand.

"Historically aircraft cost has been determined by the size and weight of the vehicle. With ACCA we are proving that while size does matter, it isn't the final determination of aircraft cost," said Frank Mauro, vice president of Advanced System Development, Lockheed Martin. "ACCA is an important step in proving that composite technologies are real game changers in reducing design and manufacturing costs along with extending life and reducing maintenance costs over traditional metallic aircraft structures."

SUMMARY

The X-55A ACCA program was a success in that it proved such an aircraft could be built at half the cost of a contemporary aircraft. It was reportedly flown fifteen to twenty times during its test phase. Its last flight was in December 2011.

Now retired, it's on display at the Joe Davies Heritage Airpark, which is next to the Blackbird Airpark outside of USAF Plant 42 in Palmdale, California. USAF Lt. Col. Joseph "Joe" Davies was a former commander of USAF Plant 42.

Top: X-55A taxis back to the ramp after its first flight. The number 3099 below the cockpit windows, abbreviated to 99 on either side of the nose, remains unexplained. *LMSW*

Above left: Nicknamed "Carbon Comet," the X-55A is a big user of carbon fiber composite materials in its structure, as shown here during its assembly processes. *LM Code One*

Above right: The X-55A under construction. *LM Code One*

217

ISIS is not a well-received acronym at this writing. Nevertheless, the Integrated Sensor is Structure (ISIS) acronym is used by the Skunk Works to describe its extreme-endurance stratospheric airship of the future, shown here in an artist concept. *LMSW*

ISIS: Integrated Sensor is Structure

It is now the year 2020, and a giant, unoccupied airship is roaming through the stratosphere some 70,000 feet above northwestern Iraq. It's been near that location for more than three hundred days, twenty-four hours a day, seven days a week. It has been operated continuously in rotating shifts by ground-based personnel at an undisclosed location. Its purpose is to provide battlefield commanders with real-time 360-degree surveillance of all enemy activities, whether they are airborne or ground-based threats. If any enemy troops or equipment move on the ground within a 190-mile radius, or any enemy air vehicle moves in the air within a 375-mile radius, the airship's immense dual-aperture radar system will detect the activities and proper action will be taken.

The foregoing is fictitious but could very well be a true event in the near future if the USAF fields what is currently known as the Integrated Sensor is Structure, or ISIS, autonomous stratospheric airship for disruptive command and control, intelligence, surveillance, and reconnaissance.

The DARPA-funded ISIS program began in 2004. By February 2008, as then projected, the ISIS program was to develop a sensor of unprecedented proportions that would be fully integrated into stratospheric airships that would address the nation's need for persistent wide-area surveillance, tracking, and engagement for hundreds of time-critical air and ground targets in urban and rural environments. ISIS was to achieve radical sensor improvements by melding the next-generation technologies for enormous lightweight antenna apertures and high-energy density components into a highly integrated, lightweight, multipurpose airship structure—completely erasing the distinction between payload and platform. The ISIS concept includes 99 percent on-station (24/7/365) availability for simultaneous Airborne Moving Target Indicator, or AMTI, (600 kilometers) and Ground Moving Target Indicator, or GMTI, (300 kilometers) operation; twelve-plus months of autonomous, unmanned flight; hundreds of wideband in-theater covert

Another view of the projected ISIS airship, clad in its all-silver livery. *LMSW*

communication links; and responsive reconstruction of failed space assets, plus continental US–based sensor analysis and operation. At the time the ISIS technology was planned for transition to the US Army Air-to-Surface Missile Defense, and USAF Joint Warfighter Space and Missile Defense Agency by FY 2011.

Earlier FY 2007 accomplishments included refined objective system concept designs enabling simultaneous AMTI and GMTI operation, one-year logistics-free operation, 99 percent on-station availability, and high-bandwidth covert communications.

Plans for FY 2008 included the demonstration of lightweight technologies for system integration (i.e., high-energy density batteries, electronic circuits on thin-film barrier materials, advanced multipurpose airship hulls, and regenerative fuel technologies).

Goals for FY 2009 included: 1) Design and simulation of new radar modes, tracking air and ground targets through the clutter notch, detection and response to rockets, artillery, and mortars; detection of dismounted enemy combatant; and "track-all-the way" fire control; 2)

Integrate and flight-test a subscale airship demonstrating launch and recovery operations, station-keeping and altitude control algorithms, and validate environmental data models; and 3) Develop a critical design for a fully operational scaled flight system demonstrating complete system integration over an extended period.

A Lockheed Martin press release dated April 27, 2009, announced that DARPA had selected Lockheed Martin as the systems integrator and Raytheon Company as the radar developer for Phase 3 of its ISIS program.

It went on to say under the fifty-two-month contract valued at just under $400 million, Lockheed Martin would lead an industry team in the design, build, test, and flight demonstration of a one-third-scale airship featuring Raytheon's new, low-power density radar. The autonomous flight test system would operate on-station for ninety days, proving several key technologies with an anticipated total demonstration of one year.

"The development of high energy density power systems, an extremely lightweight radar solution and an advanced flexible composite material were necessary to make a stratospheric airship like ISIS possible," said Eric Hofstatter, Lockheed Martin ISIS program manager. "This is an extremely advanced machine that represents a dramatically different approach to persistent real-time intelligence gathering and to the overarching utility of airships."

Raytheon's ground-breaking radar capability is an integral component of the airship structural design. The AESA antenna will transmit on UHF and X-band from within the airship.

"The operational goal for ISIS is to look for airborne and ground-based targets and to communicate directly with the battlefield from a single antenna for up to 10 years," said Michael Wechsberg, director of radio frequency systems programs for Raytheon Space and Airborne Systems.

The press release concluded, "The ISIS program will develop the core technologies necessary to demonstrate an extremely capable radar sensor package within the structure of a stratospheric airship, operating at approximately 70,000 feet. ISIS Phase 3 will demonstrate the next step to providing unblinking, mission-critical data to the war fighter from its continuous position on-station."

For FY 2010 the ISIS program was in the process of developing a radar of unprecedented proportions that will be fully integrated into a station-keeping stratospheric airship. The ISIS will support the nation's need for persistent wide-area surveillance, tracking, and engagement of all time-critical air and ground targets. Automated surveillance and tracking includes all air targets to the radar horizon of about 600 kilometers (430 miles) and all ground targets to a range of about 300 kilometers (215 miles). The radar aperture also provides track data and other communications directly to its users in-theater. The system is expected to be launched from locations in the continental United States with a multi-year operational life. No support personnel or facilities are required in-theater. Efforts will include work on the ground station and the corresponding Processing, Exploitation, and Dissemination connectivity.

According to an earlier Lockheed Martin Skunk Works information release, "ISIS will have the ability to track a multitude of targets ranging from dismounts to ballistic targets. ISIS can track ballistic targets at ranges well beyond 1,245 miles, air targets at ranges beyond 430 miles and ground/dismount/maritime targets at ranges of 215 miles. A single ISIS system can cover 5.75 million square miles as compared to a combined AWACS [Airborne Warning and Control System] and JSTARS [Joint Surveillance Target Attack Radar System] 176 million square miles coverage of the same mission space."

RQ-170 Sentinel

It is difficult to accurately report on an air vehicle that is classified. Thus, there is almost no documented information on the Lockheed RQ-170 Sentinel to share in this work. What little is known about the Wraith UAV—as it was called within the Skunk Works—is as follows.

The Lockheed Martin RQ-170 Sentinel, dubbed the "Beast of Kandahar" by the press, is an aerial surveillance drone of a pure flying-wing design that was produced by the Skunk Works. It is autonomously operated by ground-based flight crews.

The existence of the RQ-170 wasn't made public until December 4, 2009, when the USAF released an official statement acknowledging the ongoing use of this low-observable UAS vehicle and that it was built by the Skunk Works. The statement eplains, "The RQ-170 provides reconnaissance and surveillance support to forward deployed Combat Forces. The fielding of the RQ-170 aligns with [then] Secretary of Defense Robert M. Gates' request for increased ISR support to the Combatant Commanders and Air Force Chief of Staff Gen. Norton Schwartz's vision for an increased USAF reliance on unmanned aircraft."

The RQ-170 is operated by the 30th Reconnaissance Squadron, based at Tonopah Test Range, Nevada. The 30th RS (30 RS) is assigned to the 432nd Air Expeditionary Wing (432 AEW, the "Hunters"), 12th Air Force, at Creech AFB, Nevada. Both units are assigned to the Air Combat Command.

The first flight date of the RQ-170 has not been announced nor the date of its initial operational capability nor the date of its first mission. But since the 30th Reconnaissance Squadron first stood up on September 1, 2005, it can be surmised that the RQ-170 was flying as early as that time, possibly earlier.

Concerning its out-of-sequence RQ-170 designation, it's possible that it could be related to a probable Skunk Works P-number, P-170, as P-numbers are assigned to numerous ADP air vehicles such as the P-175 Polecat. The prefix P is most likely for "program" or "project." But this remains to be clarified.

Conceptual three-view as found online at Wikipedia entitled Lockheed Martin RQ-170 Sentinel. *Artwork by Marcus Aurelius Antoninus*

SUMMARY

It's unclear as to why any specific details relative to the RQ-170 Sentinel program are so elusive. But elusive they continue to be. Suffice it to say they are still classified.

DESERT HAWK III

SPECIFICATIONS

CREW: None (unmanned)

WING SPAN: 59 inches

WEIGHT: 8.2 pounds

ENDURANCE: 1.5 hours

CRUISE/DASH SPEED: 28.7/57.5 mph

PAYLOAD: Two pounds

Desert Hawk

Desert Hawk is a Small Unmanned Aerial Vehicle (MUAV) that was designed by the Skunk Works for the USAF. The USAF ordered remote controlled Desert Hawks as Force Protection Airborne Surveillance System (FPASS) air vehicles to provide air bases with surveillance inside and outside of their perimeters. In July 2002, just 127 days after contract signing, Lockheed Martin delivered the first two FPASS air vehicles to the USAF.

Six of these SUAVS, a laptop computer, a remote video terminal, and a support kit make up each Desert Hawk system.

Each Desert Hawk SUAV is hand-launched by two crewman using a modified Bungee cord. They are manufactured out of a molded, Styrofoam-like substance and each one can be fitted into and carried around in a special backpack.

Above: Original RQ-7A Desert Hawk UAS photographed with operators in 2003. *LMSW photo by Denny Lombard*

Top: The RQ-7 has evolved steadily through the Desert Hawk II to today's Desert Hawk IV, which has improved durability and is capable of all-weather operations, and the Desert Hawk EER with extended endurance and range. *USAF photo by Tech Sgt. Christopher Gish*

Since 2002 the Desert Hawk SUAV family has grown with one of the latest versions—Desert Hawk III, now in service. The Desert Hawk III carries a 2-pound payload and has an endurance of 1.5 hours.

Desert Hawk IV and Desert Hawk EER (Extended Endurance and Range) are in development. Desert Hawk IV can carry a 2-pound payload with a 2.5-hour endurance. Desert Hawk EER, which is the largest version, has 8 to 10 hours endurance and can carry a 4 to 6-pound payload.

Desert Hawk III—also used by the British Army, features a quiet acoustic signature, room for payload growth, autonomous Global Positioning Satellite (GPS) guidance, and color 360-degree electro-optic and infrared Full Motion Video that can see some 10 miles distant.

Each Desert Hawk SUAV can be assembled, programmed, and launched in under ten minutes to provide real-time surveillance of an air base's perimeter. More than forty-eight Desert Hawk systems—approximately three hundred SUAVs, have been delivered—four to the British Army.

NASA/Lockheed Martin N-Plus Aircraft Program

In a March 25, 2014, press release entitled "Getting Up to Speed," Lockheed Martin stated,

> The future of air travel is bright—and fast. Since the dawn of the jet age in the 1960s, commercial air travel has remained relatively unchanged. However, today's demand for smarter and faster technologies is driving the next generation of commercial travel with supersonic aircraft, which could potentially cut US coast-to-coast travel time almost in half.

With the commercial air travel industry expected to grow to more than five times its current size, the economic impact and significant time savings of a more efficient supersonic travel system will become increasingly important in our global economy.

One of the major hurdles of commercial supersonic air travel is the noise associated with it. At speeds greater than Mach 1, disturbances of air pressure around the airplane merge to form enormous shock waves resulting in sonic booms. For example, when you hear a car coming, you can hear it before it passes you because you hear increments of that sound continuously over a duration of time. In the case of a supersonic aircraft, you get all that sound over a very short duration of time causing a boom-like effect.

If you've never heard a sonic boom, let's just say it's quite loud. And, that's putting it lightly. Because of this, current air traffic regulations restrict supersonic planes from flying over land. For more than a decade, Lockheed Martin has been working to solve these problems.

"To achieve revolutionary reductions in supersonic transportation airport noise, a totally new kind of propulsion system is being developed," said Michael Buonanno, Lockheed Martin manager of the NASA N+2 program. "We are also exploring new techniques for low noise jet exhaust, integrated fan noise suppression, airframe noise suppression and computer customized airport noise abatement."

Buonanno explained how over the years, his team has tackled several of these technology thrust areas.

"We've developed a vehicle conceptual design and built a sub scale wind tunnel model to test the sonic boom characteristics that we predict will validate our ability to shape the airplane to generate much lower sonic boom levels."

One of their breakthroughs was being able to develop the tools and codes that allow engineers and designers to accurately predict the loudness of a plane's sonic boom. With the availability of these tools, a designer can develop an airplane concept that significantly reduces boom levels. Though it is not practical to completely eliminate noise, these advancements would result in a sonic boom that sounds much more like a distant thump rather than a sharp crack.

Lockheed Martin's design would accommodate eighty passengers and have the ability to travel more than 5,000 nautical miles with sonic boom levels one hundred times quieter than the now-retired Concorde supersonic passenger airline. The Concorde was first flown in 1969 and was one of only two supersonic passenger airliners to have entered commercial service.

"It's all about the design details," said Buonanno. "You need to able to manage the progress of volume and lift to create series of closely timed small shocks rather than one big one. Our testing has given us the confidence we need to have a good understanding of how sonic boom levels work and how to design airplanes to meet the required boom levels."

The aircraft would have to be very long, so that the volume and the lift of the plane are allowed to gradually build up and then decrease. The engine is also extremely important. Under the N+2 program, Lockheed Martin has worked with General Electric and Rolls-Royce to look at engine concepts that have high fuel efficiency and can meet the takeoff and landing noise constraints."

"The engine itself does not contribute to a sonic boom but you have to have a good integration of the engine into the airframe," said Buonanno.

Lockheed Martin's N+2 concept has a tri-jet configuration; one engine is on the top of the aircraft and the other two are located under each wing. Though not physically hidden, these locations are essentially concealed from the sonic boom because of the tailored volume and lift distribution of the plane. Therefore, the disturbance simply blends in.

And while passengers won't be buying tickets for these aircraft in the next five years, Buonanno estimates the technology will be ready around the 2025 time frame.

"We calculate that timeframe by gauging the technology readiness levels," said Buonanno. He explained that one of the pacing items would be the availability of a propulsion system. "Having something that's efficient at high speeds *and* quiet is a big technical challenge."

By choosing Mach 1.7 design, the team has been able to significantly simplify the problem of developing a propulsion system that's compatible with low emissions and takeoff and landing noise. Although slightly slower than Concorde's Mach 2 cruise speed, this enables the use of higher bypass ratio engines for lower takeoff noise and would still permit approximately a 50 percent reduction of trip time compared to today's aircraft.

"Our work with NASA has laid the groundwork for any future activity," said Buonanno. The tools we've put in place really open up future opportunities."

"It's a simple goal, really. A silent airplane that sends no carbon into the atmosphere," NASA said in February 19, 2009, of its quest to develop a silent, carbonless airplane in a three-stage process.

The three stages of the process are "N-plus-1," "N-plus-2", and "N-plus-3," said Fay Collier, then principal investigator for the Subsonic Fixed Wing Project of the Aeronautic Research Mission Directorate's Fundamental Aeronautics Program.

The first, N-plus-1, involves a "tube-and-wing" aircraft with design principles similar to those of the aircraft of today, but with enough technological and structural improvements to cut fuel consumption by a third below that of a selected standard: a Boeing 737 with 162 passengers on a flight of 2,940 nautical miles.

Then there is "N-plus-2," in which design modifications show airplanes that are hybrids: less fuselage and much more wing. Continued technological improvements and weight and flow reductions would produce aircraft that burn 40 percent less fuel and emit 75 percent less carbon with a prototype available by 2020.

The "N-plus-3" will most likely be a blended wing-body aircraft rather than a tube-and-wing airplane, according to Collier.

SUMMARY

During the 2000s, the Skunk Works released a number of interesting air vehicles that were investigated, and some that entered production and service. These included the Desert Hawk, a hand-launched reconnaissance drone; the RQ-170, a super-secret reconnaissance drone; the P-791, a hybrid airship; and the F-35 Lightning II, a dedicated stealth fighter/fighter-bomber that will serve not only the US Armed Forces but numerous other air forces throughout the world.

The 2000s featured a number of other interesting aircraft designs from the Skunk Works, such as the QSST, a proposed quiet supersonic transport; RATTLRS, a proposed triplesonic attack missile; the Polecat, the P-175 UAV demonstrator; ISIS, a proposed very-high-altitude/very-long-endurance airship; and the series of N-plus aircraft that investigated the possibility of reduced damage and noise from sonic booms.

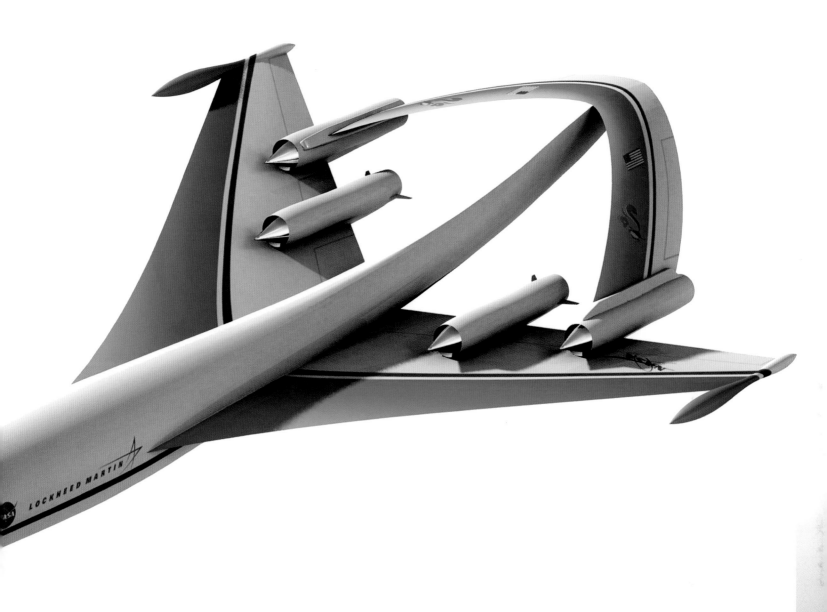

An earlier "Green Machine" concept that led to the NASA/Lockheed
N-Plus aircraft program. *LM/NASA*

08 THE 2010s: THE QUANTUM LEAPS

> ## "Hypersonic aircraft, coupled with hypersonic missiles, could penetrate denied airspace and strike at nearly any location across a continent in less than an hour."
>
> **—BRAD LELAND, LOCKHEED MARTIN PROGRAM MANAGER, HYPERSONICS**

The 75th anniversary of the Skunk Works is nearly upon us at this writing and will soon be history. During its first seventy-five years the Skunk Works has designed, developed, and produced a significant number of matchless products—most of them far ahead of their time. This trend is ongoing and will continue until the Skunk Works no longer exists.

The small cadre of highly talented aeronautical and propulsive system engineers who created the Skunk Works will never be forgotten. They created the near-frictionless machine that continues to generate many unique products today and is simply known as the ADP division of Lockheed Martin Aeronautics, Lockheed Martin Corporation.

The 100th anniversary of the Skunk Works will come on June 17, 2043. Only a higher power knows what amazing things it will be generating by then. For these near seventy-five years the Skunk Works has led the way in fielding advanced air vehicles. Such accomplishments are still being pursued, and with vigor.

Throughout the foregoing chapters of this work readers have witnessed more than a few fabulous advancements in both manned and unmanned flight, many of which are credited to the achievements of the Skunk Works. The Skunk Works produced America's first 500-mile-per-hour airplane, first 1,000-mile-per-hour airplane, and first 2,000-mile-per-hour airplane. America's first airplane to routinely fly above 70,000 feet, then above 80,000 feet. America's first attack airplane invisible to radar, then America's—the world's—first air dominance stealth fighter. The Skunk Works generated one of the world's best cargo transport aircraft, which is still in production more than sixty years later (with no

Lockheed Martin Skunk Works concept of a UCLASS air vehicle aboard a carrier at sea with its outer wings folded for storage. *LMSW*

end of its production in sight), and some of the world's most sophisticated and reliable reconnaissance satellites and unmanned reconnaissance drones.

For the near future the Skunk Works is working on several interesting projects. These include its proposed unmanned version of the U-2, touted as "optionally manned"; an unmanned hypersonic strike aircraft dubbed SR-72 that would be twice as fast as the SR-71; a high-speed strike missile to be launched by bomber; fighter and strike aircraft; advanced airships; and unmanned surveillance and combat aircraft, as well as various other types of transforming aircraft.

As the platinum anniversary of the Skunk Works approaches, one can only wonder what's next. Will it be an unmanned attack bomber or fighter, or will it be something more unbelievable? As it has done so many times in the past, the Skunk Works might create something even more incredible than what it has before.

So what's next for the Skunk Works? Only time will tell, as the old truism says.

FALCON: Hypersonic Test Vehicle

The FALCON (**F**orce **A**pplication and **L**aunch from **CON**tinental United States) project was a two-part joint project between DARPA and the USAF and was a part of the Prompt Global Strike program.

One part of the FALCON program aimed to develop a reusable, rapid-strike Hypersonic Weapon System, which was retitled the Hypersonic Cruise Vehicle (HCV), and the other part was for the development of a launch system capable of accelerating an HCV to very high hypersonic cruise speeds, as well as launching small satellites into Earth orbit.

According to DARPA, the FALCON program included: 1) The X-41 Common Aero Vehicle (CAV), a common aerial platform for hypersonic ICBMs and cruise missiles, as well as civilian RLVs and Expendable Launch Vehicles (ELVs); 2) Hypersonic Technology Vehicle 1 (HTV-1), a test

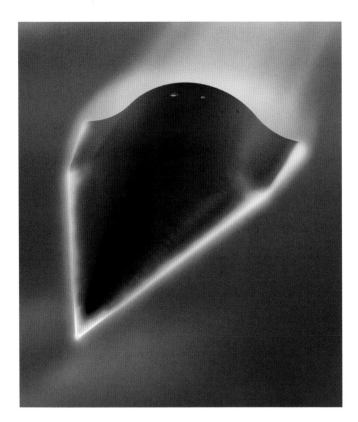

Above: HTV-2a launch on April 22, 2010. *USAF*

Above right: A full-scale engineering mockup of the Black*S*Wift Hypersonic Cruise Vehicle is pylon-mounted outside the Skunk Works headquarters building in Palmdale, California. It appears to carry civil registration number N-B645 (number 645 might be the Skunk Works P-number) and USAF serial number 09-3599. Whether these numbers are factual remains to be seen. *LMSW photo by Kevin Robertson*

Right: Another view of Black*S*Wift HCV. *LMSW photo by Kevin Robertson*

concept originally planned to fly in 2007, but canceled; 3) HTV-2, planned to fly in 2010; 4) HTV-3X: Blackswift, canceled; 5) Small Launch Vehicle, equipped with a smaller engine to power CAVs; and 6) the HCV, which would be able to fly about 10,360 miles in two hours with a payload of 12,000 pounds. It was to fly at high altitude and achieve speeds of up to Mach 20, or about 13,200 miles per hour.

The Skunk-Works-designed-and-built FALCON HTV-2 was a rocket-launched, unmanned, maneuverable air vehicle that could glide through the atmosphere at speeds of Mach 20. At such speed, flight time between Los Angeles and New York would be under twelve minutes. According to Lockheed Martin Skunk Works product information, "The Falcon HTV-2 was a multi-year research and development effort to increase the technical knowledge base and advance critical technologies to make long-duration

hypersonic flight a reality. The HTV-2 was a 'data truck' with numerous sensors that collected data in an uncertain operating environments."

In May 2003, DARPA and the USAF initiated the FALCON program—a technology development program to address high-priority mission areas, including global presence and space lift. As part of the program, DARPA and the USAF researched hypersonic aerodynamics and control systems to enable a wide variety of future capabilities then unavailable for rapid global response, including

Phantom view of proposed HTV-3X showing its scramjet-type of propulsive system. *LMSW*

high lift-to-drag technologies; high-temperature materials; thermal protection systems; and guidance, navigation, and control. The HTV-2 was just one step in a previously planned series of FALCON flight experiments to explore hypersonic technologies and their applications.

Two HTV-2 air vehicles were built and launched. These were labeled HTV-2a and HTV-2b. The first went aloft on April 22, 2010, from Space Launch Complex-8 (SLC-8) at Vandenberg AFB, California. The HTV-2 was fitted inside a special nose cone atop a USAF Minotaur IV Lite launch vehicle. The HTV-2b was launched on August 11, 2011. Both test flights ended prematurely.

The Minotaur family of launch vehicles is provided via the Orbital/Suborbital Program 2 and managed by the USAF Space and Missile Systems Center, Space Development and Test Wing's Launch Test Squadron located at Kirtland AFB, New Mexico.

The impact/recovery site was the US Army Kwajalein Atoll/Ronald Reagan Ballistic Missile Defense Test Site (USAKA/RTS) in the Republic of the Marshall Islands.

Blackswift was a program announced under the FALCON banner using a fighter-sized unmanned air vehicle that was to take off from a runway and accelerate to Mach 6 (about 3,960 miles per hour) before completing its mission and returning to base.

The MOU between DARPA and the USAF on Blackswift—also known as the HTV-3X—was signed in September 2007. The Blackswift HTV-3X did not receive the required funding for its continued development, and it was canceled in October 2008. The proposed HTV-3X was to be a little larger in size than Have Blue XST, which was about 40 percent smaller than the F-117A.

The HCV was to be the final part of the FALCON program, but the HCV project was terminated before a flying prototype was built. A full-scale engineering mockup resides atop a pylon outside the Skunk Works headquarters building in Palmdale, California.

SACD: Speed Agile Concept Demonstrator

The Speed Agile Concept Demonstrator (SACD) program officially began in August 2007, when the AFRL issued an RFP to validate the development of speed agile technologies. A number of earlier investigations had been going on since 2002, mainly consisting of smaller-scale proof-of-concept wind tunnel tests featuring a large number of aircraft configurations. This follow-on validation program had the goal of achieving a technology readiness level of at least five by 2010 on an integrated mobility configuration in the areas of high lift, efficient transonic cruise, and

Skunk Works artist concept of its Speed Agile Concept Demonstrator, of which a 23-percent-scale model was wind tunnel tested with good results. *LMSW*

flight controls, in order to support future development and acquisition activities. Specific objectives were configuration refinement, low speed performance validation, transonic cruise performance validation, and flight controls development and handling qualities evaluations. An increase in planned payload weight for the host vehicle (to 65,000 pounds) and cross-sectional size over previous concept vehicles had led to the need for a vehicle refinement. The SACD objective vehicle was to be capable of carrying the 65,000-pound payload over a radius of 575 miles. After landing on an austere 2,000-foot maximum length runway, it was to take off again with an equal payload and return 575 miles. Its maximum range with lighter payloads was to be 3,800 miles with cruise speed exceeding Mach 0.8 (about 600 miles per hour).

The Skunk Works was awarded a contract in early 2008 to validate the technologies it had been developing throughout the SACD program. To do this in part it built a 23-percent-scale wind tunnel model of its SACD conceptual STOL tactical transport aircraft, which it powered with two Williams FJ44 turbofan engines. It was tested in the world's largest wind tunnel at the USAF's Arnold Engineering Development Complex (AEDC) at Arnold AFB, Tennessee. (The actual airplane would have been powered by four high-thrust turbofan engines.) The AEDC is the most advanced and largest complex of flight simulation test facilities in the world. It operates thirty-two aerodynamic and propulsion wind tunnels, rocket and turbine engine test cells, space environmental chambers, arc heaters, ballistic ranges, and other specialized units. Nineteen of the complex's test units have capabilities unmatched elsewhere in the United States, and fourteen of them are unique in the world. AEDC facilities can simulate flight conditions from sea level to an altitude of 300 miles and from subsonic velocities to Mach 20.

The idea behind this testing was to see how well the craft's hybrid-powered lift design performed. Hybrid-powered lift means the plane combines a low-drag airframe with very simple mechanical assembly, leading to reduced weight and better aerodynamics, according to the AFRL.

SACD tests were for the most part successful through these validation programs, which ended in 2012. Hopes were then transferred to having such a system of tap for FY 2018 budgeting, the goal being to eventually replace the fleet of USAF C-130 Hercules.

UCLASS: Unmanned Carrier-Launched Airborne Surveillance and Strike

According to Lockheed Martin the Unmanned Carrier-Launched Airborne Surveillance and Strike (UCLASS) system "is to be a carrier-based unmanned air vehicle that will support long-endurance, proven Intelligence, Surveillance, Reconnaissance, and Targeting (ISR&T) and precision strike capability to Joint and Naval Warfare Commanders."

Lockheed Martin further stated that "UCLASS is a three-segment system consisting of a control system and connectivity segment, a carrier segment, and an air segment. The government will function as lead system integrator for the UCLASS system.

The system will maximize use of existing technology/capabilities to launch and control the air vehicle, transfer data, and support persistent surveillance and precision strike operations.

The system will be integrated into carrier-controlled airspace operations and will be maintained in accordance with standard fleet processes as tailored for unmanned applications."

On June 10, 2013, the US Navy released its RFP to four airframe contractors for its UCLASS program: Boeing, General Atomics, Northrop Grumman, and Lockheed Martin.

In order Boeing offered a modified Phantom Ray, General Atomics a version of its Predator C Avenger, Northrop Grumman a derivative of its X-47B, and Lockheed Martin a variation of its RQ-170 Sentinel, which it dubbed Sea Ghost.

The UCLASS air vehicle concept "integrates proven technologies from the F-35C Lightning II, RQ-170 Sentinel and other operational systems to provide both the lowest development risk and greatest Intelligence,

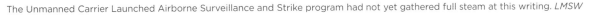

The Unmanned Carrier Launched Airborne Surveillance and Strike program had not yet gathered full steam at this writing. *LMSW*

Above: Conceptual UCLASS design flying over the eastern Pacific off the coast of California. *LMSW*

Below: Another view of a UCLASS concept. *LMSW*

Surveillance and Reconnaissance (ISR) mission capability," said Lockheed Martin.

The Naval Air Systems Command (NAVAIR) refers to UCLASS in-house as its RAQ-25, the prefix RAQ meaning Reconnaissance Attack Drone.

What eventually comes forth from the UCLASS program remains to be seen.

MUTT: The X-56A Multi-Utility Technology Testbed

The X-56A Multi-Utility Technology Testbed (MUTT) is an unmanned flight research vehicle designed and built by the Skunk Works for the USAF and NASA.

The first of two X-56A MUTT demonstrator air vehicles was delivered to the NASA-Armstrong Flight Research Center (formerly NASA-Dryden Flight Research Center) at Edwards AFB, California in late spring 2013, and its first flight was successfully accomplished there on July 26, 2013. The X-56A was developed for the AFRL to test active aeroelastic control technologies for flutter suppression and gust-load alleviation on flexible wing structures and after the initial contractor flight tests it will be turned over to NASA to support research on lightweight structures and advanced control technologies for future efficient, environmentally friendly transport aircraft.

The first flight on the unoccupied X-56A, flown by a two-man crew in a ground-based cockpit, lasted for fourteen minutes. The flight was flown at low altitude to evaluate its handling qualities at 70 knots and landing qualities at 60 knots.

The X-56A is designed to test a varied range of advanced aerodynamic concepts and technologies. It is of a modular design with an interchangeable wing assortment. With its several different wing type options, it was designed from the outset to investigate active aeroelastic control technologies such as active flutter suppression and gust-load alleviation.

SUMMARY

The first of the two X-56A air vehicles—named Fido, crashed shortly after takeoff on November 19, 2015. This was to be its first flexible-wing flight to test flutter suppression. It was its seventh of twenty flights planned

X-56A

SPECIFICATIONS

CREW: None

PROPULSIVE SYSTEM: Two non-afterburning, axial-flow, 88.7-lbf JetCat P400 turbojet engines

LENGTH: 7 ft 6 in

WINGSPAN: 27 ft 6 in

MAXIMUM SPEED: Mach 0.17 (138.1 mph)

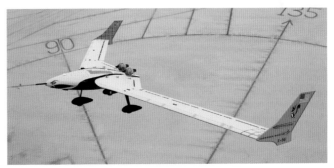

Top: One of the two X-56A Multi-Utility Technology Testbed or MUTT air vehicles taxied on Rogers Dry Lake on April 9, 2015. *NASA photo by Ken Ulbrich*

Middle: The first of two X-56As is shown here on its July 26, 2013, first flight at Edwards AFB. *LMSW*

Above: Another view of X-56A number one on its first flight. *LMSW*

Artist concept of what a Lockheed Martin Next Generation Air Dominance fighter might look like. *LM* Code One

by the AFRL before turning it over to NASA for further investigations. The aircraft was severely damaged and non-repairable.

The second X-56A, named *Buckeye*, made its first flight on April 9, 2015. It was a successful twenty-minute flight.

At this writing X-56A flight tests are ongoing.

NGAD: Next Generation Air Dominance

A Next Generation Air Dominance (NGAD) fighter will be needed in the post-2035 time period.

The F-22 Raptor is the current air dominance fighter but by the year 2035 it will have been operational for thirty years and in need of a worthy replacement.

In 2012 the USAF initiated early studies into its Next Generation Air Dominance (NGAD) fighter program. While we've heard the phrase "It'll be the last manned fighter built" countless times in the past, this time we shouldn't hear that phrase because most likely it will be an unmanned, or at least, an optionally manned fighter.

Lockheed Martin, its Skunk Works in particular, says it "has been working in unison with the DARPA, the USAF and the USN to investigate the practicable tactics involved to retain U.S. air dominance in the post-2035 world." "We are always exploring new technical capabilities and options for the development of future next generation air dominance (NGAD) air platforms, as well as potential enhancements to current platforms that are projected to be part of the future joint force structure," stated Lockheed Martin Skunk Works on its NGAD website.

Frank Kendall III, Under Secretary of Defense for Acquisition, Technology, and Logistics, tasked DARPA in October 2012 to explore concepts for the next generation of air dominance. In an attempt to break the battle space into smaller pieces, DARPA defined separate focus areas that span capabilities across the air dominance battle space.

In April of 2014, Mark Jefferson, director of Next Generation Air Dominance programs at the Skunk Works said, "This decomposition may not be perfect and will most certainly be fine-tuned over time, but it does provide a logical construct for looking at the future battle space."

He added, "The major challenge for Lockheed Martin will be integrating across the DARPA-defined domains. Adopting a multi-domain, net-enabled, system-of-systems approach to air dominance development will equip U.S. Joint Forces to achieve the freedom to conduct air operations at any given time and place."

"Given today's threats and potential emerging threats around the globe, the U.S. and its allies cannot afford to accept a status quo, or they will quickly lose their ability to ensure adequate responses to such threats," said Jefferson.

"We believe next-generation platforms will represent another quantum leap in capability," Jefferson said. "A key differentiator from previous new aircraft development programs is the need for assured universal information exchange of decision-quality information across the multiple domains of tomorrow's battle space."

"Revolutionary thinking, that's educated, but not encumbered by our past experiences will be required to produce the non-linear revolutionary combat capabilities required for success," said Jefferson. "This approach will keep us ahead of the curve."

Whether the NGAD fighter materializes as a manned platform or an unmanned platform remains to be seen. But make no mistake it will have to be the "best of the best" in the truest sense of that phrase.

VARIOUS: VTOL Advanced Reconnaissance Insertion Organic Unmanned System

VTOL Advanced Reconnaissance Insertion Organic Unmanned System (VARIOUS) is envisioned to be a stealthy Unmanned Aerial System (UAS). And like its acronym VARIOUS implies it is to be a multi-purpose platform for use by any of the US Armed Forces.

Lockheed Martin says its maximum payload will be over 1,900 pounds and its service ceiling will be above

First to Sixth Generations of USAF Fighters

The existing fleet of F-22s and the growing fleet of F-35s are considered to be the fifth generation of USAF jet-powered fighters.

The sixth generation is yet to come. But what about the first through fifth generations?

The first generation of fighters included the Bell P-59 and Lockheed F-80.

The second generation included the Republic F-84, North American F-86, Northrop F-89, and Lockheed F-94.

The third generation spawned the North American F-100 and the F-111.

The fourth generation spawned the F-15, F-16, and F-117.

The fifth generation gave birth to the Lockheed Martin F-22 Raptor and F-35 Lightning II.

Artist concept of the VTOL Advanced Reconnaissance Insertion Organic Unmanned System near its support ship. *LMSW*

235

Above: VARIOUS firing a missile from its internal weapons bay. *LMSW*

Opposite: VARIOUS hovering while it awaits targeting information. *LM Code One*

25,000 feet. It is to use interchangeable configurations to carry varying payloads ranging from cameras to cargo to weapons.

According to Lockheed Martin the capabilities of VARIOUS include: 1) Joint surface warfare operations; 2) Naval pre-assault reconnaissance; 3) Naval targeting and battle damage assessment; 4) Close air support targeting and precision weapons delivery; and 5) Precision resupply.

As a VTOL Unmanned Aerial System VARIOUS can be operated anywhere from the decks of ships at sea to forward unprepared areas without any air base facilities.

TR-X: Tactical Reconnaissance-Experimental

An unsubstantiated rumor has it that the USAF plans to retire its fleet of U-2S spy planes in 2019. On September 14, 2015, Lockheed Martin Skunk Works announced its privately funded work on a next-generation U-2 derivative aircraft, which it has dubbed the Tactical Reconnaissance-Experimental or TR-X.

No new U-2s have been built since the fall of 1989 when the last two "Dragon Ladies" built—a U-2R and a TR-1A—were delivered to the USAF. On August 18, 2015, some twenty-six years later, a new unmanned, or optionally manned, version of the "Dragon Lady"—the RQ-X, aka UQ-2—is being offered up for future production as an alternative to the Northrop Grumman RQ-4 Global Hawk series of UAVs.

J. Scott Winstead, a former USAF colonel and RQ-4A instructor pilot, became U-2 Strategic Development Manager for the Skunk Works after leaving the service and said, "Think of a low observable U-2."

HSSW: High-Speed Strike Weapon

The High-Speed Strike Weapon (HSSW) is to be a hypersonic attack missile carried by bomber and fighter aircraft of the future such as the B-21 Long Range Strike Bomber, Next Generation Air Dominance fighter, and the unmanned UCLASS. It is currently being developed in Lockheed Martin's Skunk Works.

The HSSW is to be a relatively small air-launched strike missile and with its tremendous speed very hard to defend against. It is to be used against heavily defended targets. And it will use its stealth, speed, and altitude properties to have high survivability.

And according to Lockheed Martin: "The HSSW will not only demonstrate hypersonic flight but also paves the way for future hypersonic programs, including both expendable missiles and reusable aircraft."

No further details on the HSSW have been released at this writing.

SR-72: Hypersonic Demonstrator Aircraft

On March 6, 1990, an SR-71A Blackbird of the 9th Reconnaissance Wing based at Beale AFB, California, flew cross-country from the vicinity of Los Angeles, California, to Dulles Field in Washington, DC, establishing distance, speed, and time records for a piloted aircraft. In doing so this particular SR-71A (USAF serial

LM Skunk Works SR-72 concept of an optionally manned hypersonic (Mach 6-plus) reconnaissance and/or strike air vehicle. *LMSW*

Opposite: Skunk Works SR-72 two-engine concept. *LMSW*

number 61-7972) flew 2,404.05 statute miles in one hour, seven minutes, and 53.69 seconds, and averaged 2,124.51 miles per hour (Mach 3.21). Its pilot was Lt. Col. Raymond Edward "Ed" Yeilding, who was accompanied by Regional Security Officer Lt. Col. Joseph T. "J. T." Vida. This record still stands at this writing, but its longevity might be in jeopardy if the so-called Son of Blackbird, the SR-72, eventually flies.

On November 1, 2013, Lockheed Martin announced that it was developing a hypersonic demonstrator aircraft that will go twice the speed of the SR-71. Lockheed Martin has dubbed it the SR-72.

According to Lockheed Martin, the SR-72 is to be an unmanned aircraft that would fly at air speeds of up to 4,000 miles per hour, or Mach 6.

"At this speed, the aircraft would be so fast, an adversary would have no time to react to it or hide from it," said Bradley C. "Brad" Leland, Lockheed Martin SR-72 program manager, Air-Breathing Hypersonic Technologies. He added, "Hypersonic aircraft, coupled with hypersonic missiles, could penetrate denied airspace and strike at nearly any location across a continent in less than an hour," and what's more, "Speed is the next aviation advancement to counter emerging threats in the next several decades. The technology would be a game-changer in-theater, similar to how stealth is changing the battlespace today."

Lockheed Martin Skunk Works has been working with Aerojet Rocketdyne to develop a method to integrate an off-the-shelf turbofan engine with a supersonic combustion ramjet air-breathing jet engine to power the aircraft from standstill to Mach 6. The result would be the SR-72, with an integrated engine and airframe optimized at the system level for high performance and affordability.

The SR-72 is not the first hypersonic Skunk Works aircraft. As discussed earlier, in partnership with DARPA, engineers developed the rocket-launched FALCON Hypersonic Technology Vehicle 2 (HTV-2). The HTV-2 research and development project was designed to collect data on three technical challenges of hypersonic flight: aerodynamics; aerothermal effects; and guidance, navigation and control.

The SR-72's design incorporates lessons learned from the HTV-2, which flew to a top speed of Mach 20 (13,000 miles per hour), with a surface temperature of 3,500°F.

The projected propulsive system for the proposed SR-72 is described by Lockheed Martin as a turbine-based combined cycle merged with a modified production

Four-engine SR-72 concept illustration. *Artwork by Luca Landino*

SR-72

SPECIFICATIONS

CREW: None (ground-based operators)

PROPULSIVE SYSTEM: Two TBCC units

MAXIMUM CRUISE SPEED: Mach 6.0 (3,960 mph)

LENGTH: 100 ft (approximate)

HEIGHT: NA

WINGSPAN: NA

EMPTY WEIGHT: NA

MAXIMUM TAKEOFF WEIGHT: 170,000 lbs
(approximate)

MAXIMUM ALTITUDE: 100,000 ft (estimated)

MAXIMUM RANGE: 3,300 mi (approximate)

PAYLOAD: ISR systems and/or HSSWs

fighter turbine engine with a dual-mode ramjet (scramjet) to accelerate the vehicle from a standing start to Mach 6. The turbine is to provide power up to and past Mach 3, when the scramjet takes over. A common inlet will provide air to both turbine and scramjet, with the exhaust from both also exiting through a common outlet. Variable geometry inlet and exhaust nozzle ramps open and close to match varying cycle requirements throughout its flight envelope.

While no specifics on the SR-72 have been released, its approximate size and weight will most likely be similar to that of the SR-71—that is, approximately 100 feet long with a maximum takeoff weight of about 170,000 pounds.

On December 8, 2014, NASA released a task order that stated "Task Order No. NNC15TA03T provides for a parametric design study to establish the viability of a turbine-based combined-cycle (TBCC) propulsive system consisting of integrating several combinations of near-term turbine engine solutions and a very low Mach ignition dual-mode ramjet in the SR-72 vehicle concept.

Task Order NNC15TA03T is issued under Contract NNC10BA08B on a firm fixed price basis. The firm fixed price was $892,292.00 US dollars."

To test the feasibility of the SR-72, a subscale flight research vehicle (FRV) is to be created. This FRV will be a piloted single TBCC engine air vehicle some 60 feet long, or about the size of an F-22.

SUMMARY

It's most appropriate that the SR-72 might follow in the footsteps of the SR-71, which remains the fastest and highest-flying military aircraft built to date. If the SR-72 is built. it will become the fastest and highest-flying military aircraft. And if the SR-72 is ordered into production, Lockheed Martin says that it could be operational by the year 2030.

Whether it's used strictly for reconnaissance, as a weapons launch platform, or for both duties is fluid at this writing.

HWB: Hybrid Wing Body

On March 4, 2014, Lockheed Martin announced its Hybrid Wing Body (HWB) program, which envisions an economic (more fuel-efficient) blended-wing type of aircraft that can serve as an airlifter (strategic and tactical) and as an aerial refueling tanker.

According to Lockheed Martin, "In 2010 alone, the USAF spent $10 billion in fuel, with mobility aircraft being the biggest gas guzzler."

John R. "Rick" Hooker, Skunk Works manager of the AFRL's Revolutionary Configuration for Energy Efficiency program, in March 2014 said, "The cornerstones of our Hybrid Wing Body (HWB) concept are efficiency, affordability, and compatibility. Designed with an eye to the future, the HWB program would save 400 million gallons

Inboard view of proposed Lockheed Martin Skunk Works Hybrid Wing Body aircraft with two fuselage mounted engines. *LMSW*

HWB concept with two above-wing-mounted engines. *LMSW*

of fuel per year and would be capable of dual use as both an efficient transport and tanker." Hooker added, "Saving even one percent is a huge amount of fuel and a big reduction in cost."

As pictured in several artist concepts, the HWB aircraft looks to be highly aerodynamic (to help reduce parasite drag) and uses two engines for its intended propulsive system.

"We constantly work with major engine companies to ensure that our designs include the latest engine technologies and concepts for greater efficiency and reduced fuel burn," said Edward A. "Ed" DiGirolamo, Skunk Works research and development engineering manager. "Those technologies include engines with higher pressure ratios for engine thermal efficiency as well as higher bypass ratios for propulsive efficiency.

The next-generation engines even promise to reduce fuel burn by as much as 35 percent for the same amount of thrust."

No additional information was gleaned from this program at press time.

LBFD: Low Boom Flight Demonstrator

By federal law, there can be no commercial supersonic transports traversing the contiguous United States. This is the primary reason the government canceled the US SST program in May 20, 1971, and the reason the doublesonic British/French Concorde SST wasn't allowed to cross over US territory when it was operating.

NASA—in particular its NASA-Langley Research Center in Hampton, Virginia—has continued to investigate the flight of aircraft with low sonic boom levels as part of its Structures, Materials, Aerodynamics, Aerothermodynamics and Acoustics Research and Technology (SMAAART) program. To do this in part, it tasked the Lockheed Martin Skunk Works with low sonic boom technology work with the award of a contract on June 11, 2014. This contract calls for the creation of a Low Boom Flight Demonstrator (LBFD) aircraft. The Boeing Phantom Works was a competitor on the LBFD aircraft program, but its design wasn't accepted.

The Lockheed Martin LBFD aircraft is to be a piloted air vehicle that will be flown to measure sonic boom levels over select communities. Under the NASA SMAAART program it is hoped that federal regulations governing acceptable sonic boom levels can be developed through the flight testing of the LBFD air vehicle.

No further LBFD details were available at this writing.

ARES: Aerial Reconfigurable Embedded System

This reference is loaded with acronyms. While some of these acronyms seem to make sense, there are a number of others that seem a bit far-fetched. The acronym ARES used here is one of these. When this particular acronym is spelled out—Aerial Reconfigurable Embedded System, it makes all the sense in the world.

As Lockheed Martin said on its ARES webpage,

Difficult terrain and threats such as ambushes and improvised explosive devices can make ground-based transportation to and from the frontline a dangerous challenge. While helicopters can easily bypass those problems, they often present logistical challenges of their

Low Boom Flying Demonstrator concept from Lockheed Martin Skunk Works. *LM* Code One

Happy 75th Anniversary, Skunks!

The Lockheed Martin Corporation will celebrate the 75th anniversary of its legendary Skunk Works on June 17, 2018. June 17, 1943, is considered to be the birthdate of what became the Skunk Works because this was the date when Kelly Johnson received the official go-ahead on the XP-80 program under the highly classified USAAF AMC Secret Project MX-409.

In its seventy-five-year history, the Skunk Works has manufactured a flock of exceptional aircraft as well as many other interesting products. Some of these products were brilliant diamonds, some were still in the rough, and many other gemstones are still in the works as still uncut diamonds.

The future of the well-oiled Lockheed Martin Corporation machine, proudly called the Skunk Works by its dedicated cadre of "Skunks," depends on many things. But first and foremost it's the *need for* and *funding for* whatever comes forth that will always be the bottom line. In the same vein, unsolicited ideas and inventions will almost always be presented by the Skunk Works in its ongoing attempt to produce advanced development programs and to generate money from sales.

From the XP-80 of yesterday to the F-35 of today and the who knows what of tomorrow, the ADP arm of the Lockheed Martin Corporation has and will continue to impress.

Though a bit premature, since this book was scheduled for publication before the official 75th anniversary of the Skunk Works, this writer felt compelled to congratulate each and every Skunk that reads it.

Just exactly what will emanate from the Lockheed Martin Skunk Works beyond the 2010s? While we can see what's already visible, it's the invisible that generates our deepest curiosities. And just what will the dedicated cadre of Skunks come up with?

PODS—the cargo-carrying version of the ARES VTOL system. *LMSW*

own and can subject flight crews to different types of threats. Additionally, they are expensive to operate and the supply of available helicopters cannot always meet the demand for their diverse operational services.

To help overcome these challenges, DARPA unveiled the Transformer (TX) program in 2009. Transformer aimed to develop and demonstrate a prototype system that could provide flexible, terrain-independent transportation for logistics, personnel transport, and tactical support missions for small ground units. In 2013, DARPA selected the Aerial Reconfigurable Embedded System (ARES) design concept to move forward.

Lockheed Martin's Skunk Works is leading a team with Piasecki Aircraft to develop the next generation of compact, high-speed vertical takeoff and landing (VTOL) delivery systems under the ARES program. ARES VTOL flight module is designed to operate as an unmanned platform capable of transporting a variety of payloads. The flight module has its own power system, fuel, digital flight controls, and remote command-and-control interfaces. Twin tilting ducted fans would provide efficient hovering and landing capabilities in a compact configuration, with rapid conversion to high-speed cruise flight.

It is envisioned that the flight module would travel between its home base and field operations to deliver and retrieve several different types of detachable mission modules, each designed for a specific purpose.

Example modules include: Cargo resupply, casualty evacuation (CASEVAC), and intelligence, surveillance, and reconnaissance (ISR).

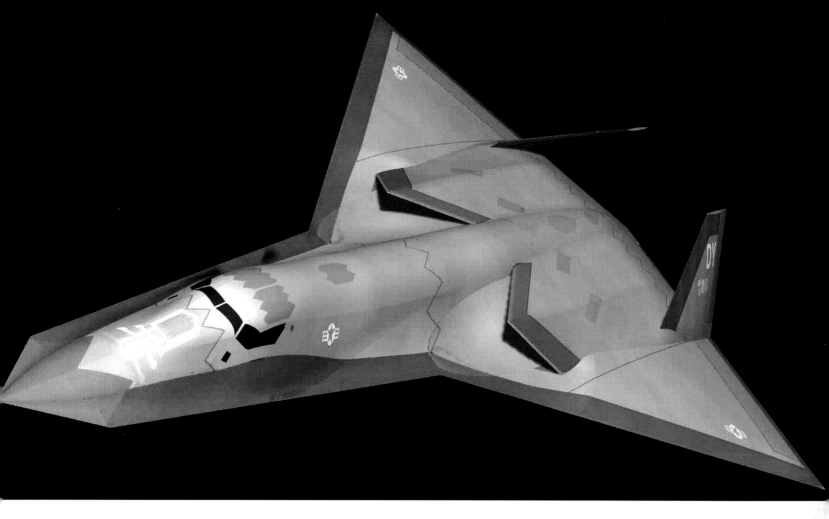

Skunk Works long-range bomber concept, circa 2003. *LMSW*

LRSB: Long Range Strike Bomber

The Air Force announced on October 27, 2015, the contract award of the EMD and early initial production phases for the Long Range Strike Bomber (LRSB) to the Northrop Grumman Corporation.

On February 26, 2016, Air Force Secretary Deborah Lee James released an artist concept of the Northrop Grumman LRSB, which closely resembles the all-flying-wing B-2A Spirit design. At the same time, she announced that the LRSB has been designated B-21 to reflect its debut as the first new bomber of the twenty-first century. She added that an official name for the B-21 would be selected with input from service members and that the winner of the "name the plane" contest, as well as the name of the B-21, would be announced at a later date.

Still highly classified, according to the USAF, no specific details on the LRSB were released at that time—not even its designation nor its propulsive system, or a photograph.

Earlier, on January 25, 2008, team members Lockheed Martin and Boeing announced their agreement to co-develop what was called the 2018 Bomber. As agreed by both parties, Boeing was to be the prime contractor, taking 60 percent of profit, while Lockheed Martin would be the principal contractor, earning the remaining 40 percent.

The 2018 Bomber was previously known as the Next Generation Bomber (NGB). Earlier still was the so-called 2037 bomber, which was for the most part a flash in the pan because its debut would be too far off. This short-lived program quickly evolved into the "Regional Bomber," "Interim Bomber," "2018 Bomber," "2037 Bomber," and "Next Generation Bomber" programs.

The design of the 2018 Bomber came from the Boeing Phantom Works with support from the Lockheed Martin Skunk Works. The 2018 Bomber program evolved into the LRSB program.

This announcement was of course bad news for the LRSB team of Boeing and Lockheed Martin (primary teammate), who had teamed up on the LRSB program on October 24, 2013. Boeing's Phantom Works and

245

X-47B

On February 4, 2011, the Northrop Grumman X-47B Unmanned Combat Air System-Demonstration (UCAS-D) made its first flight at Edwards AFB. Since then it has successfully launched from and landed on an aircraft carrier numerous times, proving not only that it works but that it works well. Its evaluations are ongoing.

Lockheed Martin, specifically its Skunk Works, is a "teammate-subcontractor to Northrop Grumman on the X-47B," and its "workshare includes development and fabrication of the arresting hook, flight control surfaces, and edges, including the engine [air] inlet lip," according to an April 6, 2011, posting on the *Code One* magazine website of the Lockheed Martin Corporation.

Lockheed Martin's Skunk Works were heavily involved in the LRSB program and collaborated throughout.

The USAF had released its RFP on July 9, 2014, regarding the LRSB. The details of the RFP had not been disclosed at this writing. In all likelihood, it required the use of an advanced propulsive system, survivability (stealth), avionics, and ISR.

The LRSB is to be a long-range strategic bomber for the Air Force Global Strike Command. It is to be a stealthy heavy-payload bombardment aircraft capable of carrying and precisely delivering any air-dropped weapon in the US arsenal. Its initial operational capability is expected in the mid-2020s. The USAF plans to purchase one hundred LRSBs at a cost of $564 million each in FY 2016 dollars.

A protest was filed by Boeing, but it was denied on February 16, 2016. Thus, the Lockheed Martin/Boeing LRSB proposal was not accepted and their respective parts in the program are history.

Artist concept of what a Lockheed Martin Next Generation Air Dominance fighter might look like. *LM* Code One

LRASM: The AGM-158C Long Range Anti-Ship Missile

The Long Range Anti-Ship Missile (LRASM) program began in 2009 but has just recently come to fruition. It was in 2009 when two types of LRASMs were planned: 1) the LRASM-A, a subsonic cruise missile based upon Lockheed Martin's AGM-158 JASSM-ER; and 2) the LRASM-B, a high-altitude supersonic version. The latter was canceled in 2012.

Lockheed Martin received a contract for an air-launched LRASM-A version on October 1, 2012. Another contract dated March 5, 2013, called for tests on both air- and ground-launched versions of the LRASM-A.

On July 11, 2013, Lockheed Martin completed its captive-carry tests using a B-1B Lancer. On August 27, again from a B-1B, the company conducted the first successful launch and test flight. Halfway through this first flight flight, the LRASM-A changed from following a preplanned path to autonomous guidance. It then autonomously detected its moving target, an unoccupied 260-foot boat—one of three in the area—and hit it in the desired location with an inert warhead.

On November 12, 2013, on only its second test flight from a B-1B, it scored another direct hit on a moving naval vessel.

AGM-158C

SPECIFICATIONS

CREW: None

PROPULSIVE SYSTEM: One non-afterburning, axial-flow, 700 lbf–class Williams F107-WR-105 (Model WR19) turbofan engine

LENGTH: 14.0 ft (without booster)

WINGSPAN: 7.87 ft

GROSS LAUNCH WEIGHT: 2,000 lbs (approximate)

MAXIMUM RANGE: 580 mi

MAXIMUM SPEED: High subsonic

MAXIMUM ALTITUDE: Sea-skimming

PAYLOAD: 1,000-pound conventional high-explosive blast-fragmentation warhead

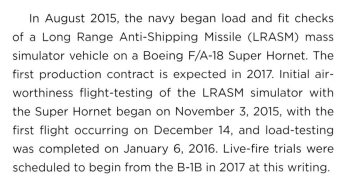

New Vice President and General Manager of the Skunk Works Appointed

Dr. Alton D. "Al" Romig Jr. joined the Skunk Works in January 2011 and in June took the reins from longtime ADP Vice President and Assistant General Manager Frank J. Cappuccio. During the January–June time period both Cappuccio and Romig reported directly to Ralph D. Heath, executive vice president of Lockheed Martin Aeronautics Company. Heath retired on April 1, 2012, and Larry A. Lawson became executive vice president on that date.

In August 2015, the navy began load and fit checks of a Long Range Anti-Shipping Missile (LRASM) mass simulator vehicle on a Boeing F/A-18 Super Hornet. The first production contract is expected in 2017. Initial airworthiness flight-testing of the LRASM simulator with the Super Hornet began on November 3, 2015, with the first flight occurring on December 14, and load-testing was completed on January 6, 2016. Live-fire trials were scheduled to begin from the B-1B in 2017 at this writing.

SUMMARY

With the AGM-158C LRASM now in production, the JASSM series of air-, surface-, and ship-launched missiles have come full circle.

SUMMARY

The 2010s are far from over as this reference goes to press. Yet the always-inventive Skunk Works has already generated a number of interesting programs and aircraft proposals.

On tap within Lockheed Martin ADP are a variety of air vehicles that range from very low and slow types to very high and fast types. Among these are high-flying, long-endurance airships, transforming air vehicles, an optionally manned tactical reconnaissance aircraft, an optionally manned hypersonic strategic reconnaissance-strike aircraft, high-speed strike weapons, unoccupied combat aircraft, and even a supersonic airplane that promises quite sonic booms.

Appendix A
Timeline

6/17/43, Lockheed given the go-ahead on the MX-409 (XP-80) program—recognized as the birthday of what would become the Skunk Works

6/24/43, Letter Contract received for a single XP-80 (TDN L-140) airplane

1/8/44, XP-80 first flight—pilot, Milo G. Burcham

6/5/44, XP-58 first flight—pilot, Joseph "Joe" Towle

6/10/44, XP-80A first flight—pilot, Anthony W. "Tony" LeVier

9/13/44, YP-80A first flight—pilot, Tony LeVier

6/45, XP-80B first flight—pilot, Tony LeVier

2/46, P-80R first flight—pilot, Tony LeVier

6/19/47, P-80R established world speed record of 623.738 miles per hour, pilot—USAAF Col. Albert "Al" Boyd

3/22/48, TP-80C first flight—pilot, Tony LeVier

4/16/49, YF-94 first flight—pilot, Tony LeVier

6/3/49, XF-90 first flight—pilot, Tony LeVier

1/19/50, YF-94C (ex YF-97A) first flight—pilot, Tony LeVier

3/4/54, XF-104 first flight—pilot, Tony LeVier

4/22/54, Kelly Johnson applied for patent on his F-104 design; patented for fourteen years on 12/4/56

6/16/54, XFV-1 first flight—pilot, Herman R. Salmon

6/54, DOD/CIA/USAF Bald Eagle program: CL-282 design with a single J73 engine was rejected in favor of the Bell X-16 design

8/23/54, YC-130 first flight—pilot Stanley "Stan" Betz

11/19/54, DOD/CIA/USAF Bald Eagle program: CL-282 with a single J57 engine selected; program was codenamed Project Aquatone

7/55, The CL-282 design was designated U-2

7/25/55, U-2 (Article 341) was delivered to Area 51 via C-124D transport

7/27/55, Tony LeVier performed first taxi test on the U-2 taking it to 50 knots

8/1/55, LeVier performed second taxi test to 70 knots, and the U-2 became airborne, to his total surprise; he landed as soon as possible

8/4/55, LeVier flew first "unofficial" flight on U-2

8/8/55, LeVier flew first "official" flight on U-2

2/17/56, YF-104A first flight—pilot, Herman Salmon

9/4/57, JetStar first flight—pilot,

4/26/62, The "unofficial" first flight on A-12—pilot, Lou Schalk

4/30/62, The "official" first flight on A-12—pilot, Schalk

8/7/63, YF-12A first flight—pilot, James D. "Jim" Eastham

12/22/64, SR-71A first flight—pilot, Robert J. "Bob" Gilliland

12/22/64, Mated M-21/D-21 first flight—pilot, William C. "Bill" Park

4/66, Skunk Works initiated F-X (F-15) studies

6/17/67, 25th anniversary of the Skunk Works

7/67, U-2R first flight—pilot, William C. "Bill" Park Jr.

8/68, Skunk Works ended F-X (F-15) studies

11//70, The CL-1200-1 Lancer program was terminated when the Northrop F-5E Tiger II won the International Fighter Aircraft competition

4/72, The CL-1200-2 Lancer—a further development of the X-27—was entered into the Lightweight Fighter (LWF) competition

3/72, The CL-1200-2 (X-27) program was terminated when the prototype General Dynamics YF-16 and Northrop YF-17 aircraft were selected to compete in the LWF fly-off

10/75, Lockheed and Northrop won the first phase of the competition to produce a VLO aircraft

1/76, Lockheed and Northrop 1/3-scale RCS VLO aircraft pole models evaluated the Gray Butte RCS Range in the Mojave Desert

4//76, DARPA announced that Lockheed won the VLO aircraft competition and would build two flying prototypes

5/76, The NASA/USAF X-24C (TDN L-301) hypersonic research airplane program was launched

7/76, Construction on VLO aircraft number one (HB 1001) began

9/77, The NASA/USAF X-24C (TDN L-301) hypersonic research airplane program was canceled

11/16/77, Have Blue XST number one (HB1001) was transported to Area 51 via C-5 transport

12/1/77, Have Blue XST-1 (HB1001) first flight—pilot, Bill Park

5/4/78, Have Blue XST-1 (HB1001) crashed to destruction near Area 51—pilot Bill Park survived the ordeal

7/20/78, Have Blue XST number two (HB1002) first flight—pilot, USAF Lt. Col. Norman Kenneth "Ken" Dyson

11/1/78 (OR 11/16/78), Lockheed received a contract to produce five FSD F-117A aircraft

7/78, Senior Prom first flight

7/11/79, Have Blue XST-2 (HB 1002) crashed to destruction about 35 miles from Area 51—pilot Ken Dyson survived

12/3/79, full-scale engineering mockup of an F-117 was completed in Burbank; its construction began 1/1/79

7/80, F-117 FSD-1 was scheduled to make its first flight in July 1980, but the program had slipped; since it was scheduled to fly at this time the airplane was numbered 780 (signifying July 1980)

1/17/81, FSD-1 number one (780)—the premier F-117A, arrived at Area 51 via C-5

6/18/81, YF-117A first flight—pilot, Harold C. "Hal" Farley Jr.

8/81, TR-1A first flight—pilot, Art Peterson

10/89, the last production U-2R and TR-1A aircraft were delivered—one of each

9/29/90, YF-22 PAV-1 first flight—pilot, Dave Ferguson

10/30/90, YF-22 PAV-2 first flight—pilot, Tom Morgenfeld

4/23/91, Lockheed Martin won the right to produce the F-22 ATF

6/17/93, 50th anniversary of the Skunk Works

1/97, Lockheed was selected as one of the two companies to participate in the JSF CDA phase of the JSF competition

9/7/97, Raptor 01 (EMD F-22A number one) first flight—pilot, Paul Metz

10/24/00, X-35A CTOL first flight—pilot, Tom Morgenfeld

11/22/00, X-35A completed flight test program and returned to Palmdale to be converted to the X-35B STOVL airplane

12/16/00, X-35C CV first flight—pilot, Joe Sweeney

3/11/01, F-35C completed flight test program

6/23/01, X-35B first flight—pilot, Simon Hargreaves

8/6/01, F-35B completed flight test program

10/26/01, Lockheed Martin was awarded the JSF SDD contract

2/05, P-175 Polecat UAV demonstrator made its first flight

7/18/06, Existence of the P-175 Polecat announced

12/15/06, First SDD F-35—and F-35A, made its first flight—pilot, Jon Beesley

12/18/06, The P-175 Polecat crashed to destruction

1/25/08, Boeing (prime contractor) and Lockheed Martin (prime teammate) joined forces on the 2018 Bomber program

6/2/09, X-55A ACCA first flight

12/4/09, USAF acknowledged the existence of the RQ-170 Sentinel UAV

7/26/13, X-56A MUTT first flight

10/25/13, Boeing (prime contractor) and Lockheed Martin (prime teammate) joined forces on the LRSB program

11/1/13, Lockheed Martin unveils its plan to produce a Mach 6–capable reconnaissance/strike aircraft dubbed the SR-72

7/9/14, USAF released its LRSB RFP to the industry

10/15/14, Lockheed Martin Skunk Works announced its ongoing development work on a compact fusion reactor that could be ready for use in about ten years

12/8/14, NASA awarded Lockheed Martin a design study contract to investigate the parameters on its proposed SR-72

7/31/15, First squadron of USMC F-35B Lightning II aircraft declared ready for deployment

8/19/15, Lockheed Martin proposed an unmanned and/or "optionally manned" version of the U-2—the TR-X (formerly RQ-X/UQ-2), with a higher payload as an alternative to the Northrop Grumman RQ-4 Global Hawk

10/27/15, it was announced that the LRSB would be built by the Northrop Grumman Corporation; teammates Boeing and Lockheed filed a protest

2/16/16, The LRSB program protest filed by Boeing and Lockheed was denied and Northrop Grumman got the nod to continue its EMD processes on the B-21 as the LRSB has been designated

6/17/18, 75th anniversary of the Skunk Works

Appendix B
Skunk Works Related Patents

Airplane. Patent number: Des. 119,714. Filed: June 27, 1939. Date of patent: March 26, 1940. Inventors: Hall L. Hibbard, and Clarence L. Johnson. Assignee: Lockheed Aircraft Corporation, Burbank, California. (Patent for XP-38)

Gas Reaction Aircraft Power Plant. Patent number: Des. 2,540,991. Filed: March 6, 1942. Date of patent: February 6, 1951. Inventor: Nathan C. Price. Assignee: Lockheed Aircraft Corporation, Burbank, California. (Patent for L-1000 turbojet engine)

Airplane. Patent number: Des. 136,352. Filed: October 5, 1942. Date of patent: September 14, 1943. Inventors: Hall L. Hibbard, and Clarence L. Johnson. Assignee: Lockheed Aircraft Corporation, Burbank, California. (Patent for Constellation)

Airplane. Patent number: Des. 143,820. Filed: October 4, 1943. Date of patent: February 12, 1946. Inventors: Hall L. Hibbard, and Clarence L. Johnson. Assignee: Lockheed Aircraft Corporation, Burbank, California. (Patent for XP-58)

Airplane. Patent number: Des. 140,795. Filed: November 26, 1943. Date of patent: April 10, 1945. Inventors: Hall L. Hibbard, and Clarence L. Johnson. Assignee: Lockheed Aircraft Corporation, Burbank, California. (Patent for Constitution)

Airplane. Patent number: Des. 143,822. Filed: June 5, 1944. Date of patent: February 12, 1946. Inventor: Clarence L. Johnson. Assignee: Lockheed Aircraft Corporation, Burbank, California. (Patent for XP-80)

Aircraft Engine and Fuselage Arrangement. Patent number: Des. 2,504,422. Filed: April 25, 1946. Date of patent: April 18, 1950. Inventor: Clarence L. Johnson, Willis M. Hawkins Jr., and Alonso B. Storey Jr. Assignee: Lockheed Aircraft Corporation, Burbank, California. (Patent for P-80 aircraft engine installation/removal)

Rocket Nose Installation. Patent number: Des. 3,026,773. Filed: January 26, 1950. Date of patent: March 27, 1962. Inventor: Clarence L. Johnson, and William A. Reed. Assignee: Lockheed Aircraft Corporation, Burbank, California. (Patent for housing rockets in F-94 nose section)

Airplane. Patent number: Des. 179,348. Filed: April 22, 1954. Date of patent: December 4, 1956. Inventor: Clarence L. Johnson. Assignee: Lockheed Aircraft Corporation, Burbank, California. (Patent for F-104 Starfighter)

Airplane. Patent number: Des. 172,969. Filed: October 1, 1953. Date of patent: September 7, 1954. Inventors: Clarence L. Johnson, Willis M. Hawkins Jr., and Eugen C. Frost. Assignee: Lockheed Aircraft Corporation, Burbank, California. (Patent for C-130 Hercules)

Rotatable Radomes for Aircraft. Patent number: Des. 3,045,236. Filed: September 28, 1954. Date of patent: July 17, 1962. Inventors: Philip A. Colman, and Eugene C. Frost. Assignee: Lockheed Aircraft Corporation, Burbank, California. (Patent for upper/lower rotatable radome applications on Orion and Constellation type aircraft)

Directional Controls for Propulsive Jets. Patent number: Des. 2,952,123. Filed: May 25, 1956. Date of patent: September 13, 1960. Inventor: Benjamin R. Rich. Assignee: Lockheed Aircraft Corporation, Burbank, California. (Patent for GE J79/F-104 propulsive system applications)

Airplane. Patent number: Des. 183,657. Filed: March 5, 1957. Date of patent: October 7, 1958. Inventors: Clarence L. Johnson, and William H. Statler. Assignee: Lockheed Aircraft Corporation, Burbank, California. (Patent for JetStar II)

JASSM MISSILE. Patent number: Des. 417,639. Filed: August 3, 1998. Date of Patent: December 14, 1999. Inventors: Grant E. Carichner, Stephen P. Ericson, Stephen G. Justice, Joseph M. Wurts, and Scott D. Van Weelden. Assignee: Lockheed Martin Corporation, Palmdale, California. (Patent for JASSM)

Reverse Engine VSTOL. Patent number: Des. 4,901,947. Filed: February 27, 1989. Date of patent: February 20, 1990. Inventor: Daniel P. Raymer. Assignee: Lockheed Corporation, Calabasas, California. (Patent for RIVET)

Supersonic Airplane. Patent number: Des. 201,062. Filed: May 15, 1964. Date of patent: May 4, 1965. Inventor: Clarence L. Johnson, and William H. Statler. Assignee: Lockheed Aircraft Corporation, Burbank, California. (Patent for Supersonic Transport)

Vehicle. Patent number: Des. 5,250,950. Filed: February 13, 1979. Date of patent: October 5, 1993. Inventors:

Richard Scherrer, Denys D. Overholser, and Kenneth E. Watson. Assignee: Lockheed Corporation, Calabasas, California. (Patent for Hopeless Diamond/Have Blue XST)

Exhaust Nozzle for a Turbojet Engine. Patent number: Des. 6,000,635. Filed: October 2, 1995. Date of patent: December 14, 1999. Inventor: Stephen G. Justice. Assignee: Lockheed Martin Corporation, Palmdale, California. (Patent for F-117 exhaust system)

Unmanned Aircraft. Patent number: Des. 382,851. Filed: May 28, 1996. Date of patent: August 26, 1997. Inventors: Eric D. Knutson, Joseph M. Wurts, and Michael H. Pohlig. Assignee: Lockheed Martin Corporation, Bethesda, Maryland. (Believed to be the patent for the P-420 LightStar; similar to RQ-170)

Partially Buoyant Aerial Vehicle. Patent number: Des. 418,804. Filed: June 22, 1998. Date of patent: January 11, 2000. Inventors: Edsel R. Glasgow, and Grant E. Carlchner. Assignee: Lockheed Martin Corporation, Palmdale, California. (Patent for P-791)

Appendix C
L- and CL-Numbers and Associations

L-133, proposed turbojet-powered pursuit aircraft

L-140, XP-80

L-141, XP-80A

L-153, XF-90

L-161, YC-130

L-1000, XJ37

CL-225, Low-altitude nuclear-powered bomber

CL-278, G2, G2A flying-wing

CL-282, U-2 proposal, original

Appendix D
Lockheed Model Numbers

22, P-38 Lightning series

75, Saturn

80, P/F-80 Shooting Star series

83, F-104 Starfighter series

89, R6V Constitution

90, XP/XF-90 and XF-90A

Appendix E
Chief Skunks— Presidents, Executive Vice Presidents, and General Managers of the Skunk Works

President

Clarence Leonard "Kelly" Johnson, June 17, 1943, to December 31, 1974

Benjamin Richard "Ben" Rich, December 31, 1974, to January 1, 1991

Sherman N. "Sherm" Mullin, January 1, 1991, to March 1, 1994

Jack S. Gordon, March 1, 1994, to November 1, 1999

Robert T. "Bob" Elrod, November 1, 1999, to January 1, 2003

Executive Vice President and General Manager

(There was a realignment within the Lockheed Martin Corporation whereby an EVP/GM would be the head of all operations within ADP.)

Frank J. Cappuccio January 1, 2003, to January 1, 2010

Dr. Alton D. "Al" Romig Jr., January 1, 2010, to July 29, 2013

Robert F. "Rob" Weiss, July 29, 2013, to time of writing

Bibliography

Books

Boyne, Walter J. *Beyond the Horizon: The Story of Lockheed*. Thomas Dunne Books. 1998.

Carey, Alan C. *Lockheed F-94 Starfire*. Air Force Legends Number 218. Ginter Books. 2015.

Cefaratt, Gil. *Lockheed: The People behind the Story*. Turner Publications Company. 2002.

Crickmore, Paul F. *Lockheed F-117 Nighthawk Stealth Fighter*. Osprey Publishing. 2014.

Johnson, Clarence L., with Smith, Maggie. *Kelly: More than My Share of It All*. Smithsonian Books. 1989.

Merlin, Peter W. *Area 51*. Arcadia Publishers. 2011.

—*Mach 3+: NASA/USAF YF-12 Flight Research, 1969-1979*. Monographs in Aerospace History Number 25. 2002.

—*Unlimited Horizons: Design and Development of the U-2*. NASA Aeronautics Book. 2015.

Miller, Jay. *Lockheed Martin's Skunk Works*. Revised Edition. Midland Publishing. 1995.

Pace, Steve. *Lockheed Skunk Works*. Motorbooks International. 1992.

———. *Lockheed F-104 Starfighter*. Motorbooks International. 1992.

———. *F-117A Stealth Fighter*. Motorbooks International. 1992.

———. *F-22 Raptor: America's Next Lethal War Machine*. McGraw Hill. 1999.

———. *Lockheed SR-71 Blackbird*. Crowood Press. 2004.

———. *The Big Book of X-Bombers and X-Fighters: Jet-Powered Experimental Aircraft and Their Propulsive Systems*. Zenith Press. 2016.

Rich, Ben R., and Janos, Leo. *Skunk Works*. Back Bay Books. 1996.

Suhler, Paul A. *From Rainbow to Gusto: Stealth and the Design of the Lockheed Blackbird*. American Institute of Aeronautics and Astronautics. 2009.

Magazine Articles

Hehs, Eric. "Super Hustler, FISH, Kingfish, and Beyond (Part 1: Super Hustler)." *Lockheed Martin Code One*, www.codeonemagazine.com/article.html?item_id=67; posted March 15, 2011.

———. "Super Hustler, FISH, Kingfish, and Beyond (Part 2: FISH)." *Lockheed Martin Code One*; www.code-onemagazine.com/article.html?item_id=74; posted July 16, 2011.

———. "Super Hustler, FISH, Kingfish, and Beyond (Part 3: Convair Kingfish)." *Lockheed Martin Code One*; www.codeonemagazine.com/article.html?item_id=89; posted November 4, 2015.

———. "Super Hustler, FISH, Kingfish, and Beyond (Part 4: Beyond Kingfish)." *Lockheed Martin Code One*; www.codeonemagazine.com/article.html?item_id=92; posted March 9, 2012.

Pace, Steve. "Fighter on the Fringe." *Airpower*. 1987.

Papers

Johnson, Clarence L. *SR-12 Log (Abridged)*. Lockheed Martin Corporation.

———. *A-12 Log (Abridged)*. Lockheed Martin Corporation. April 1993.

Merlin, Peter W. *Design and Development of the Blackbird: Challenges and Lessons Learned*. AIAA. 2009.

Mullin, Sherman N. *Winning the ATF*. Mitchell Institute Press. Mitchell Paper 9. Air Force Association, June 2012.

Telephone Interviews by Author

Brown, Dr. Alan. May 4, 1991.

Farley, Hal (Bandit 117). July 24, 1991.

Merrit, USAF Lt. Col. Mike (Bandit 180). June 6, 1991.

McCloud, USAF Lt. Gen. David J. (Bandit 201). November 11, 1992.

LeVier, Tony. January 22, 1991.

Rich, Ben. September 4, 1991.

Index

Quarto is the authority on a wide range of topics.

Quarto educates, entertains and enriches the lives of our readers—enthusiasts and lovers of hands-on living.

www.quartoknows.com

First published in 2016 by Voyageur Press, an imprint of Quarto Publishing Group USA Inc., 400 First Avenue North, Suite 400, Minneapolis, MN 55401 USA. Telephone: (612) 344-8100 Fax: (612) 344-8692

quartoknows.com
Visit our blogs at quartoknows.com

Voyageur Press titles are also available at discounts in bulk quantity for industrial or sales-promotional use. For details contact the Special Sales Manager at Quarto Publishing Group USA Inc., 400 First Avenue North, Suite 400, Minneapolis, MN 55401 USA.

10 9 8 7 6 5 4 3 2

ISBN: 978-0-7603-5032-4

Library of Congress Cataloging-in-Publication Data
Names: Pace, Steve, author.
Title: The projects of Skunk Works : 75 years of Lockheed Martin's advanced
    development programs / by Steve Pace.
Description: Minneapolis, Minnesota : Voyageur Press, 2016. | Includes
    bibliographical references and index.
Identifiers: LCCN 2016015398 | ISBN 9780760350324
Subjects: LCSH: Lockheed aircraft--History. | Lockheed Advanced Development
Company--History. | Aeronautics--Research--United States--History. |
    Aeronautics, Military--Research--United States--History. | Research
    aircraft--United States--History.
Classification: LCC TL686.L6 P334 2016 | DDC 623.74/60973--dc23
LC record available at https://lccn.loc.gov/2016015398

Acquiring Editor: Dennis Pernu
Project Manager: Jordan Wiklund
Art Director: James Kegley
Cover Designer: James Kegley
Book Designer: Bradford Foltz
Layout: Rebecca Pagel

Printed in China

Acknowledgments

Dana H. Carroll (Skunk Works Integrated Communications, Lockheed Martin Aeronautics), Giuseppe De Chiara (artworks), Ryan Crierie (Alternate Wars/Standard Aircraft Characteristics Archive), Harold C. "Hal" Farley Jr. (Skunk Works chief engineering test pilot, retired), Jozef Gatial (artworks), James C. Goodall (photographs and research support), Eric Hehs (Editor, *Code One* magazine, Lockheed Martin Aeronautics), Heather H. Kelso (Skunk Works Integrated Communications, Lockheed Martin Aeronautics), John R. Kent, Senior Manager, Media Relations Lockheed Missiles and Fire Control; Scott Lowther (Aerospace Projects Review), Luca Landino (artworks), Tony LeVier (Skunk Works Director of Flight Test, retired), Denny Lombard (Skunk Works photographer, retired), Sandra Lee Mabra (proofreader), USAF Lt. Gen. David J. "Dave" aka "Marshall" McCloud, Alan Radecki (photography), Jeffrey P. Rhodes, associate editor, *Code One* magazine. Lockheed Martin Aeronautics; Kevin Robertson (Skunk Works Promotional Photography), Kevin Ronaldson (research support and proofreader), Eric Schulzinger (Skunk Works photographer), Chad Slattery (© 2013 Chad Slattery. All Rights Reserved / www.chadslattery.com), J. Scott Winstead (Strategic Development Senior Staff, Lockheed Martin Skunk Works).

Illustration Credit Key

LM/Code One, *Code One* magazine published by
    Lockheed Martin Corporation
LMSW, Lockheed Martin Skunk Works
NASA, National Aeronautics and Space Administration
NMUSAF, National Museum of the United States Air Force
USAF, United States Air Force
USN, United States Navy

Image credits

On the front cover: The SR-72 soars above the atmosphere.
    LM Code One
On the back cover: The XP-80 holds a special place in the
    history of the Skunk Works. *LM* Code One
On the endpapers: The U-2 prepares for takeoff. *Getty*
On the title page: The SR-71 prepares for takeoff.
    LM Code One